Policy Analysis,
Education, and
Everyday Life

Policy Analysis, Education, and Everyday Life

An Empirical Reevaluation of Higher Education in America

David Schuman
University of Massachusetts, Amherst

D. C. Heath and Company
Lexington, Massachusetts / Toronto

This is Barbara's book.

Foreword

The general intellectual level of textbooks has declined—for whatever reasons—in the last decades. David Schuman's texts are an exception to this trend. They encourage students to think, they discourage rote responses, and they question the basic assumptions of political science, public administration, and policy studies. He has stirred my anger time and again by raising issues that I considered settled and by attacking assumptions I took as basic truths. His books are notable in their respect for the reader's intelligence. Students will be challenged by this book—on every page and with nearly every sentence.

Schuman's radical empiricism (of the William James variety) is one of the most exciting features of the book. It points a way out of the current intellectual embarrassment of the social sciences. At present, we see the disciplines of political science, sociology, psychology, and economics fragmented by conflicting perspectives, approaches, and methodologies. Wider observation of social phenomena has been restricted by endless debates over whether or not human action can be studied scientifically, with ancillary squabbles over what is or isn't scientific and what is or isn't human. Schuman's departure is to avoid the a priori discussions typical of such "methodism." Attempting to find the practical difficulties and actual limits of social investigations, he has proceeded to carry out innovative research. "What is the impact of college education on everyday life?"

he asks. To answer that question, he spent many hours with a few people, listening patiently to the stories of their lives and their educations. Nothing could be more direct, simple, and yet thoughtful and complex.

To place Schuman's efforts in context, consider the rough parallel with the pioneering works of Niko Tinbergen and Konrad Lorenz in the young science of animal behavior called ethology. They (and others) found animal behavior so multiform and complex that it supplies evidence in support of any theory or hypothesis imaginable. Thus they argued that the facts about animal behavior must be carefully observed, described, and classified before any explanations are attempted. Their methodological motto became "First observe what is going on and then look for causes."

Many, if not most, social scientists consider this an impossible directive. The view of research prescribed by philosophers of science maintains that theory and hypothesis are prior to and necessary for observation; and philosophers of science are the authoritative source of canons of scientific procedure, for political scientists in particular.

Schuman doesn't initiate a new debate on epistemology (although he does explain his epistemological assumptions in a late chapter), nor does he claim possibilities for a unique approach. The strength of this book is that it carries out a distinctive research idea. The insights emerge from the process of an actual investigation. The social sciences will mature only when we go about discovering the limits and the utility of our investigations without the direction of philosophers and even the advice of scientists from other fields. First the observations, based on our problems and interests, then some explanations, and finally a reconstructed logic of investigation should be the plan of attack.

The book is organized first to present the details of the study, then to explore the emergent patterns of behavior Schuman discovers, and finally to discuss the implications for methodology and policy studies. This format allows the reader to confront Schuman's understanding of the data with a variety of interpretations. The reader can learn much from the study without agreeing with the author.

In my own case, I found compelling both Schuman's data and his arguments that direct, certain, and complete knowledge of social life is impossible. But I found also that he sometimes assumes a special knowledge of the nature of the reality of the social world. He insists that social reality is a process, and a messy process at that. He can't have it both ways. Knowledge cannot be uncertain and incomplete yet contain statements about a certain and complete reality, even if that reality is declared to be a messy process.

Schuman's commitment to his messy vision, however, and the

thoroughness with which he puts forth and explores that vision avoid easy relativism. He persuades me not to ask him to give up his partial view of the world but to put forward my own vision with the same dedication and enthusiasm he demonstrates. Discarding the older metaphor of a marketplace of ideas with its implications of monopolies of truth and rejection of the marginal, he suggests that we explore other models of intellectual interactions, such as the concert hall, the seminar, the stage, and, most appropriate here, the gallery.

How do the insights of this project apply to the study and evaluation of education policy? Too often the study of policy has become a matter of seeking correlations among the various available quantified data. We can find easily the number of years a person has spent in school. We can ask for and get a reasonably accurate report of his or her annual income. In turn, we find that income is related to years of schooling. What this means is not clear, since the correlation may result from factors and causes other than those we have considered and measured. The correlation, however, looks like hard, reliable, scientific data. It appears especially "hard" when compared to older ideas that education promotes maturity, good citizenship, and competence, since indicators of those characteristics are not easy to find. The unfortunate result of this aura of scientific reliability is that many parents begin to consider higher education a means of guaranteeing their children's future income. Many students begin to choose courses in light of their parents' expectations. Finally, educators adapt to these demands by designing courses and programs geared to training future employees for job slots. Not only are the results lamentable for higher education, they are based on a simplistic view of methods and an arrogant ignorance of detail. But the mistakes involved may not show up until society finds itself without sufficient mature and competent citizens to perform the necessary tasks of nurture, maintenance, and production. While we can sympathize with the attempt to bring precision to the study of public policy, we can also appreciate Schuman's scorn and contempt for the crudities of such methods of policy study.

He proposes, as an antidote, to study policy from the "bottom up." His study is an exploration of the intersection of the personal and subjective with the institutional and abstract. His findings challenge the policy scientist seeking exact measurement to consider what is important to measure, and the policy scientist trying to formulate causal explanations to ground them on empirical observations. It won't do, his study shows, for us to measure only what we can count or for us to explain the results only on the basis of plausibility.

Down newly cut paths lie difficulties, I have warned. I'm not sure whether Schuman means to reform policy studies or to abandon them. Sometimes I am appalled by the messiness of the new trail and the seeming pride in ambiguity with which Schuman defends it. The man is human. It is just this combative and stubborn individualism that enables him to appreciate people—singular, willful, and complex—as the subjects and not the objects of social research. Schuman's pictures and stories of social life are always sharp, always detailed, and always unsettling. They are hard to dismiss, and they will leave tracks of unanswered but important questions in the reader's mind. When so much academic debate is riven now by party lines, his cranky but distinctive voice is most welcome.

Larry Spence
The Pennsylvania State University

To Acknowledge

Mostly, this is Barbara's book. But before the details about why, there are many other people to thank.

The discussions about a research project on doing policy analysis in a different way began in the early seventies in Ken Dolbeare's dining room. There were several of us involved, and we finally came up with a wonderfully expensive plan to study the effects of the economic depression in Seattle. We decided we needed a million dollars. I don't think we even submitted the plan to a funding agency.

A couple of years later, Ken and I received a grant from the National Institute of Education to refine our thinking about policy analysis and to conduct a study on the effects of post-secondary education.

Ms. Lee Scheingold helped us with the interviews, and did a fine job. Ms. Carolyn Wallace and Ms. Barbara Peterson not only typed the interviews but helped us sort out many of the everyday problems of continual interviewing.

It was, of course, a treat to interview those people. They were unfailingly kind and open and tolerant. They reconfirmed my basic sense that many people are heroes/heroines in their own times. Given the state of the world, it is nice to be reassured.

Sadly, I have neither seen nor heard from any of the people interviewed since 1975. I can only speculate about how they are and what they are doing now. Certainly my hope is that each one is alive and well and prospering. If this were a world of unlimited grants, I would apply for one in order to go back and visit them.

Teaching graduate courses in a school of education was an intense indoctrination into a whole mix of realism: The range reached from remarkable insight to a variety of hard- and soft-headed foolishness. Many of the students were first-rate, and those classes were always good for me. My colleagues Ralph Hummel, Patrick Sullivan, John Brigham, and Earl Seidman were always encouraging.

Thinking through how to use the material and how to write the book took time and effort and worry. And worry. I got help in indirect ways. For example, at a convention I gave a paper that used part of the research. I was attacked in all kinds of ways: My motives were challenged, my methods were suspect, my morals were called into question, and my work was demeaned. Or so I thought. When it stopped hurting I was encouraged to continue. I was told that there must be merit to a work that was so threatening.

Much better than indirect help was the advice I received from many people who read some or all of the manuscript and who encouraged me not only to continue but to rethink and rewrite. Bob Waterman, Larry Spence, and Ricka Schwartz were remarkably helpful. While I know none of them agrees with all I have argued, each must accept responsibility for friendship and kindness.

Getting the book from where I am sitting to where you are reading was no simple task. Ann Knight signed the manuscript in spite of its less-than-mainstream approach. Susan Didriksen made certain it got from one place to another in spite of what the lawyers said. Finally, in the editing of the manuscript, everyday speech came up against the rules of grammar. The temptation of "perfect" was resisted in favor of reality, and for that I would like to thank Sylvia Mallory. She also helped save *A Preface to Politics* from many unkind cuts and changes.

All three were unfailingly kind and helpful. Each, in her own manner, treated me and the manuscript in special ways.

But mostly this is Barbara's book. Not simply because she read and made suggestions, which she did. Not simply because she periodically made certain there was relative quiet in the house, which she did. Not simply because she was sympathetic with some writing-related grumpiness, which she was.

No, this is Barbara's book because every time I wanted to quit or go back on what I thought best, she simply would not consider it. Much of her integrity went into this book. That is a remarkable gift.

David Schuman
Spring 1981
Northampton, Massachusetts

Contents

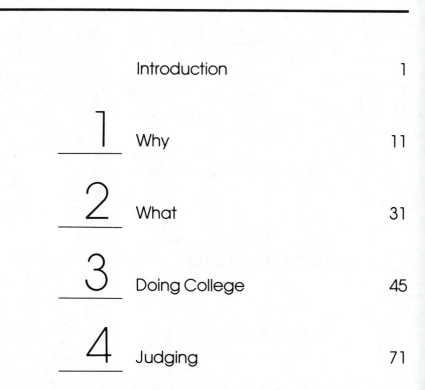

Men, though they must die, were not born in order to die but in order to begin.

—Hannah Arendt

Disorder is simply the order we are not looking for.

—Henri Bergson

"Life," he said to no one in particular, "is marvelously peculiar." He enjoyed another bite of croissant.

—Thomas Gifford

Introduction

...you merely demonstrate your subservience to a thinker when you spend your time attempting to disprove him. The way to fully refute a man is to ignore him for the most part, and the only way you can do this is to substitute new fundamental categories for his own.... Such categories represent the only hope for a genuine escape.

—Louis Hartz

The three topics that need introducing—method, subject, and style—are common enough. Most writers need to explain themselves right away, and these three topics make explanations more manageable. I would like to ask that you read what follows just a little more carefully than you normally might, as these topics introduce some of the central problems and tensions of the book.

Method

It seems reasonable to tell a story. It is an updated and more complicated version of the philosophical problem of the ship of Theseus.[1] I repeat it not in search of an answer but to get into the spirit of another problem.

We begin with a ship, an all-wooden ship, which we shall call Ship A. There is a second ship, identical to A: This one, all-aluminum, we'll call Ship B. One day, a wooden plank is taken off Ship A, and the piece is replaced by an aluminum one from Ship B. Still the same ship, with one slight change.

But the change continues day after day, and we finally reach the time when Ship A is made *entirely* of aluminum. One could now argue, and be on strong ground, that the aluminum ship *is* the wooden ship we started with. Ship B *is* Ship A. Oh my.

To make things more complicated, let us say that we saved all the wooden planks from Ship A. We saved them and put them back together. In other words, we rebuilt Ship A. Now we have an impossible situation: We have two Ship A's. Of course two ships cannot be the same ship; two things cannot be the same thing.

But—and here is the question I want to think about—when does one thing become another thing? When did Ship A stop being itself? When it was 50 percent aluminum? 80 percent? 100 percent?

Now, think about social analyses. There are, it seems to me, at least three parts to them: There is the event (or whatever) being studied; there is the studier; and there is the method used to do the study. Each is critical to what is being done; none should be overly dominant or forgotten. Let us take up each one in order.

We know that whatever is being studied—whatever the data are— is never self-evident. Events do not speak for themselves, and meaning is not a natural occurrence. Context and perspective help give meaning; so we do not have to be overly nervous about an event that will wholly dominate our analyses.

Next is the studier. The person doing the studying—the analyst— sorts out what is to be included and excluded according to a number of personal and professional reasons. In rare instances, the person doing the study becomes the center of attention. To take extreme examples, Norman Mailer and Hunter Thompson seem to be the focus of most of what they write. Others, of course, dominate under the cover of neutral and objective language.

Finally, there is the method being used. This third part, the method that is chosen, seems to have the greatest potential of dominating any study.

For example, if this study had been done by an Eastern European Marxist,[2] it would be fair to say that both I myself and the event would become something different. Or, if I were using strictly capitalist/liberal biases and categories, at what point would I disappear? Or, if only quantitative methods were employed, when would my judgment be totally overwhelmed and much of what now appears as data be replaced with things that could be quantified?

It seems to me that there should be some balance among the three parts of social analyses. None should assume extraordinary importance. The data should not become the method; the individual doing the study should not become an instrument; the method should not be ignored or left out as being unimportant.

This book, then, is an attempt to work out a way of doing social science research. It is an empirical study of a sort that does not conform to the way the term is generally used.[3]

Method in Particular

For two years I worked with a group of advanced doctoral students. It was a diverse group in terms of age, background, and experience. Happily, the people were nice as well as intelligent, and much of the work was first-rate.

One underlying theme was repeatedly discussed: How can we do social science research better? By the end of the second year, we were able to critique Newton and Descartes and easily come to agreement about the shortcomings of current research. There was a corresponding fact that I found both curious and sad: We could never talk about doing social science research that would include values in ways that seemed right.

Each of us understood and readily admitted that for all of us, almost all of the time, values were central to our actions. It was agreed that judgments of right and wrong are made constantly. Yet, when we asked how that fact could be incorporated into research, the answers were a mixture of anger and denial.

Put bluntly, we could never reach the point of getting our research to reflect life.

Put personally, if I could not get a class to talk about values, what was it going to be like to write a book in which values were important?

There is a way to conceptualize the problem that may be helpful. There is, I believe, some level or layer of knowledge that runs between the purely personal and the notions of general concepts. It should not be thought of in a hierarchical arrangement but probably more as the range in which most of life occurs. The purely personal and the learned notions of general concepts are always part of the mix of the activities in which we engage.

Psychologists make it their business to explain the personal; social scientists who use quantitative methods are always in the market for more inclusive general concepts. In most studies, then, the range of conclusions seems polarized around the uniqueness of an individual (in the best cases, depicting how that may illuminate the world around that person), or conclusions are polarized around concepts that may explain a little about a lot of us.

We do not know what that layer of knowledge about everyday life sounds like when it is analyzed, or what might be gained by it if we put it to specific use. To put that in question form: What advice can we give policymakers? What conclusions can we come to, what will they sound like, what might we be able to learn?

And, equally important, how do we judge the research?

Judging research depends (I know this will seem redundant) on the research being judged. There are some instances in which the method itself is judged. We can ask such questions as: Was, the method carried out correctly? Was the method appropriate to what was being studied? Were the numbers accurate? Was the sample correct? And, finally, did we prove something that has not been proven before?

The method dictates much of what is studied and, it follows, much of what is learned. There is something reasonable about judging the method in those cases.

Because this is research into the way people live in this society—and into the way education may or may not affect those people—method becomes of secondary importance. Method is not unimportant, but it is not of primary importance.

There is a tension in this study that is, I believe, a key to most studies about people and how they live. When one tries to describe the points at which people and society and organizations and values are constantly being worked out, the descriptions are bound to be messy and full of multiple and often contradictory truths. If there can be an elegance and beauty in what is real, then there should be a kind of elegance and beauty in parts of this study.

Empiricism

In an empirical work that involves human beings, the whole notion of objectivity is important for this reason: It is something the researcher should never claim.

The warning is necessary because it would be possible to make claims about the objective way in which the people in this study are presented. After all, the bulk of many of the chapters is the words of the people themselves. Words from their mouths to the tape recorder, to the typists who transcribed the tapes, to the rough draft of the manuscript, to here. Also, I tried very hard to be accurate and honest and fair.

But none of that is really objective.

At least twice in the process there was serious involvement by others. First, each person was generally interviewed by two people. It is impossible to calculate when—at which points—the straight talk was the result of the interaction of the three people. At the very least, answers are in part the response to a question someone else thought was important.

Second, there were at least three hundred pages of transcript for each person. Why I chose and edited the way I did probably has as much to do with preconscious stuff as it does with conscious decisions. The "straight talk" of these people reveals facts not only about themselves, but also about me, which you may see very clearly but to which I am blind.

What you read, then, is not simply an "objective" presentation of individuals talking about themselves and the world. In an empirical work, there is just too much to report. Being objective is neither interesting nor possible.

Subject

In the course of working out this method, it was reasonable to do it about something. If the way we study is more instructive than normal study or is instructive in different ways, that is all for the good. When we move into the world in which decisions are made, policies are set, and lives are influenced and changed, then it is best to know as much as we can.

Generally, any policy study begins with policymakers and the policy made, and works down to the people affected. In this study, we begin at the bottom, with the end of the process, and work our way up. The trick is to begin with the individual but have the study be something other than wholly personal and individualistic.

The subject, then, becomes important. Higher education—what a college degree/education might mean—seems a worthwhile topic for several reasons. Education is enormously important in the United States. Let me be more specific. Education, and particularly higher education, is something almost everyone in the United States has to come to terms with. There is a myth of higher education that affects us all, and its effects are not easily understood. The effects are different from things like social status, economic gain, job mobility, and so forth, which we know about. The subject of education helps connect the individual to his or her world. That is only part of why I chose the subject.

The other part stems from more personal concerns. I can get at those concerns most easily by beginning with my job. Teaching, like so many other jobs and professions, is full of lessons that can be learned simply by doing it for a number of years and trying to figure out the right question. Let me offer an example.

There are a surprising number of problems in directing dissertations. The problems are well beyond the obvious ones of editing and encouraging. While teaching at a professional school, I found this curious fact: Dissertations (in outline and sometimes even in draft form) could be technically perfect but somehow wrong. Basically, the problem was, I didn't know quite what was being written about.

After some straightforward but fairly wrongheaded attempts at being helpful, such as, Why are you writing this?, I got to what appears to be a right question. In one or another form, the question is this request: "Tell me a story about why you're writing this dissertation." When the story gets told, when the person begins to understand the basic emotion behind the basic question being asked, then the writing makes a good deal more sense.

It is in this spirit that I offer the following three stories.

Story One

When I was an undergraduate and was going through a particularly bad time emotionally, it became clear that I wanted to teach in the university. A relative—an older, rich man who was interested in the appearance of being learned as well as the reality of wealth—and I had a long talk.

In the course of the conversation I told him that I planned to be a professor. He was very pleased and gave me a little talk about how wonderful and important education was.

His last line was this: "But what are you going to do for money?"

Story Two

My mother was always a little surprised that I survived growing up and even made it through college. Graduate school was a shock. By the time I was in my late twenties, I was living in Seattle, had published a book, and was fully involved in an academic life.

Mother lived in Texas, and we visited each other at least once a year. They were good visits. During one of my trips to Texas, she was extremely happy because of my book. I was that curious mix of pleased and embarrassed/appalled at what a mother would say about her son.

One Saturday afternoon I excused myself and went into the TV room. After all, the football game was on.

As I was getting settled for serious watching, I heard her say to some family friends who had dropped by: "Isn't it wonderful, he hasn't changed a bit. He's still just like he was when he was growing up."

In the original version, the above two stories were meant to explain many of my motives for writing the book. It was my sense that the stories contained enough tensions to provide you with a kind of emotional starting point. I was wrong.

People who read this introduction convinced me that more was needed. So, instead of using a "real" story, I made one up. Those who read it liked the story and urged me to include it.

Story Three

In essence, this has the same beginning as Story Two. I get to Texas, friends come over, Mother brags. At that point I stand up and say: "Please excuse me, but I must go to the study and read Kant." I leave the room and mother says: "Isn't it wonderful how much he has changed now that he is a scholar."

That is the *expected* story, but one that leads us to all kinds of wrong questions based on wrong assumptions. School may make us change or aid us in changing in some ways, but not so much that we disown the self that helped get us to school. The fact seems to be that the true story is the right one. Mother saw that in many ways I had not changed, and that insight was somehow unexpected and unexplained.

Style

In most of the things I write, I purposely leave some parts blank, some vague, and some open to interpretation. There are several reasons for this kind of writing. I often leave things blank when I do not know an important detail, like a fact or an answer. And I often leave things vague or open because I understand the world in these terms. If there are many right answers to a question, and if I can live with most of them, it seems silly to limit anyone's choice to one answer. To put the idea in a different way, it sometimes seems that what I write is exactly as interesting as what people read. That is fine with me.

There are parts of this book written in that style. Other parts are not "open" like that at all. There are three very distinct sections of the book; the aim and style of each section are different.

The first section, four chapters, is mainly concerned with introducing the dozen people who participated in the study. The way they are presented is, appropriately enough, by quoting them at length. To read these chapters might lead one to believe I have simply presented some unedited reflections of the people I talked with. While an interesting observation, it would be wrong. This chatty/interviewee style begins to change in the second section and disappears in the last section.

In section two there are different themes. Topics such as work, bureaucracies, and politics form the focus of the various chapters. While people are still important, they are now placed in the context of a theme of American life. The style is different from the first section, if for no other reason than that there is more analysis.

The third section is about methodology, policy analyses in general, and higher education in particular. It is the kind of work that sometimes appears as speculation at the end of a book, with this suggestion: "Some study utilizing these ideas should be made." What this section is concerned with is why the study was conducted as it was, what I think was learned, and how that fits into the arguments about how we should do research and how we might think about a college education/degree. Clearly the style of this section must, by definition, be different from that of a section that aims at introducing people through their own words.

Style and content are interrelated in important and, for me, almost un-understandable ways. Hopefully, the three different styles will ultimately help make the contents of the book more interesting.

Advice

With all of the above, the fact remains that there have been only hints about what to expect. It is fair to be more explicit.

There are two threads that run through the book. The first is this question: What—if any—is the effect of post-secondary education on everyday life? What does it mean to have a college education? What does it mean not to have gone to college?

The second thread has to do with education and those who are professionally involved in it. The basic question is simple enough: Knowing what we know from this empirical work as well as from the literature in the field, can we do something better?

The answer, by the way, is yes.

Or so it seems.

1. Meredith Michaels first told me the story. This updating comes from Roderick Chisholm, "The Loose and Popular and the Strict and Philosophical Senses of Identity," in N. S. Carr and R. H. Grimm, eds., *Perception and Personal Identity* (Cleveland: Case Western Reserve, 1969), pp. 82–84.
2. For a good critique see Jean-Paul Sartre, *Search for a Method* (New York: Vintage Books, 1968).
3. Or, to misquote Louis Hartz just a little, I "could not help lapsing into the empirical mood" as I looked around.

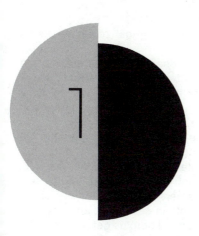

Why

Just Because, and Other Reasons

I have a hard time separating, obviously, how I felt then and how I look back on it now.

—Carol

When I get in a perverse mood—maybe with a touch of masochism and a pinch of paranoia—I read those short pieces of research that appear in obscure academic journals. On a scale from my children's classic comics at one end to classic literature at the other, most of the studies are only a step or two above the comics.

There is, you can well imagine, an enormous amount of research about college. But the more I have read about college, and the longer I have participated in the everyday activities of the university, the less and less certain I have become about what it all means.

Meaning

If I understand correctly, meaning is a subject too rarely at the core of academic activity. There are, it seems, good reasons for that, as it is not at all easy to think about and study meaning. But, regrettably, meaning does not disappear simply because it is not studied. It would be wonderful if I could truthfully write that what follows reveals the true meaning of college. The best I can offer is this: There is no single "true meaning" of college. That is the good news.

The bad news is this: Many of the "true meanings" of college seem to be hurtful to people.

I am getting ahead of myself. The next chapter is a full description of what the book is about, where the ideas came from, and where they seem to be going. In this chapter it makes sense just to start. Not only is it—I hope—more interesting that way, but it will give you an idea of what much of the book is like.

The topic of this chapter is simple enough: Why do people go to college? Those earlier-mentioned short pieces of research are straightforward enough about it. People go to college, we are told, for jobs, status, and the like. Even if that were true, and I'm not certain that it is, what does it mean for the person making the decision? What would we need to know about people in particular, and environments in particular and in general, that would help us get to meaning?

We begin with people in particular. Four people. Two graduated from college, two did not. This chapter is about their getting to the point of—and making a decision about—whether or not to go to college. In later chapters we will see whether that decision made much of a difference in their lives.

The "Because" Case

Me: "Hm. O.K. You were gonna go to [Big State University]?"
Carol: "Yes."
Me: "Because . . ."
Carol: "Just because, yes."

CAROL

If we are ever to get even a glimpse of what meaning is about, we must try to understand what is built into each person's idea of "normal." The woman about to be introduced, Carol, could truthfully say she went to Big State U. "just because."

In many ways she was a larger-than-life example of why many of us go to college. The decision to go and the place to go to were so *obvious,* so *normal,* so reflective of everyday pressures that everything seems preordained. It is those pressures—family, school, peer, and the like—that we will study. Later, we will see how this woman was living, how even the strongest socialization and parental pressure could be worked through, rejected, or analyzed out.

Let me try to describe Carol, since much of what follows is her words, and you might want a mental image of who is talking. She was, simply, a lovely person. She was in her mid-thirties, maybe 5'4" tall, and medium weight. But it was her face that was most striking. Clearly, Carol had experienced difficult things, and she was a gentle and sympathetic person possibly because of that.

She had lovely eyes, bright and active; a good mind, a ready laugh, and a sharp tongue.

We can begin to understand her by listening to what she had to say about her grandfather:

"He was one of your great barons of the early twentieth century in that he went out and made money which everyone is now living off of.

"He went into banking and was also into aeronautics and was one of the directors of [a major airline], and he just had his hand in everybody's pie, and his own pie, and he was also in mining . . . [which my] father went into.

"I remember him as a fairly cold, frightening grandfather . . . never your warm, up-in-the-arms sort of person. He and my grandmother were very much into living the way their money would allow them to live."

If her grandfather was a baron, of the capitalist sort, her father was an autocrat—of the military sort. He *ran* the mines, and he *dominated* the home. Some examples:

"[home life was] very structured. . . . We [my sisters and I] took piano lessons. . . . We could not practice when my father was in the house . . . we could not look at the paper until my father was done with it . . . when we played a lot in the living room, we used to get chewed out if we were too noisy. One time, my sisters brought some friends home when they were at the university, and brought them into the living room. . . . And when they left my father was so pissed . . . that they had come into his sanctuary; and [he said] they should have taken their company elsewhere.

"And one time I was in Europe . . . and I had wanted to stay . . . and I wrote this wonderfully logical letter, and I said, 'Can't I stay?' You see . . . I couldn't make the decision on my own. He didn't write me back for several cities, and I guess I wrote and asked him a second time, and his response to me was again in three or four sentences, saying, 'I wish I didn't have to write this letter, because you should be able to come to this decision on your own, but you have to come back and finish school.'

"You didn't discuss the pros and cons . . . you make this decision and you go along with it."

Or, put more simply: "Because he was [a military school graduate], and because of his own family and because of the way he was reared, he was an incredibly strong-minded, unloving, uptight individual."

It is important to remember that even authoritarian parents exist in a social/political/economic context. For most of Carol's first fifteen years, she lived in a small mining town in the Northwest. The family lived in a big house in the area where management lived. They were segregated by power and money and the distance between the top and the bottom of the mountain.

On military bases, especially in the navy, there are areas of bigger, prettier houses. There are also barracks and smallish apartments for those of lesser rank. The military, leaving nothing to either chance or imagination, posts signs around the area of the big houses, which read *This Is Officers' Country.* The family of the man who ran the mines and who would someday inherit them lived in the biggest house in "officers' country."

And his youngest daughter? What was it like to go to school with the children of the miners? To be bright and pushed by her parents? Listen:

"All my friends' parents were the muckers in the mines. If I got bossy on the playfield, they'd say, 'Just because your dad bosses us around, that doesn't mean you can boss us.'

"I also remember lots of the striking that went on, and I was always reared to believe that the conditions were so good, how can—how can they complain? And one time my father—they'd been out for several weeks, and my father came home and said, 'Well, we're just going to starve them, and when they're hungry, they'll come back to work.'

"I went through this period where I always seemed to choose the poorest kid in the classroom to befriend. . . . Who knows what was going on in my head? . . . I'd go off to these friends' houses, and for some reason or another I was rude enough to stay through dinner and watch them eat, which of course I wasn't supposed to do . . . and I'd come back, and they'd [my parents] say, 'Well, you're late. . . .'

"I'd say, 'Well, they were having dinner, and I stayed and talked to them.'

" 'You're not supposed to stay to dinner! What did they have for dinner?'

"And I'd say, 'Well, a plate full of peas.'

" 'Is that all?' "

Life for her friends was filled with going to "forage in the dump" and spending years living in a cellar while trying to build a small cabin, or coming to school so undernourished that they did not have the energy to concentrate. Their lives were not full of skiing lessons, braces for crooked teeth, or cabinets full of sterling silver.

Academically, Carol did well. She was moved up a grade because she did so well.

"One thing I—one small thing [*laughs*] I remember in kindergarten is that already I was very interested in getting my strokes and all this, and being an achiever."

Achiever? Ah, yes.

"I was achieving well. And my parents were always [pushing us]; it was very important to them that we got all pluses and few minuses and no zeros certainly, and we always got a nice dollar if we came home with perfect cards.

"The achieving was [easy], things came easily, and even if I was in the highest reading group, I wanted to be the best in the highest reading group. And I do remember pushing myself incredibly. . . .

"But the one thing about this achieving is, and I'll make this statement about my *entire* education, is that it was an empty achievement. And, you know, come to these judgments about—the little train that could [*I laugh*] type of thing [*Carol laughs*]. This wonderful, forceful attempt to achieve on the part of the train, right?"

And high school, what were those days like?

"I've pretty effectively blotted out that. . . . Painful, painful years . . . adolescence and high school: Just everything falls upon you and what the expectations are and whether you can meet the expectations and if you can't meet them, God! You know, you've disappointed *everybody*. What difference does a single personality make? It's a network. . . .

"I think the high school days were very beneficial for me and also very traumatic. [I] didn't have any trouble with the schoolwork, because I learned everything in two years . . . and I could just slide through my last two years . . . *and so the social thing was of tantamount importance*."

There was never any doubt about *if* she would go to college and not really much doubt about where. "What I probably felt then I think, again—it was probably playing out a written script." I suppose that may be an accurate statement in this case. In a true sense, for Carol the world was a stage and—to that point—the players read from a finished script.

To get a better understanding of where this came from, we should take another look at her family, beginning with her mother.

"My mother came from a struggling newspaper family." Yet, from this struggling family, all seven daughters graduated from Big State University. "My mother—her university days were incredibly successful, being the belle and the queen and everything else . . . and she said: 'Look upon these days—these school days—as the best years of your life.'"

Like mother (in some ways) like daughters: "I have two sisters, both older, two years apart. Both my sisters were highly successful . . . it was inbred in us that you must succeed and do your best. And we all came to [Big State U.] and we all pledged to my mother's sorority."

As we will see in later chapters, what has happened to this woman after college could not have been scripted and is simply a remarkable story. But the focus here is why people go—or don't go—to college. What we now know is that "just because" is a correct and simple answer that is the result of years of effort.

College Because It Is Easier

Me: "Did you enjoy college?"
Chuck: "Not particularly. Again, we'd still be talking about a struggle."
Me: "Yeah, but this struggle you won."
Chuck: "Oh, so what?"

CHUCK

From what I heard in discussions with the people I interviewed for this book, the first twelve years of school were difficult. (They probably still are.) Either socially or academically or both, school—and the growing up during those years—was tough.

The number of things that go on—the sorting out of family and friends; the general learning about how to come to terms with the world; baseball and jacks and sex; reading and gym and the summer—is as overwhelming as it can be fun. Or awful.

And it all takes place when you are relatively short and certainly powerless.

The trite phrase is that youth is wasted on the young. As I get more involved in the problem, I am becoming convinced that a better trite phrase would be this: Only in your youth are you strong enough to be young. If you enjoy having only a limited say in a world almost entirely not of your making—and you lack the ability and knowledge to do many things even if you do have a say—then being young is dynamite.

As we saw with Carol, one way to get through being young is to be rich and to have your life "tracked" in a fairly acceptable (middle-class American, to be sure) way. The man about to be introduced was neither rich nor tracked in that way.

Chuck was a man of medium height and weight. He had brownish hair, thick glasses, and seemed nervous. He appeared to be in good health, although it was clear he neither spent much time outside nor engaged in sports. I believe that Chuck was fairly intelligent and successful at what he was doing; yet he was a college graduate who was hardly able to read. Much of his life had been affected by a specific learning disability, which had led him to consider his environment in a particular way.

We can begin to understand Chuck by listening to what he said about his parents.

"My mother is from Tennessee and, as she said, she was raised in the hills of Tennessee and her biggest thing—she got out of it. I think at sixteen she got married, which is a way that gals get out of it."

The family lived in a large midwestern city; and when Chuck was three or four, his parents were divorced. It was the depression, and his mother was too poor to take care of her three children, so "I went to live with a . . . religious family. I went to a Lutheran school for the first year, grade school—I mean, I had a real tough time in the school. Very tough time. . . . And then my mother remarried when I was about seven or eight."

His stepfather ("He was a very good guy; I can't imagine why anyone would take on three kids") moved the family to the Northwest. But that is getting ahead of ourselves. While still in the Midwest, Chuck worked. At the age of eight or nine, he was working the cash register in the drugstore where his mother worked. Also, by the time he was ten, he was going alone to the movies at night.

He was an independent young person who was, in his own words, always a "good boy." Yet:

"Probably one of the most difficult things then, as it was always, was school. . . . I often wonder *why* it was so difficult, and I wonder, now, there is a good possibility (and I'll *never* know) that it could be, maybe, possibly, eyesight. I didn't get glasses until I was probably in the second grade. I will reverse numbers, you know—even words, when I glance at them, they can be various—anywhere close to what it should be, and I would never detect someone else misspelling it because I can't spell—I can't hardly—even now. Someone will—someone will give me something to write . . . and I'll—maybe I'm thinking too far ahead or something, but I can't even begin to spell. I mean, I just—so whether or not the spelling, which would be the eyesight to some extent—I don't know, whatever the reason, I did have a very tough time in school."

To hear his stories about school is to believe it was tough. Chuck understood that school is a top-middle-bottom arrangement, and his was a view from the bottom.

"In every class that I can remember . . . you can tell pretty much who's the top student and who's the bottom student, right?

"For some reason, I don't know why, there was always one person in class dumber than me. When I say dumber, he would always be the low one in class, mainly because he couldn't—he was totally dumb, or, not totally but almost—slow. Now, I always came up second. . . ."

A story: "One teacher I remember, a science teacher. She had within the class—she had the ones that could not do the work, and she always put them at one table—I think she called it the pansy table—and naturally I was the president. You know—I mean, I remember her."

It got to this: "I didn't like—this was—I did not join in: Very few things would I join in. I didn't do it, and I did not like [it]. . . ."

It is necessary to say that there were, of course, good stories about growing up. But there always seemed to be an edge to those stories. After talking about the friends Chuck played with, we had this exchange:

Me: "Do you figure those were happy years? Pretty good years?"
Chuck: "O.K. I don't know what happy is, but it was O.K. I wouldn't want to go back."
Me: "O.K. O.K."
Chuck: "But I don't think many people would want to go back."
Me: "Were the holidays big things? Birthdays, Christmas?"
Chuck: "Christmas—all parents make a big deal out of Christmas —I never really—Christmas Day, even now—and I never really did like it that much. O.K. Fine, you open up your presents—that was nice, but to me holidays are nonproductive. I feel kind of a letdown because I'm generally going and doing things. But I don't think it is just me; I think it's many, many people."

So much for carefree, happy youth. Like just about everyone, Chuck was passed from one grade to the next. He went to high school, but not for very long. "Half a year. And then I quit . . . and I went to cooking school. I was sixteen then. I just turned sixteen . . . you had to be at least sixteen to get into trade school." He enjoyed cooking and found a school that taught it. The trade school was better for him than a regular academic program. He stayed for almost two years and, at the age of seventeen, joined the navy. Why the navy? For what sounded like good reasons:

"The army would be worse, because you sure wouldn't want to march around and camp out; I'm not a camper. The marines would absolutely have killed me, and I recognized that at an early age. The air force—again, sight—not that that would have mattered much. I actually tried to get in the coast guard first. Boy, am I glad I did not, because I'm sure I would've been seasick. Fortunately, they did not take me."

The military was, it seems, a mixed experience for Chuck. He went into the service as a trained cook but was put to work in the commissary. The logic of that decision is lost on all but a military mind. For him, one important thing that came from the navy experience was that he came into contact with college-educated people.

Me: "And the people who had been in college—you wanted to be more like them?"

Chuck: "Well, not necessarily more like them; well, maybe more like them. Leastways, *I didn't want to have the hassles of the noneducated.*"

An interesting thought, but hardly his only one about a college education. Here are four more:

"I'm against education in some ways, but I know we have to have it, because if you go to the other extreme, that's no good.

"Everyone was coming out of the service; then you automatically started going to college. Even though I'm sure I decided to do it, . . . the reason maybe why I decided to do it was because everyone else was doing it.

"In order to get a job in that period of time and maybe even today, you must have a college degree. I mean, it's a must. . . . How do you get a job? You get a degree first; now it really doesn't matter which degree. It can be in BA [business administration], it can be in science, and you can go down and work for a bank. But if you don't have a degree, you don't go to work for the bank.

"Like I say . . . as an undergraduate, you went to get a degree. And —and for no other reason, really."

After the navy, he went back to trade school; and this time, instead of learning a trade, he took college prep courses. English and the like. He worked hard and did all right. Soon, Chuck applied to, was accepted at, and attended Big State University.

Not Going

"... and I thought, 'Well, gee whiz, I'll go to college and I'll learn something.' "

ALFRED

To have seen Alfred's hands—they were soft, uncalloused, and seemed a little disconnected from their owner—one might have guessed he made medieval musical instruments. That would have been a good and an accurate guess, but like most facts, it would have left out more than it revealed.

Alfred made his living as a longshoreman. He was in his thirties, about six feet tall, as muscular as you might expect, and was a nervous, sensitive man. As we shall see, his growing up was unpleasant, his schooling possibly worse, and his eventual life in the world something of a personal triumph.

He was enrolled in and attended classes at two different community colleges, but it is safe to say he was not college-educated. That is not to say he was not exposed to all of the pressures and myths about post-secondary education. In fact, he felt all of the pressure and made all of the decisions most Americans have to make about college.

Alfred's grandparents were not native to the Northwest. Of his father's parents: "My grandfather . . . he was Irish; . . . my grandmother was German, a fat German lady." His maternal grandmother was from Norway and his grandfather was from America. Both sets of grandparents were poor, as were his parents. His mother and father came to the West Coast because of work.

His family moved around a great deal, looking for work. "I guess they had some financial problems and things like that, and I remember sleeping on the road down in California, and living in a motel kind of thing. I lived in [another place] which was then a housing project for very, very poor people. . . . They were very poor, very trashy people. . . ."

In the early 1950s the family settled in a large city in the Northwest, and Alfred's father became a longshoreman. That, naturally enough, meant a change for the family. The change was not a particularly good one.

About his father: "He had gotten into the union, so he had more money, but I've always had a father that would go out and drink and come home drunk. See, at this time . . . a typical longshoreman—to be a longshoreman you wore a white hat and you drank like hell and you were a drunken longshoreman. It was a longshoreman's social thing, and it wasn't until, I believe, that I got into the union that the old-time real drinkers stopped. There were a few old-time drinkers left, but they . . . the young fellows aren't drinking like that; they smoke a lot of dope, and drop a lot of dope."

The family moved, he said, "from one ghetto to another ghetto," most of the time he was growing up. His parents were unhappy with each other, and his father—always rough with his mother—finally stopped physically abusing her when she began to call the police.

It was from that environment that Alfred went to school. It might be useful to begin by summing up.

> *Me:* "In those first six grades—through elementary school—were they good years, did you have a good time?"
> *Alfred:* "Well, no; not really. I don't think I had a good childhood; I really didn't like it."

And moving, for a young person? "Most of the time I was the new kid, and I . . . like one time . . . there was an incident. I was nominated to be class president or something like that, *and I could hardly believe it.* I wasn't elected, but that was—I made an impression on some people. I think . . . my first impression of people—no, their first impression of me—they like me until they get to know me."

About school in particular: "I think it was in, like, sixth grade, I kind of decided that I was going to live my own life and not be affected by other people's life as far as my lunch was concerned. The rule was you didn't go off the lunch room . . . and, well, gee whiz, I sure would like to have a, a banana split; so I went off to this place and had a banana split and that was nice. And the school lunches weren't really that great. And another rule was you ate your plate—no matter what was on it, you ate it."

The combination of bad food and wanting to be himself got Alfred into trouble:

"There was this teacher in charge and she said something to the effect, 'Well, you aren't getting your money's worth if you're not eating this.' 'Well, you mean I don't have to pay—I don't have to buy all this? O.K.' 'Oh no, oh no—you gotta pay the whole amount.' 'O.K. —I'll pay the whole amount.' We finally got around to it—I'd pay the whole amount, but I wouldn't have to eat all this, and I wouldn't eat that. And she said, 'Well, if you don't eat your plate, you can't eat here.' 'O.K.'

"Well, other teachers and the principal was called in. She said to somebody else who relayed it to me that I was the most obstinate child that they'd ever come across. And I think my principal said that also, but *they really couldn't understand.*"

The stories he told of grade school through high school carried much the same theme. His efforts to be independent were not understood.

His self-evaluation: "I was just a kid that went to school, and then came back, you know, just to be a good kid—back and forth, back and forth."

And his evaluation of school: "Well, let's put it this way, when you wanted to be responsible for yourself, well, you couldn't be responsible—there was no outlet. You went out at recess time and played and you came back . . . just repetition, repetition, everything was repetitious in school. And if you didn't learn it—repetitious, repetitious, repetitious, all over again, and it wasn't even in a new form or anything."

By the time he got to high school, Alfred ". . . wanted to be a scientist, because they did this and they did that and they knew a lot of stuff, but I wasn't really that good in science. I took some science courses in high school, and I really didn't ̣o that good. . . . I was a very poor learner.

"Maybe it was [in] grade school that I started reading. Well, when my mother would stop reading her comic books, I would start reading them; so I could read comic books. I could never spell too good, which I think was really a hindrance as far as school work went—I couldn't spell, so I couldn't do anything."

It seemed overwhelmingly wrong and difficult; so, "I started asking questions about what good is this going to be after I get out of high school, and no one had the answer. . . . You know, how does this relate to what I'm going to do . . . I would start asking those kind of questions, and a lot of the answers in high school would really turn me off to high school, but I just went to high school, and that was that."

The fact for Alfred was this: "If you [were] just physically there, they'd pass you . . . you just keep going there and eventually they'll pass you . . . and that's more or less what I did. Overall it was really disgusting. The closer I got to graduation, it was like I really hadn't accomplished anything and frankly I didn't. . . ."

Those years were not entirely trauma-filled. There were some courses he enjoyed: art, drama, and machine shop. Alfred had a friend, and together they worked on old cars. Also, during that period he became a longshoreman: "I was eighteen . . . and I started on the waterfront. I went to an executive board meeting and it was, 'Son of bitches, bastards, cocksuckers!' The whole—all those words and worse, and 'I'll throw you out of this window. There's been more than one guy who's been thrown out this window!' And they were actually threatening lives of each other."

He hated it, and was repulsed by it. As we will see later, much effort had gone into getting distance from his work.

He went to two community colleges and did not do very well. But the interesting question is, why did he go? Why, after all that was ugly in public school, would he want to continue? His reasons:

"I came out of high school and I didn't learn a damn thing, and I didn't want to live with my folks the rest of my life. Besides, they might die, and well, here I was, and I thought, 'Well, gee whiz, I'll go to college and I'll learn something.'

"Some of my friends were going there, and I decided that I might as well go to college myself. I couldn't get into the classes I wanted; so I took choir or something like that.

"I didn't want to go to some college that was near my—I didn't want to live at home, let's put it that way, but I wanted to go on to college. I really couldn't get into the [Big State University]; so I figured I could get [into a community college]."

I think we are still left with the question, *Why?* Certainly what Alfred said was true, but there was more. Hopefully, as we get more deeply involved with the idea—the myth—of education, we will get closer to understanding the *why* questions.

Computers, But Not College

"If you want something, you just hammer at it long enough; you're going to get it."

CARL

We saw Carl in his office; at least we did most of the time. He was the head of a company that provided a computer service to retail businesses. When we saw him, his desk was always clear, his office neat, and his attention on our talks.

Carl was in his early thirties, of medium height and weight. He dressed in doubleknit coats and wore ties that did not always match. He appeared much like the stereotype of his position: a middle-class businessman. But, as we know, that kind of statement is neither a very helpful nor a very accurate description. A story may help make Carl clearer to you.

Carl, like everyone we talked with, was nervous during our discussions. He was more articulate than most, and very good to talk with; but he was very insecure. That was in his office. We had one group meeting, and he was relaxed and quite funny. Yet, in his office, he never failed to apologize about how he felt or how little sleep he had had the night before. There was always a reason for his "not being very sharp today."

In fact, he seemed quite sharp.

He was from a small town on the coast of Washington State. His training was in computers, and he was very much involved in being a businessman. His ideas of education revolved around technical training for a career, and in a very direct way he made decisions based on that idea. First, his past.

Carl's family had lived in the Northwest for some time: "My [maternal] great-grandfather was one of the first settlers in the area. On my father's side, let's see—I was adopted when I was about a year old. There are some things that I'm still kind of sketchy on, that I don't know. But I only met my real father once."

When Carl was young, his family moved around a great deal. They moved down and up the West Coast as his father worked in a service station, in a butcher shop, on a log boom, and on the harbor. Finally he worked in a mill.

The family settled on a small farm, and his father worked in the mill: "Well, we hit hard times out there; if we didn't farm, we wouldn't have eaten. My Dad just got started with the mill and the mill wasn't making it, and they worked for nothing a couple of weeks like that, and then they reached the point where they worked for $1.50 an hour. So the farm was our real salvation . . . we even raised pheasants one year, and a garden."

The moving from place to place was difficult: "I think there's a problem with moving a lot. You don't get involved in things and you don't get established: you don't get recognized by the kids; it's very frustrating."

Towns came and went, but his family stayed the same.

His father:

"He was very hard; you know, strict discipline. He believed in a good spanking, I mean a good one; so when he said to do something, by God, you did it and didn't think twice about it. I had a father that was very hard, and if I wanted to do something, I had to learn how to work him so that I could do what I wanted to do. . . .

"Oh, I think he really cared, but he didn't know how to show you. Well, I know he did. But he didn't know how to show that he really cared. He had no affection. . . . No, once Dad got mad, that was it; you'd best just shut up."

His mother: "Well, my mother is somewhat contained, a little bit reserved. She likes people. My brother-in-law, for example—now that my sister died and so forth, he finds he's able to talk to her. She's the kind of person that you can sit down and really talk to. She's a mother, quote, unquote."

His sisters: "I had three sisters; so I had somebody to manipulate. O.K.?"

Carl's schooling, in his estimation, was hurt by moving. He had been to four schools by the fourth grade. Beyond the "getting established" problem of moving, there were many academic problems: "They could never figure out what my problems were. That's another problem: Your problems are never defined."

And there were some troubles: "I was better at arithmetic than at reading or spelling and English. I was very, very bad; reading I was poor, and spelling poor. I did reading and spelling poorly. And arithmetic, I was good, not excellent."

His attitude about going to a remedial reading group in junior high school gave an interesting insight into who he was: "Well you know [pauses], as I recall, I don't recall that I had to go to class, it was just requested that I go or something. I thought it was a good idea. I believe we got involved with counselors then. And I realized that it was needed, and so I went; but I really didn't like it. But I think I had one advantage, that I was able to realize my faults and did go and do something."

Carl's family was involved with his schoolwork: "My father would put on a lot of pressure: You know, you'd come home with a report card and he'd get all upset; and if you got C's you shoulda got B's, and if you got B's you shoulda got A's. You'd sit through a four-hour lecture and really not accomplish anything, and it was really frustrating. Not the kind of pressure you need, not the supportive-type pressure."

And Carl's attitude: "I always found it pretty easy to pull down a C. If I pulled down a C, that's good."

When he was in high school, Carl was very busy. He made his C's, finally lived in a place long enough to be known and became popular, and he worked.

Worked at home: "I'd get up at six in the morning and build the fires. . . . We had a fireplace in the living room, a wood heater in the den, and a wood cookstove in the kichen. I'd build a fire in all of them. Get the fire going and then about 6:30 go out and milk the cow . . . so that by the time I got the fires built and the cows milked and the chickens fed and everything, it was time to get ready and catch the bus for school."

Worked for money: "You know, the twelfth grade I worked four hours a night after school in the foundry."

He was, not surprisingly, subjected to pressures about attending college. "Primarily, when I left high school, as everyone finds true, the pressure is to go to college. From home and society and the whole bit. . . . But I just really wasn't that interested in school, you know, and I—school wasn't my thing."

After high school, he did leave his parent's house, and he did attend a community college.

Carl: "I left home after I graduated from high school."
Interviewer: "So that was a fairly big moment?"
Carl: "Yeah. I can't remember what took place, a big argument or something, not with my folks but with my sisters. I went into my room, packed my clothes, and left. I had a job; I didn't have to stay there."

And he got married.

Interviewer: "So, you left home, your house, first, and you got yourself a place . . . and you were still dating your wife?"
Carl: "Yes."
Interviewer: "When did you get married?"
Carl: "When she told me we'd better get married!"

For a while Carl studied engineering at Small Town Community College. That, and he worked while his wife finished high school. But he did not enjoy school. In his words: "School just wasn't the thing." Work became more important.

"I was working on the paper machine which, if you enjoy the work, is a very good job. You can work your way up to a fairly well-respected job. But it still wasn't what I wanted to do, and I still didn't really know what I wanted to do. So I was talking to a lot of my friends and so forth, and some of them were taking data processing. And that sounded very exciting; so I immediately signed up for trade school and data processing."

And he went to a data-processing school, and he prospered. The details come in later chapters.

There is one last important topic. It has to do with Carl's basic understanding about his relationship to the world. It can be seen clearly enough in the following statements, which he made to describe his attitude about three different events in his life:

"I [have] a lot of stick-to-it-iveness, you know. Just get in there and just hang on and just keep pounding away after something, and you'll get it.

"If you want something, you just hammer at it long enough; you're going to get it.

"I always try to work with the philosophy that where there's a will, there's a way."

What Do We Know? Is It Helpful? What Can We Say?

The question of this chapter is, roughly, why do people go—or not go —to college? Are we any smarter now? Just what do we know, and is it helpful?

Earlier I mentioned all of the studies on why people go to college. It makes some sense to review that material now as a counterpoint to what you have just read. To make the studies a little more manageable, we should divide them into two categories. The categories are motives for doing things; one is the *because* motive, the other is the *in-order-to* motive.

The terms, which come from Alfred Schutz,[1] certainly need explaining. Schutz writes that we can begin to understand why people take actions by examining their motives. One type of motive has to do with a person's surroundings and the pressures produced by people therein. These are because motives. For example, a person goes to college *because* his or her parents demand it, or *because* everyone else is going, or *because* it is the "normal" thing to do.

The other kind of motive, the in-order-to, has to do with the end product of an action. In other words, the reason for doing something takes place in the future perfect tense. A person might go to college, then, *in order to* have a degree. The idea of college, the time and energy and process itself, is really not considered. The reason that a person goes to college, given this motive, is to reach the final state of being a college graduate.

The in-order-to motives studied the most have to do with money. More exactly, the assumption is made that people go to college *in order to* get high-paying jobs when they graduate. Serious scholars are capable of writing, ". . . [the educational system] is best understood as an institution which serves to perpetuate the social relationships of economic life through which these patterns are set, by facilitating a smooth integration of youth into the labor force."[2]

If that is true, and the value of college is truly a dollar value, then one could study parts of in-order-to motives fairly easily. Let me give some examples:

"Education and Performance: Some Problems." In this study, we learn that "people with college degrees do not necessarily get higher salaries or more interesting jobs."[3]

"Are We Overstressing the Returns from a College Education?" Here, we are warned about the possibility of diminishing and "even negative returns to investment in education at the margin."[4]

"What Good Are the Liberal Arts?" Well, people with liberal arts degrees can "sell" themselves on the job market as being special because of their "in-depth" educational background.[5]

"The Declining Value of College Going." This indicates you might not make as much money as you had hoped after getting a degree; it does not indicate whether the things you learn in college might help you in other ways.[6]

"The Decline in Economic Rewards to College Education." A monograph on "the deterioration in the job market for college graduates."[7]

"Is the Value of College Going Really Declining?" An effort is made to be more "optimistic" about a college education.[8]

I remember very clearly my first reaction to this debate about the value of a college education. It was simple enough: The whole thing depressed me. Then I became fascinated that the debate was going on at all. Finally, I became convinced that people actually believe in the importance of college as a future-moneymaking activity. (Or, I suspect it is more accurate to say, as a future-moneymaking investment.)

As we interviewed people about themselves, their educations, and their lives, the economic element of education was never as clear as it seemed in the studies. Economics, in fact, was only a part of a much larger myth of education. We will see that more fully in the next chapter.

Let's go on to the because motives. These are concerned with the pressures to go to college. Here is a list of reasons (variables, if you will) concerning why people do or do not go to college.

1. Ability and parents' socioeconomic status appear to have the strongest influence of the three factors investigated. Family income is the least important.[9]

2. Economic factors are indirectly related to attending college, as they affect the "environmental conditions" that "give rise to significant personality variables."[10]

3. One major reason for not attending college is a preference on the part of the individual for going to work.[11]

4. Immediate family and other relatives consistently rank first as the group urging the decision to go to college.[12]

5. People whose fathers were in skilled or semi-skilled occupations are more interested in vocational training than in college, than are those whose fathers were in professional positions.[13]

6. Some important data: Parental encouragement is an indepen-

dent variable, not an intervening one.[14] (Odd, it never feels that way when you are a parent.)

7. Parents exert greatest influence on sons; peers exert more influence on young women.[15]
8. The more education the father has, the greater the likelihood that the daughter will go to college.[16]
9. Young men with low grades are more likely to attend college than young women with low grades.[17]

I certainly do not mean for you to have the idea that this is an exhaustive list. But this is, I believe, a good enough sample to give you a sense of the facts available to us. It is not easy to correctly characterize the studies. They are accurate, but not right; they are not wrong, but certainly you could not call them correct.

The strain is simple enough to understand. Each little study is such a very small part of reality that it is wrong because of gross exclusion. When what we do not know so overwhelms what we do know, what we do know loses meaning. Put differently, without a context, it is difficult to give a fact much meaning. In such cases it is common for us to assume our own context so that whatever the fact is automatically has the meaning we have implied it should have.

What I would like to argue is that to know what college means to people, one must understand both their way of seeing the world and the world in which they are living. For example, we know that it does not seem to matter who you are, how much income your family has, or whether you want a job or not—if you live in America there is an enormous amount of pressure on you to attend college.

That is a fact of the world we live in. How each of us handles that pressure has to do with each individual's understanding of the world.

Of course there are relationships between being able to afford college and attending college, but to dwell on those relationships really obscures what goes on. College—at least the decision to go to college—is often a monument to social pressure. It is a living reminder that there are promises and dreams built into the idea of a college degree, and we all must deal with that fact.

The myth seems as strong for those who are rich and make good grades as for those who are poor and can neither read nor spell.

It seems to me that if we begin to understand the reasons why it is "natural" that we must decide about going to college, we will know something about the United States. If we can figure out some of the effects of college—not financial effects but rather the effects on the quality of our day-to-day lives—we will know more about ourselves. Depending on what we find, we can begin to think about what college is and what it might become.

But before all that, we should have a sense of the context and some of the working assumptions of the book.

NOTES

1. Alfred Schutz, *The Phenomenology of the Social World* (Chicago: Northwestern University Press, 1967). See Chapter 2.
2. Samuel Bowles and Herbert Gintis, *Schooling in Capitalist America* (New York: Basic Books, Inc., 1976), p. 11.
3. Ivar Berg, "Education and Performance: Some Problems," *Journal of Higher Education,* March 1972.
4. Edward Renshaw, "Are We Overestimating the Returns from a College Education?" *School Review,* May 1972.
5. John Munschauer, "What Good Are the Liberal Arts?" *Journal of National Associations of College Admissions Counselors,* April 1974.
6. Richard Freeman and Herbert Holloman, "The Declining Value of College Going," *Change,* September 1975.
7. Richard Freeman, "The Decline in the Economic Rewards to College Education," *Change,* February 1976.
8. David Witmer, "Is the Value of College Going Really Declining?" *Change,* December 1976.
9. Sandra Christensen et al., "Factors Affecting College Attendance," *Journal of Human Resources,* Spring 1975.
10. Benjamin Bailey, *Characteristics of High School Seniors as Related to Subsequent College Attendance* (Morgantown, West Va.: West Virginia University, 1966).
11. Leland Medsker et al., *The Influence of Different Types of Public Higher Institutions on College Attendance from Varying Socioeconomic and Ability Levels* (Berkeley: Center for the Study of Higher Education, 1965).
12. Edward Harris, "Consistency of Group Influence and College Attendance," *College Student Survey,* Winter 1970.
13. Colorado State University, *A Continuation of the 1963 High School Graduates Follow-Up Study* (Ft. Collins: Colorado State University Press, Sept., 1966).
14. Richard Rehberg et al., *Educational Orientations and Parental Encouragement—An Intervening or an Independent Variable* (Eugene, Oregon: Center for Advanced Study of Educational Administration, 1966). Can you imagine arguing that parents are not an intervening variable? Somehow, the technical language of variables is richer in irony than in information.
15. New York State Education Department, *A Longitudinal Study of the Barriers Affecting the Pursuit of Higher Education by New York State High School Seniors, Phase One* (Albany: August 1969).
16. Charles Werts, "A Comparison of Male-Female College Attendance Possibilities," *Change,* March 1967.
17. Ibid.

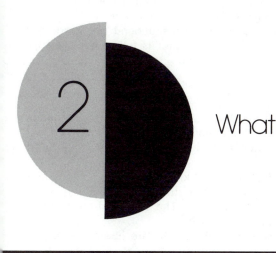

2

What

Yet for all of us there were moments when *the game we were agreeing to play* could not stand up to events. . . .

—Doris Lessing

Don't ever bet against paradox, ladies. If complexity doesn't beat you, then paradox will.

—Tom Robbins

Every week, once a week, Friday to be exact, I get paid. It is only a modest amount of money and is certainly unimportant to all but my family, but it is a fact.

More to the point, I work at and am paid by a university. I get paid for teaching, and people actually pay to learn. Most of the time I know what I say and why. It is, of course, impossible to know if or what the students learn. There are more problems than that.

None of us, I am more and more convinced, knows what post-secondary education means. Of college, that special segment of post-secondary education, we know even less. If a technical school teaches you to be a technician, what do you think college does?

In order to even begin to answer that question, one must consider and reconsider an incredible number of issues. What follows is an exercise in considering, choosing, guessing, and general searching for the meaning, or meanings, of a college education.

Answers depend on questions. Questions depend on where you begin and which way you look. This chapter is full of the assumptions that form the background of the book.

Ways and Whys

Please excuse this line, but for all of its simplicity it says what needs to be said very accurately: Generally, people study what is most easily studied. They may choose difficult methods, but at its heart the study is easy.

More needs to be said than that. We know that the questions of a study will reflect not only the method of studying but also the prejudices of the cultural setting of the study. The setting of the study is influential in a number of important ways.

Our surroundings, the setting of the study, are liberal/corporate/capitalist ones. Major themes—among others—that seem so natural to us are equality, money, enterprise, competition, law, and the like. It would seem quite sensible that our study would reflect these concerns. If we were consciously to ignore these themes, we would be ignoring reality. Not only that, we know they are concerns that we may quantify fairly easily. Yet, if we quantify, we again fail to get a full and accurate account of our particular world.

Our study of a college education could legitimately center around how much money a college-educated person might expect to get, or even the effect of "open admissions" on equality of opportunity. We might even expect a socialist critique of education beginning with many of the same questions but with a set of biases all their own.

Such studies are informative. Not only do we get the results of research, but we also learn about the kind of questions built into how we study as well as the "natural" questions that are a product of our cultural, political, social, and economic setting.

I am not arguing that all such studies are wrong or bad or ignorant. Some of them may, in fact, be interesting and helpful. What I am arguing is that we do not know enough to judge if they are helpful studies.

We know so little about what having a college degree—or not having a college degree—means that we do not know what questions to ask. Only after we have a sense of the right questions will we start to know what kind of studies will be helpful. It seems reasonable to say that what the world does not need now is another super-sophisticated questionnaire given to a carefully selected representative sample of 250,000 people.

In any study, the *terms* and *focuses* are easily as important as the results. In a remarkable work, Hannah Arendt explores the costs of modern research that ultimately takes us from the realm of a common-sense world, the world that surrounds us, and puts us into ourselves, into our own intellectual concepts. She writes:

> ...we deal only with the patterns of our own mind, the mind which designed the instruments and put nature under its conditions...in which case the hands of an evil spirit who mocks us and frustrates our thirst for knowledge, so that wherever we search for that which we are not, we encounter only the patterns of our own minds.[1]

The desire for order, for answers, for truth is a strong and seemingly natural one. When we deal with anything—but especially when we deal with human beings—it is a desire that moves us away from seeing the multiple realities and general messiness of what goes on. Given this condition, will and belief and action become important. How analyses go on becomes central.

If we are going to begin to find the "right" questions to ask, we must start behind our current methods and our most easily quantifiable questions.

Myth

This section is concerned with something big and amorphous and real—culture—and something small and specific and singular—the individual. The tie is myth—obvious if you read the heading.

If we were involved in strict definitions, the word *myth* could never be brought up. I am not talking about "formal" myths; not those from the ancient Greeks or South Pacific natives or even Johnny Appleseed. Those are somehow too epic to apply.

Myth is used differently by anthropologists and political scientists. While an anthropologist assumes that a myth will explain the mystical origins of the world to a particular culture, for a political scientist a myth is much less grand.

Basically, I am using *myth* in the less grand way. *Myth,* as I am using it, forms part of the cultural/political/economic values of a society. It justifies, promises, encourages, and glorifies certain behaviors. For example, in the United States we can talk about the myth of free enterprise, or the myth of individualism. Even after understanding the particulars of each myth—in terms of historical fact and empirical data—we would not have a full understanding.

A myth is bigger than the sum of its parts. A key part of any myth is how much an individual believes in it. We should begin to understand and work with education as one such myth.

You know the myth wherein the poor (but honest) young person goes to college (and works!), marries his or her college love, studies hard, graduates, gets a job, raises a family, gets rich, retires, has grandchildren, moves to a sunny climate, and lives happily ever after.

Lives happily all the time. And all the sons and daughters and grandchildren go to college. And are happy. And successful. It is the American dream. Or at least, it has come to be the American dream.

The dream is firmly rooted in fact and myth. It is easily as true as it is false.

Let me try, in a straightforward way, to describe the American myth about college. The parts are these: an entry into the "degreed" class; an increased opportunity for employment; greater income, status, mobility; greater knowledge; a more rational thought process. Deeply buried is the idea that one somehow is a *better* and certainly a *happier* person by virtue of having had a college education.

Myth, in our telling, is what anthropologists understand as a "sacred tale." While never quite formalized or authorized in either telling or writing, it is a tale that permeates our surroundings. From the vague peer pressure of *Which college are you going to?* to the straight-ahead "track" for college you are put on in high school, the myth lives.

One of the more curious aspects of myths is that they contain a mix of truth and—for want of a better term—ungrounded promise. Let's take up our myth, in a very cursory way, in that order.

Truth. There is every kind of good evidence that should convince us that a person can make more money if he or she gets a college education. Further, there are whole sets of vocations that require "higher" education of their members. In broader context, our documentedly technological society needs highly educated individuals to keep it in repair and make it more refined.

It seems silly to suggest that there be apprentice nuclear physicists or journeyman biochemists. No, our society needs "higher" education, and those who have it are on the track of getting ahead.

Not only does it lead to money; it leads to power. Those who do not become scientific technicians can always become attorneys. Lawyers are often simply social technicians who amass both money and power. Since the Mayflower Compact, our social affairs have been put in legal language. The Constitution is our sacred text; our judges wear robes.

Those parts of our myth concentrated on economics are mostly true. Even the studies mentioned in Chapter 1—the ones containing data about the "declining value" of college—argue that the decline is relative to a time when a smaller percentage of people got degrees. A person can still expect to come out economically ahead if he or she attends college. Put a little differently, there is some economic truth to our education myth.

Beyond that truth, where myth is full of fancy, there is trouble. The groundless promises somehow sound simple-minded when they are laid out. We know that to have more money does not automatically ensure more (or less) happiness. We know that spending time in college (even if it is spent studying) does not mean that a person will be wise or knowledgeable. I suspect that good parents will still love you and good friends still like you even if you do not happen to have a college degree.

But it never *seems* like that.

The myth is full of misleading implications about and correlations among happiness and money and friends and wisdom and God knows what all.

The most instructive parts of the myth are largely those untrue elements that hold so much promise. What we shall see is that it takes some effort to re-view post-secondary education without using the normal, everyday, some-true, some-false myth that permeates our American culture.

The Obvious and a Warning

The question or, more accurately, an important question we are asking has to do with this: What does higher education mean? A question of values is not necessarily a question of money. Economics is not the basis of this study of education.

It will take some explaining simply to talk about how to get at the question of meaning. I am, in order, going to do the following: (1) say the obvious; (2) write about what I am not doing; and (3) explore some of the pre-judgments that form the background of the study.

The obvious. While the exotic is often fun, it makes sense here to simply start with the obvious: Higher education is surrounded by myth. In order to get at meaning, we must take that myth as a fact of our lives. We are carriers of the myth; it lives in and through us. Certainly we can get over it, be cured of it, even have another myth replace it; but no matter what the case, the myth has meaning for us and an effect on us.

It is possible to make the focus sharper. One way to get at and more fully understand the implications of a myth is to study the life of an individual, or, more properly, the lives of individuals. But *people.* One at a time. If we are really good at it, we might study those people as they go through a day. The ingredients of such a study are seemingly easily come by—we each are affected by myth and we each have a day. Implied (so much for simplicity) is a universe of unexplained and unknowable happenings.

Let me stop the obvious here, and try to make clear one thing I am not doing. I *will not* argue that, in a day in the life of an individual, higher education is the most important element of that day. No, no, no. I am not making that argument. Any day is a complex of events and memories and futures and strange actions that have little to do with education.

But formal education *is* a part, a piece, a slice that adds to or subtracts from our day. It is more important for some people, less so for others, but rarely the most important part for anyone. As we get more involved with the discussion, I will repeat the warning. Perspective, after all, is not all that destructive if only periodically invoked.

Meaning and Prejudice

Near the end of the book there is a full discussion of what, intellectually, informs the method used for this study. It is fairly particular, it is critique as well as things more positive, and one does not need to read it first to understand what comes before. However, it is important that there be a few pages of explanation about the world and people and education and about how those may be fit together.

Put differently, it is necessary for you to know something about my prejudices. It only makes sense to know the context of what is being said, for—I suppose this is a very primary prejudice—meaning depends in critical ways on context.

The words *incompleteness, movement,* and *uncertainty* convey a certain sense of the world we live in. The past keeps imposing on us, the present is a clutter of events no one can control, and the future seems to constantly and unpredictably pull us places we cannot imagine. And as long as we live with others, that will be the state of our affairs. "God's will" has lost its viability as an explanation for events, and even scientists, who sometime seem to play God, readily admit that the essence of reality is a mystery to us.

The world around us—our reality—should not be thought of as static, as a still life, as a color photograph. They are appealing images, just misleading (read *wrong*). We can see that even at a simple level. Just look around at the room (I assume you are in a room) you happen to be in and try hard to convince yourself that reality, at some stage, is little more than a still life.

But to look at that room is to invest it with meaning. The meaning you now have, the meaning you have gathered over all the years you have lived, the future you want—that is the meaning I am talking about. Your past, your intentions, your present mood all interact and help make the reality of the room you are in. Even the "still life" of a reading room is full of activity and meaning.

Directly across from me (I am sitting on the left-hand side of the sofa in my living room) is a clock on the fireplace mantel. Beyond its moving parts and its "telling" me the current time, it helps me open up my past and future. The clock was my grandfather's wedding gift to my parents. The clock is full of my growing up, my parents, my wishes for my children. It evokes more thoughts than I can consciously deal with.

The clock is an extreme example. Yet, it is difficult for me to think of this—or of *any*—room as a still life. Each object and its arrangement are at least in part subject to my memories, fantasies, projections, and more and more.

If we are at all interested in accuracy, it seems necessary to "picture" reality by using words of emotion and/or movement.[2] The language of philosophy is sometimes centered on words of change and away from static descriptions. Even language itself is understood as a creative activity.[3] This language has now become a familiar part of our common reality and is mentioned here simply to help you know the background of this study.

We begin in a world that has been unstuck.

The world of people is as confusing and complex and muddled as any part of reality. Maybe more so. One way to make getting through life (or, equally difficult, a day) easier is to be a member of a culture. In an overly simple way, people get together and agree on how they are going to understand reality; what will be given reward and punishment; what is right and wrong, good and bad, true and false, important and unimportant, meaningful and meaningless.

Institutions are set up to enforce and re-enforce those things. As numbers of people increase and issues become more complicated, more and more institutions with specialized power come into being.

Also, and equally important to ongoing cultures, there are the stories of justification and promise that people share. These stories, or myths, are good guidelines for knowing what is expected in any given society. The institutions as well as the stories and myths of a society help tie things together, help us make some sense of the diversity and contradiction that surround us.

In other words, from physical force (police, punishment, and the like) to fantasy (Are you *certain,* deep in your heart, that George Washington *never* told a lie? Or that always telling the truth is a virtue anyway?), we learn what the world *should* be, according to the standards of those around us. That "should be" is a people-created set of values that helps make life more comprehensible.

While the above description is correct enough, there are bothersome problems with it. Something is left out, and that something—individuals—is central to meaning. We know that people are more than carriers of myth and mindless furtherers of cultural biases. In our Western sense of things, the striking elements of humanity are plurality and diversity.

We are much the same, each of us; yet we are never the same: never have the same past, experience, or certainty so that we share the same meanings or feelings. This endless diversity in the setting of ultimate chaos leads to no great optimism when one thinks about how to study and understand people and their social, political, economic, and cultural setting.

"No great optimism" is misleading. We can be sure people are exposed to (even schooled in) certain common experiences and pressures. We can be sure that there is a multiplicity of truths and meanings that surround us.[4] I'm always pleased to think we can learn some of those truths and meanings.

Even given our more modest aims in our search for meanings, how do we do it? Where do we look? What do we do?

People in Particular

To find meaning, the kind that is apparent every day but seemingly so hard to find in a formal study, one must somehow study individuals as they seem to themselves and as they interact with the people and institutions around themselves. Also, to always remember that actions take place in a cultural context. I am not suggesting therapy for 230,000,000 Americans so they can adjust to society, nor does it make much sense to begin by changing society without knowing why, or for whom, the change is being made.

In order to write about people, one must do at least two bits of background work. The first has to do with biography and stories,[5] the second with the notion of wisdom.

Each life is an incomplete story, one that is tied into others' lives, others' stories and events, and tied in unknowable ways. These ties and connections help form fabrics and meanings that are central parts of our reality. While that seems self-evidently clear, it is not always easy to study the self-evident. There are at least two parts of people's stories important for us to remember.

The first part involves the interrelationship of stories. When a person does something—especially something involving speech or action—there is no way to know its consequences. Even the reasons for actions and the intended results are never wholly clear. As we saw in Chapter 1, a simple decision about attending college can be remarkably complicated. Much of human interaction may be realistically understood, in part, as many series of events stemming from multiple reactions to the same thing. More to the point, a person has no control over how a personal act is perceived. The other half of that point is that an individual is responsible for his or her actions.

We come to a curious conclusion. An individual is known by his or her actions—or stories—yet has little say over how they are understood. Human interaction is partially the activity of acting on stories that each of us understands in different and sometimes unique ways. I will come back to this in a few paragraphs.

The second part of what we should remember involves the idea that life is an incomplete story. We have seen some of that. We do not know the full effect of any one action. We may partially know how it begins, what the underlying motivation was, the initial audience, and so on, but we can never know all of the places it goes, all of the meanings it is given, all of the effects it has.

This is equally stark, maybe even more so: While we are alive, our stories have not ended. If we live in a world that is constantly unsettled, we too stay unsettled. Our stories, and their meanings, may change as the context is changed. We may see this most easily in politics, in which someone is periodically "resurrected." For example, Harry Truman became more popular for his honesty and straightforwardness as Lyndon Johnson and Richard Nixon became less and less popular for the lack of them. Or, to put it in a more homey way, your parents become smarter as you get older. The lesson is the same: Context gives a story meaning.

Even those among us who seem to "never change" have had to fight hard against new and probably strange forces to stay the same. And what we know is that even those who "never change" are, in fact, different from what they were before.

There may well be main themes and major influences in an individual's life. A horrible event or a parent or an illness or an amazing triumph or experience may be given a central place in the understanding of an individual's actions. But in only a very, very few cases does an event dominate a whole life.[6] The complexity of our setting and of ourselves simply overwhelms any single factor.

But in doing *any* study that searches for meaning, one cannot know everything. It is only possible to concentrate on pieces, on parts of what make up an individual. We can only tell some of the stories and remember their contexts.

The second part of this discussion has to do with how we can better understand an individual on his or her own terms. Somehow, real people must appear real; they must be seen in their own settings, as active, living, breathing individuals. What needs to be developed is a combination of common sense and mystery that will allow us to study a person better.

While trying to work out various ideas,[7] I encountered different sets of problems. "Formulas" seemed to ignore important nuances, while the studies that had concentrated on individuals were blind to obvious social realities. Equally bothersome was the fact that some focuses of study were simply inappropriate for the subject of higher education. Not only was there nothing ready-made and perfect; I could not even find something imperfect that made much sense for what I was trying to do.

Let me list a combination of aims and important points I wanted to consider:

1. to know people on their own terms
2. to understand the world as changing and messy and impinging on the individual
3. to understand that the myth of higher education is a part of our environment, and that it is something with which we must come to terms
4. to acknowledge that an individual acts (and has stories), and that these actions have important meanings
5. to understand that as a social scientist, as a policy analyst, I should sort facts, make judgments, and deal with meanings and implications of social policy.

In Chapter 4 I have used the idea of wisdom to try to combine these five points. A short description of wisdom, I am convinced, is *worse* than no description at this point. It is important to say that one key to the chapter is, in Jean-Paul Sartre's words, "to reintroduce the unsurpassible singularity of the human adventure" into our understanding of the world.

It is clear that my sense of the world permeates the judgments made—from the original judgment about the importance of judgments to the stories I choose to repeat about the people with whom I have talked. My hope is that by using as much material from the talks as possible, I will minimize the imposing of my will.

Of course, this is not a unique problem. Let me quote:

> Thus science is much closer to myth than a scientific philosophy is prepared to admit. It is one of the many forms of thought that have been developed by man, and not necessarily the best. It is conspicuous, noisy, and imprudent, but is inherently superior only for those who have already decided in favour of a certain ideology, or

who have accepted it without ever having examined its advantages and its limits.[8]

Our tasks, then, are these:

1. We must deal with people in particular. People one at a time.
2. To best do this, we must know their stories, through their accounting of past ideas and actions as told both in the present and projected into the future.
3. We must not forget that we are studying Americans in America. We are listening to stories from people who are in a particular political/economic/cultural/social setting that produces powerful sets of demands.
4. Finally, we are interested in focusing on one set of demands—one set of demands firmly based in reason and promise—the demands contained in the myth that surrounds higher education.

I think it is only fair to add that these tasks are impossible. Of course, that is a petty, even silly reason not to experiment—not to see how much can be learned. One of the most endearing virtues of science is that no experiment is a failure. Each experiment teaches something. It was Edison who, after a thousand failures at trying to invent the electric light, said without dismay that he now knew a thousand ways not to make an electric light. Or at least that is the story.

In this kind of study failure is not the most obvious alternative to success. When people and myth are at the center of a study, the calculation has more to do with illumination, degrees of light and darkness, and clarity and murkiness than with the more reassuring standards of finding a truth or a bunch of lies.

I am fully aware that I am suggesting odd standards for judgment, that they seem a poor basis for any policy analysis. But I think they make sense, and for the rest of the book I hope I can make that clear.

In the final chapter there are conclusions and suggestions that it seemed fair to draw from the evidence of the rest of the book. The punch line is this: The debates about liberal arts versus technical education may be interesting but often ignore very important points. Whether one has a liberal arts or a technical education in college may not be an overwhelmingly critical variable.

What I will argue is that colleges and universities should reorganize around unified principles—or ideologies—in order to help students make more sense out of the world. The reorganization would affect all aspects of schooling.

Like most punch lines, everything makes more sense once you have heard the whole story. Certainly this is not the place to present an in-depth defense of my conclusions.

The Basics

There are some practical details—as well as decisions based on taste—that should be explained. The easiest way of doing that is to relate a few details, then quickly review the order of the book.

The people we talked with lived in Seattle, Washington. I assume that some still live there. In all, we talked with fifteen people for about twenty hours apiece. The details of our talks will be taken up later. All the talks were recorded and transcribed. Most of the people we interviewed grew up in lower-socioeconomic-class families. There was an approximately even number of men and women, and about half the people had college degrees. Most were between the ages of thirty and forty-five.

The details of each person's life have been changed to protect his or her confidentiality. Each gave the research project a great deal of time and energy, and each was remarkably honest and open about issues that were sometimes emotionally painful. Everyone worked hard and deserves both praise and protection.

Some are dealt with in more detail than others: As it turns out, fifteen people are too many with which to work.

What to expect. We will first deal with the combination of the myth of higher education and how it is lived through people. More to the point, within the context of the myth we will see how people act and react.

By chapters. You know that the first chapter is concerned with why people go or do not go to college, and that the second chapter covers some of the assumptions of the book.

The following chapter takes up a discussion of the experience of college itself, with examples of what it was like for those with whom we talked. Chapter 4 deals with the consequence of education/no education. Here, finally, we get a more whole sense of a person's stories. We will be able to begin to talk about the idea of wisdom and its possible relationship to education.

By Chapter 5 all of the people will be introduced, and we will start to study the social/political/economic context of their actions. We will see how they act in different aspects of their worlds, and we will make judgments about education and the everyday lives of individuals.

There are three "theme" chapters. The themes are overlapping and certainly important parts of the web in which we live. The topics are these: work, bureaucracy, and politics. They were chosen in part because they are domains controlled by the "highly" educated. Our job, in part, is to understand just what that means. There follows a first concluding chapter.

The last three chapters—9, 10, and 11—will deal with more specific issues of public policy analysis. Chapter 9 will give a full description of the philosophic base of the study. In Chapter 10 the details of the project will be presented. Finally, the concluding chapter will re-focus on higher education and on the literature in the field, and will offer recommendations and the general tying-up of loose ends for which last chapters are famous.

Enough background. Back to college.

NOTES

1. Hannah Arendt, *The Human Condition* (Garden City, N.Y.: Doubleday Anchor Books, 1959), p. 260.
2. Some of my pop culture West Coast friends were forever using the image of "my movie." The language of pop psychology often suffers from the same kind of sloppiness. For a wonderful book that accurately describes the phenomenon, see Cyra McFadden, *The Serial: A Year in the Life of Marin County* (New York: Alfred A. Knopf, 1977). The book is better than the film.
3. I am thinking of philosophers such as Edmund Husserl, Henri Bergson, and William James.
4. For an interesting epistemology by an anarchist, see Paul Feyerabend, *Against Method* (London: Humanities Press, 1975).
5. Arendt, *The Human Condition.*
6. Even something as focused as Freudian analysis does not claim that a single factor is wholly controlling. At least Freud did not make that mistake.
7. The most useful idea came from Jean-Paul Sartre, *Search for a Method* (New York: Vintage Books, 1968). In the book Sartre uses the concept of *project* and explains it, in part, like this:

   > Only the project, as a mediation between two moments of objectivity, can account for history; that is, for human *creativity.* (p. 99)

   and:

   > Finally, the project never has any *content,* since its objectives are at once united with it and yet transcendent. But its *coloration*—i.e., subjectivity, its taste; objectivity, its *style*—is nothing but the suppressing of our original deviations. (p. 106)

   The idea of project was useful as it opened up various ways of studying. Regrettably, while it seemed right in principle, it did not quite work out in practice.
8. Feyerabend, *Against Method*, p. 295.

Doing College

One began at last to see that a great many impressions were needed to make a very little education.

—**Henry Adams**

Generally, in social analyses, people doing the studying formulate general categories so that the experiences of many may be understood at a glance. The more interesting the experiences, the longer the glances. For example, it would be possible for us to label—as ideal types—the following four stories thus: "The Party-Goer," "The Engineer," and so on. To do that would, I think, take something away from the truth of the matter.

As we shall see, each person "did college" in his or her own way. Each clearly came to terms with school as an activity and later had to come to terms with school as a past event—an achievement or whatever.

What you are in college is not necessarily what you are going to be later. But it does have an effect; to attend college may possibly be an important factor.

The focus of this chapter is four people who graduated from college. To steal from William James, this will be a chapter on varieties of college experience.

While it is always helpful to learn from similarities, it is equally important to learn from stories of uniqueness.

SARA

"I was into boys and beer in college—that was my whole trip in college, dating and drinking and dancing."

Sara was a craftsperson when we talked with her. I have no doubt that she still is. She was good at her trade; she worked hard at it and was clearly very involved with her work. Sara was an attractive woman, with dark hair and an interesting combination of intensity and good humor. She carried herself in a way that somehow indicated that she used her body; she seemed strong and healthy.

Her clothes were practical for her work as well as what was then called "counter-culture." Sara was a bright, articulate, interesting person to talk with.

Sara was anything but counter-culture growing up. She was, in her words, an "Eisenhower teenager" and a "typical 50s coed" in high school and in college. Clearly, she had changed a great deal; the conversations we had with her had an interesting tinge of detachment to them. To quote: "I tend to forget it sometimes, I tend to discount all the years before 1970 as unimportant, and they really were important—they were just different. . . . It's good for me to remember back and compare experiences and bring back that part of my life and remember the good things about it."

Sara talked of her parents in many ways:

"My mother came from an old New England family . . . my father came from a Philadelphia family, kind of a working-class family. . . . When they met, he was working in a country club that she belonged to, and they met in the stables and it was all very romantic. . . . She thought she was marrying beneath herself.

"Whatever my mother might have had was really crushed by her being first a school teacher, which she didn't like, and then a housewife, which she hated . . . she just despised it. She really loved us individually, but she didn't like spending her day taking care of three kids, and I don't blame her; and she started drinking, and my father started drinking and the whole thing—my whole childhood really— well, my family life was not very happy. My brother and I were deliriously happy together and were always off on adventures."

"You know . . . they both . . . they would just come home and sit down and drink. And my father didn't like his job—he was selling cars.

"I thought everybody drank, but . . . she was depressed all the time. . . . Now, looking back now I can really sympathize. They finally separated in '55, I guess, and I think that was better . . . but I stayed with my father. My two brothers went with my mother, but it never occurred to me to leave; and my mother and I were just starting to get into adolescent . . . our adolescent agonies and clashing with each other and competing, and it was really yucky. He was really pretty good for a parent for an adolescent.

"My father was really a loner—he hardly liked anybody. . . . My father never got . . . support from his environment, and he . . . always, somehow or for some reason, had the feeling he was taking on the world singlehanded, which is a real shame . . . you know. My father's outward strength was a real weakness of his."

And Sara—how did she do in all of this?

"I was always, was always approved of or was special or something like that . . . I was just top dog all the time. In my younger childhood I was oblivious to my parents' relationship, and what was important was their relationship to me. I guess that I always felt that I was special.

"Then there was that couple of years that were pretty grim, and then the first year after my mother left was traumatic; you know, I just cried a lot for no reason. . . ."

The story of Sara's parents was striking and difficult and layered with meaning. But her childhood was much more than the sum of her relationships with her parents. It is useful to trace her childhood in her school experience now that we know something of her family.

When Sara started school, she remembered "being absolutely terrified the first day, panic-stricken until I got there, and then I was fine. I don't remember very much about it."

The family moved twice when her father was in the navy. The big move was from a rural area ". . . into the city in Philadelphia, and I was suddenly dumped into a very, very large two-story city elementary school, which threw me into a state of shock that didn't end until college. I felt left out and unrecognized; and I did get to know people, but I somehow never got back on my feet socially." All of that was in the first couple of months of the first grade.

"The school was so big and my part of it was so small that it just felt like being in the army or something . . . I still have nightmares about that building. I was always treated kindly because I was shy . . . I wasn't super-competitive academically, you know; I wasn't a hand-raiser. I never found it particularly thrilling, but it wasn't awful either."

The social structure was unusual: "The social group in the school was arranged not in cliques but in a sort of hierarchy. There was one girl who was agreed by everyone to be the most popular girl in the class, for no particular reason."

From Sara's stories, it was clear her trips to and from school were what was most fun. There was, she said, a wonderful and rich fantasy world, first with her brother, then with her friend on the school bus. The grade school years were undramatic; they were certainly without lasting trauma and surely happy enough.

Sara went to a brand-new junior high school. It was exciting to be part of something that was just beginning: "We felt that it was our school; the other kids that came along later, you know, it wasn't anywhere near as much theirs as it was ours."

By the ninth grade "it had broken down into a very definite social order." There were, it seems, the academics and the others. There were two academic classes, "those who were taking Latin and the ones taking French." Sara was in Latin, and it seemed those in French had more fun.

High school had its worries: "Oh, the whole class-changing procedure was kind of anxiety-producing for me . . . I still have nightmares about it, . . . you know, of not being able to get my locker open and not finding my next class and things like that . . . and having a test you're not prepared for. . . . I finally ended that anxiety by saying, 'I don't want to take this test!' and walking out in one dream, and I never had it again."

There was, of course, another social group, which Sara and her friend called "the Stuckups." One imagines the name was accurate enough. The two criteria for getting into this "satellite group" were to be either "very smart or very athletic." Sara was not athletic and did not try to be "very smart."

About the whole experience? Said Sara:

"God, high school was really a rich experience, just incredibly so; thinking back on it now, so much went on. . . . It seems to me I was in love most of the time . . . [my friend and I] just constantly loved someone or other and were getting one heartbreak and always recuperating very quickly. When boys had cars, we'd meet them at dances and neck in the parking lot and things, and . . . I managed to have a steady boyfriend, which I found was a very convenient social thing.

"I thought I was terribly ugly, in a way, but then I thought I was probably also sexier than most of the girls I knew."

She did well in school: "I'd say I was probably in the top 10 or 15 percent of the class. I got a National Merit Scholarship. I was a great test-taker, they never made me anxious . . . I never went into a panic, and I invariably remembered everything that I had studied. In fact, I think it was kind of a detriment in my whole academic career that I always knew that I could bail out before a test."

College? There was never a doubt.

> *Interviewer:* "Can you pinpoint when the idea that you would go to college emerged?"
>
> *Sara:* "All right, always. O.K., I can remember being maybe, let me see, six. . . ."
>
> *Interviewer:* "Six years old?"
>
> *Sara:* "There was not the slightest shred of doubt in my mind when it came time . . . that I was going to college."

Before we do Sara and her thoughts about college and her college experiences, there is one important detail. In a discussion about school, not about her family, she described her parents' divorce: "I'm sure that [*long pause*] that it made me feel inferior; you know, I'm not sure I was embarrassed by it . . . divorce back in those days was fairly uncommon, and . . . I imagine that it kept me from being open with a lot of people, and probably a lot of my feeling of being excluded was brought on myself."

Back to college. We saw it was always a fact, but the question is why. There were reasons.

> *Interviewer:* "If I had talked with you the day you graduated from high school, would you have said you were going to attend college to get a husband?"
>
> *Sara:* "If I'd been honest about it, which I wouldn't have been, yes [*laughs*]."

And more reasons.

"There was also just a whole—a thing about being educated; the difference between educated people and people who weren't was pretty obvious to me. Also, people who were educated made a lot more money. Not always, but usually, and [they] had fewer children and less oppressive lives, it seemed to me; more options [*long pause*]. And I don't think I was not looking forward to the academic aspects of college, but it wasn't the major pull.

". . . and it was the people with educations that got the more interesting jobs and had more interesting lives, knew more interesting people; and I still buy that, not quite as much as I used to, I'm still buying it. There are in my circle of friends now a number of people who haven't gone to college, and they're just as interesting as the rest of my friends."

Or less. In another part of her conversation, Sara told the story of a "really, really bright" young man who quit high school.

"My father was just crushed because he'd been really fond of this boy and recognized his very, very lively mind immediately, and was just heartbroken that he'd gone off to be a steel worker.

"I'm sure that he managed to get someone pregnant and got married and has three kids and drinks a lot of beer and is miserable; that seems to be the pattern of a lot of people's lives."

College allowed you to, just possibly, miss the beer and the kids and the misery.

There seemed to be no particular reason why Sara chose her state's Big Public University over the other schools that had accepted her. Her guidance counselor was of no help: "She was really an old bag, unfortunately; she was a totally uninspiring woman." So Sara chose a school "which was just a country club school—its reputation was that you went there to have a good time, and there were parties and fraternities all the time—[this] seemed to me like a very good reason for going."

Just how did Sara think and talk about her alma mater? An introductory list should be useful:

"It was an inactive college; I think its attitude was pretty midwestern . . . [it] wasn't a very intellectual college at all.

". . . a cow college in central Pennsylvania.

"Sports were really big. There certainly was, at least among the people that I knew, very little in the way of intellectual discussion.

"It was called a country club college.

"There were a lot more men than women at that school. . . . Oh, yeah, I think the ratio was maybe five to one or something like that.

"Gosh, there were fifty parties every weekend, or maybe even a hundred!"

After spending "my last summer of freedom," an excited Sara went to college. One of the first things she did was ". . . manage to find myself a boyfriend who was an important athlete very early on, which I think helped a lot." Academically, she found classes "very easy, very easy, compared to high school . . . I started getting good grades on tests right away.

"I also really liked the anonymity of large classes. I liked the lecture system; I never liked participating . . . it made me feel kind of on the spot. I didn't get too involved intellectually; I would kind of sponge, I was really soaking up everything I could learn. I was paying tuition to a professor who was theoretically an expert in his field, and I wanted to hear what he had to say; and there were some of my classes where that was very much the case, and they were probably the best. I really enjoyed good lectures.

"When I finally changed majors it was to a program called General Arts and Sciences. It's just like penny candy: a little history, a little geography, and a little, you know, whatever.

"I still look at rock formations and remember things from geology class, and look at flowers and remember things from botany; and that was probably the best thing, academically, about college . . . that sampling of so many different things."

There were things other than classes. "Dorm life was silly for the most part—I guess there was probably a lot of tension and we released it by being foolish, and it was very friendly. Anyway . . . maybe in the middle of my sophomore year I went through rush and got into a sorority."

Sorority? "Being in a sorority to me was—I was being sophisticated and was being accepted and so forth; and wearing the blue was being ostracized and feeling childish and foolish and of course the whole sorority rigmarole—I don't know why I bought that. I guess I was just so excited about being accepted. I really enjoyed living in the sorority dorms. . . . For me . . . I think it was a necessary passage . . . it was an artificial bond of friendship which in the end fostered real friendship."

The sorority caused some tension between Sara and her best friend from high school, who was also attending Big State U. "Her friends kind of looked at me as straight and dumb in my kilt and circle pin, and my friends looked at her . . . crazy in her black tights and fuzzy hair." Their friendship survived.

During the summers Sara worked. Generally she was a salesperson in fancy stores. One summer she worked with a woman whose "orientation was much more intellectual, much more anti-middle class, anti-*Time* magazine, and so forth; and I remember at the time being confounded by her. I couldn't—I kept thinking, 'What's wrong with *Time* magazine?' and not understanding at all what she was talking about."

Politics came along later for Sara.

Her father remarried. Her stepmother was a journalist, and Sara was influenced by this woman who had her own career. By her senior year Sara declared herself an inactive sorority member. "You know, I just got tired of what seemed to me to be the childish social life of college . . . and I decided to just accelerate and just go straight through, which I did." Sara spent much time with a boyfriend in New York City, went to summer school, and graduated in December.

Grades: "A 3.2-something; it was respectable. I didn't feel that it was worth spending all my time on grades—there were other interesting things to do, and my tendency was to spread out."

Reaction: "Relief. I was really through."

WILLY

"Well, the best I can give you is a sort of all-over marmalade-type memory."

"... if you can promote this idea again, it's a brilliant idea ... opening up and being a sponge. Let somebody throw it into your head."

Willy, in his early fifties, was the oldest of those we talked with. When we met him he had just separated from his wife and was living with his high-school-aged son. The marriage had lasted a long time, and the separation was a traumatic one for him. Naturally enough, it was a time of intense self-reevaluation.

Willy was an articulate, vigorous, loud man. He smoked a great deal, lighting one cigarette from another; and I do not remember seeing him relaxed. Willy had short, almost all-gray hair and was of medium height and weight. He worked as an engineer (an "inventor," in his words) for a local airplane manufacturer.

Willy was born in New England of New England parents. His mother ("old New England stock") was raised on a farm in New Hampshire. Willy's grandfather, "apparently a very stern man," divorced his grandmother when it was not in fashion. Because of this Willy's mother, sixteen or seventeen at the time, spoke but two words to her own father for the rest of her life. He spoke none to her. Willy's grandmother remarried seven times. She died when she was ninety-seven or ninety-eight, "a real bag; strong, loud."

About his father's family: "My father was an only child—they say his father died when he was still unborn. His mother remarried." These grandparents lived in a "beautiful place, beach with clams and fish and a yacht;" and Willy "spent, generally speaking, a month to six weeks there every summer."

All of the grandparents, naturally, were New England Republicans: "Cal Coolidge, there was a man; there was a man. Best. Grace Coolidge was the ideal President's wife [*laughs*]."

Willy's mother, one of four daughters, was a registered nurse when she was married. She gave up nursing, and "she didn't work during her entire married life, at anything, except at being a housewife."

Willy's father, an only child, worked for the YMCA when he was married. To Willy, he was "a real good guy, honest and whatnot, very good at his work, without guile, without any, the all-American male of 1927. And with his personality and whatnot, everybody told him, 'You're a born salesman, Paul, you're a born salesman ... 1927.' "

So he sold his home, and the family moved for the first of many times. By the time the market crashed and depression was an admitted fact, Willy's father was selling insurance. While things were "tight" for the family, they made it. What is interesting is how the same facts were seen by each parent.

For example:

"According to my mother, during that period things were always bad. But, remembering back, he [Dad] apparently brought in enough money to pay for the—we got behind on the rent, which she thought was pure tragedy. She thought it was immoral rather than economic to get behind in rent. I can remember she once took a vacation . . . and he got a little bit teed-off, and he bought linoleum for the kitchen floor, and he bought a suit of clothes for me and a suit of clothes for my brother, and, I don't know, some goodies of some sort. Cookies or something. Mother came back and hit the roof. 'You're spending all of our money.' Well, he was probably pissed-off at living cheap and decided he could swing a few bucks; so he did."

Of his home and early years:

"It was a very good but limited place to live. Limited intellectually, limited artistically, nothing of driving demand on anybody.

"There was a lot of dissension about money [during the depression].

"[Mother] saved dimes, and she was very meticulous about Christmas presents for seventy-eight people. She had a wide correspondence . . . she had an incredible ability to make friends with people.

"It was very—this is probably—it was a very homey home."

Me: "Would you eat supper together every night?"
Willy: "Oh yeah; all meals all of the time."

Of himself and his school?

"And I was a very nice little boy . . . I was very dutiful about all assignments. In fact, I did all the extra work as well.

"No, I don't think I've ever felt 'normal.' Because I wouldn't know what it was. That—there were times that I felt very good and strong and friendly, and other times I felt lonesome and friendless. I would guess the experience of almost every pre-adolescent, adolescence, would have to be a period of turmoil and mixture; and I don't think that—well, observing my kids' friends—that anybody feels normal.

"I did not feel 'special'; I enjoyed learning and I enjoyed some stinking emotion called pride when I got an A [*pause*]. I only thought

I was special in that I was myself and not necessarily better or worse or I speak differently. I don't know.''

Willy had an older brother and a younger sister: "The story on getting the sister was that my brother and I were fighting, and they thought that a new child would eliminate the argument, because we'd both have something to love."

Me: "Ah, how did it work out?"
Willy: [*With emphasis*] "They believed it! They believed it!"
Me: "No, I was just wondering what the punch line was; did it work out like that?"
Willy: "Oh, shit, no. Of course not."

Of more lasting interest and importance was Willy's relationship with his brother: "We had personality conflicts all our lives, except we both like each other a lot because of many mutual interests. It's something that still isn't resolved today. He still has the real urge to feel that whatever elements of superiority that I have are because I'm *his* brother, he led me. . . . But, nevertheless, I'm still the younger brother and capable of being *told* [*pauses*]—how to get with it.''

Willy was a better-than-average student. He read a lot, listened to the radio, and even went to Boy Scout Camp some summers. By high school the family had moved from Providence to a small town in New Hampshire.

"So probably the best years of my life, as far as pleasant, non-conflicting, my junior and senior year in high school. . . . An extensive social life, with the 'upper-middle-class' high school kids. A party every Saturday night. No pot, no nothing. But it was fun.

"The classes in the high school were uniformly interesting. In English my compositions were very pleasing to me. . . . I was very successful in chemistry, physics, math [*pause*], and also, oddly enough, economics, which was taught by the basketball coach. It was very interesting because it was supposed to be a snap course for the jocks, which it *was;* and I would doze in class, which would make him angry, and he would wake me up with a question and I would read him back the answer with indulgence, which made him *angrier* [*laughing; long pause*].

"It would be no value for your record to recite the names, but I can remember perhaps thirty, or maybe forty, of my friends from that time."

Those were good times—the best times—for Willy. There were the big bands and his brother's (then his) friends and even a nearby quarry where everyone could swim. In the American tradition, then came college.

"Well, a lot of kids weren't going to college at the time unless you were wealthy, and we weren't wealthy. None of my high school friends actively talked about going to college. Except the very wealthy ones.

"I graduated in '37. My grandfather, I think, decided—he had not, as I recall, urged my father to go to college at all, but [*pause*]—decided, almost independently, that I should go to college and selected a school for me on the basis of the recommendation of our minister at the church in Providence, Rhode Island, whom he liked. I always thought he was kind of phony, but my father liked him.

"I don't think I wanted to go to college. It was sort of *the* thing to do, the *right* thing to do or the natural thing."

So, Willy went to a medium-sized state university in Ohio. "It was actually, it was a big bus. ed. school, drawing students from both Cleveland and Cincinnati." Willy's grandfather paid tuition and his father paid "maintenance, room and board, with precious little left over."

And this college experience?

"Perhaps, for the first time, I was out and *entirely* upon my own.

"I did well in my classes and enjoyed them. I belonged to the drama society.

"I had some good friends. My first roommate was a ding-dong. [*He laughs; clock chimes; everybody laughs.*]

"I didn't like life in a dormitory because there was a great deal of very stupid competition among the guys as to who had the richest parents, the most knowledgeable, the best connections in New York City. . . . As I look at it at *that* time, I was miserable, lonesome, lost, left out. Nobody asked me to join their fraternity.

"The whole atmosphere of the place did not appeal to me. A great deal of false pride, all over the place."

It was, as it turned out, an atmosphere Willy would not have to endure for more than a year. That year, his freshman year in college, Willy's grandfather, and then his father, died. With no money and no real interest in returning he quit school and returned to the East.

For a year or two he did some work; lived at home with his mother, brother and sister; and "did a whole lot of reading." Finally he joined the navy. "Navy guys don't have to hike X number of miles, nor do they camp out in the rain; you may get sunk by a torpedo, killed one way or the other, but it's more comfortable."

It was the navy that provided Willy with another shot at education. In a very real sense this education, sandwiched between the two colleges he attended, was Willy's most important one. There is, at least for me, a fascination about how the military trains people.

First, Willy was given a series of tests on which he scored well. To find technicians, the navy seemed to "pick the smart kids... don't make them officers, make them radio technicians." Willy then took another test (algebra and trigonometry) and with many others went to "what was called pre-regular for a month, which was a one-month intelligence test. With instruction in D.C. electricity and mathematics. They flunked out 50 percent at that point. You went on to primary school, which is a three-months course. They flunked out 50 percent of what remained there. Then you went on to secondary school... and in the first month they flunked out another 50 percent." After four months in the navy, "... having received a 90 average, I got second-class petty officer, which is the fastest grade increase the United States Navy or any military organization has ever given."

Me: "Did they keep tally? Did they?..."
Willy: "Strictly on averages. Put the carrot right out and you can get the carrot."

For Willy, the former navy man/engineer, that experience was what school should be about:

"You're in school eight hours a day, 8 to 5, with an hour out for lunch. In general, classroom four to six hours, and lab either four or two. And it's work, work, work, work. And you get sort of into the habit of working this hard in your head. It was remarkable, the ability of the class itself to absorb the amount of material thrown at them. As far as higher education goes, if you can promote this idea again, it's a brilliant idea, getting into the *real* habit of opening up and being a sponge. Let somebody throw it into your head."

The method, he claimed, could be as effective with Shakespeare as with electronics.

"To continue higher education, we go from leaving the navy to dumping my mother in Providence. She, incidentally, got a job in a laundry, ironing shirts. Physically and mentally she loved it. She led a very sorry life—I don't know why."

Willy enrolled at the University of California, Berkeley ("I was deeply in love with a dame in San Francisco"). "I told myself at the time, you get all of your V. A. rights, it's free, the government's paying for it, you're to expect nothing from [college]." Basically, he had "no intention, necessarily, of it serving any benefit in my later life."

And college, this second college—how did he "do" it? "So I struggled through with about—just under a 3.0. Something like that: 2.8, something like that. I commuted all four years from San Francisco. I took part in no college activities whatsoever. Zero. No football games, no sociables, no dances, no nothing."

What he loved was San Francisco and the music and the theater and the wine and the talk and the friends. And school? This is what he and his classmates decided:

"College had not given us, in any way, the quality of education we'd expected.

"It wasn't well enough organized.

"The teaching ability of the professors, I think, was in the main poor.

"I don't know if you know about the college of mechanical engineering in universities in this country, but they're dull. They're dull, dull, dull!"

So he spent time in San Francisco building hi-fi's, enjoying himself, and traveling three hours a day round-trip to Berkeley. And his education, what effect has it had?

"Well . . . the education didn't impinge that heavily, to begin with or while it was happening or since. With the one exception of the fact that I do have a degree. It makes no difference to me, but it makes a great deal of difference for them."

Them?

Another Introduction

In writing, there are always problems simply not worth dealing with. Other problems have a solution that seems so obvious that it is embarrassing to write about them. There is another category of problem that needs to be discussed. It is the kind that contains an important tension.

This study is about education and politics and doing research and people. The first concern, as has been made clear, is the people. The emphasis so far is on how each has worked at growing up and living in the United States. That is a reasonable enough thing to say, *except that when we begin with people and their problems, the tendency is to shift from social analysis to psychology.*

I have no desire to "analyze" these people in a psychological way. That is neither my interest nor my wish. In fact, part of what I would like to explore is what we can find out about people when we do not use psychology as the central way of understanding and knowing. But we do need to acknowledge that psychology forms a part of our social setting.

We now have whole generations that have grown up hearing the words of psychologists used freely in everyday life. We are "repressed" and "hostile" and "depressed"; and, on occasion, we "act out" all kinds of unconscious stuff. Many of the people we talked with had been in therapy, and one finally became a social worker.

The next two people in this chapter use the words of psychology well, and each understands much of his life in those terms. I believe it is accurate to accept what each says as true, and also to accept that particular psychological vision of the world as an interesting—and certainly not a neutral—social fact.

TED

"Everything was geared toward heaven."

Ted was a nice-looking man, a little over forty, with dark hair and eyes. He was almost six feet tall, and his "desk job" was beginning to add some fat to his former runner's build. Ted was a very kind and concerned person who had suffered much.

He was certainly easy to talk with—sometimes, it seemed, almost too easy. Much came out like well-rehearsed answers. No doubt that had a great deal to do with his years in therapy. Ted was both well informed and insightful. He had several degrees; and one reason why his college experience is interesting to us is its high personal cost.

Ted was born in a very small town in the Northwest. His paternal grandfather was a dentist in Seattle and a Christian Scientist. His maternal grandfather was a farmer and an educator. There was no mention of either grandmother. Ted's father wanted to be a veterinarian but never finished college; his mother graduated and was a teacher. He was one of seven children.

His father was a very "dynamic" man.

"I was very idealistic . . . I worshipped my father.

"My father was a very strong man with lots of vociferous ways, very flamboyant.

"You could never win an argument with him. He was always right. The first time I ever really consciously said no to my father, it so shocked him that we talked for two hours with my continually asserting no."

Interviewer: "And how old were you at that time?"
Ted: "I was about thirty-three."

And the wife of the "dynamic" man?

Interviewer: "You haven't said much about your mother."
Ted: "An analyst told me that once [*laughs*]."

"My mother . . . was the type of woman who I'm sure let Dad talk her into a quick marriage and talk her into everything else since. My mother is hard-working, [and] let herself be satisfied pretty much with the raising of the family. My mother was generous to us children [there were seven; Ted was in the middle], but not particularly demonstrative in her affection. She constantly criticized my father—she always was very critical of his church decision. Also, he was the type of man with whom work came first, and she always criticized him for this."

When Ted was nine his father's "church decision" was made. The effects, as will be clear, were powerful and long-lasting. It is interesting to take some time to see such an example of the American revival/religious tradition in action.

"My father went to a revival meeting at the Nazarene Church. He got converted, and from then on we went to church twice on Sunday and two or three times during the week.

"My mother was very opposed to it. Her family became very opposed to my father at this time, because he wanted to convert everybody—it's a very evangelical-type faith.

"My father was the type of man who is very intent and serious in some ways, and as I look back now I think he's covering up some guilts for an early age, because he's always making sort of oblique references to the fact that he led sort of a wild life when he was a teenager.

"He has since departed from this Nazarene faith and is now into something even more fundamentalist: Only God is perfect, and no one else can be but they're supposed to be."

The "main tenet" of the church, according to Ted, is that "each person has a work of grace which takes away the desire to sin. . . .

"Dancing and card playing were taboo; in fact anything that was at all pleasurable was, when I was growing up, identified with sin.

"Everything was geared toward heaven.

"I had my first so-called conversion at age nine. I don't think I resisted very long."

Ted went to a small grade school and was happy. There were four teachers and eight grades. "I don't particularly remember school being hard. I think of those more as really idyllic years and lots of fun. I think the family years then were lots of fun then, too. This was before we got tied up with the fundamentalist church."

His first school trauma came in the fifth grade, when the family moved from one farm to another—in the same area but in a different school district. Ted did not get into trouble at school until the seventh grade, and then only seldom after that. He was, compared to his brothers and sisters, "more of a goody boy than any of them."

The idea that he would be a minister was clear to him "right from the start . . . everybody was to become a great teacher or evangelist or preacher. I can remember one incident. My mother . . . prepared some [bible] verses for memorization and threw the piece of paper away, and it somehow ended up in the coal bucket. . . . I went out to fill the bucket, and each time I dumped some coal in there, this piece of paper would float around. I finally looked at it, and read it, and thought that it must be God's voice to me to become a preacher."

Ted's high school experience was an interesting one. In the beginning, he was popular, good in sports, but not interested or outstanding in anything academic. Serious about God, he and his friends prayed for their classmates at lunchtime. At the end of his freshman year, Ted remembered ". . . seeing this ceremony and determining that I was going to get into the National Honor Society. And did the next year. It wasn't the getting of the grades but it was the recognition; recognition was always very important to me."

Ted played basketball, ran the mile, was a boy scout, had a paper route, and made good grades. Yet his social life existed not in school but in church ("Church was a separate society"). Also, there was tension.

"For instance, I could not go to shows; other kids went to shows. I began to see other kids interested in dances; I wasn't able to go to dances, that was supposed to be taboo. I started sneaking off and going to movies and doing some of these other things and not considering myself a Christian anymore. It was such an escapism that I never even was smart enough to look up what movie it was and go at the time it started. I just tried to sneak off, and I'd go. So I'd usually go in at the middle and watch it through to the middle. I can remember Esther Williams movies—oh . . . my idol as far as feminine at the time."

There are, I believe, two stories that capture a great deal of Ted's high school life. The first has to do with his reconversion and the second with what it means to be a mile runner. First (always first in those days) was religion.

"I was definitely a backslider as far as the church was concerned. I can remember many revival meetings, where, you know, at the end of the meeting the preacher would, say, have what they call an altar call, and those who are backsliding are supposed to come forward to what they call the mourner's bench and publicly pray and confess and get miraculously converted. I can remember for about a year-and-a-half period I resisted all these altar calls. And it was kind of an interesting sort of negative pleasure, because everybody crowds around you and tries to get you to go forward to the altar, and you sit there stony-faced and resist, and the evangelist would use tricks. . . .

"The technique, the pressure, the psychology would always work on many people. I can remember being very rebellious and just determined I wasn't going to go . . . I remember going to the movies. I went to one or two dances; I think I remember going to a Halloween party that ended up as a dance out at a place. I remember cussing during this time but feeling very guilty about that."

Then, one summer at a religious camp, "they had the big push and I guess I caved in; and I can remember supposedly having a glorious conversion and going home and telling my father that I'd been converted and how pleased he was.

"I was going to be a preacher; I was going off to a Nazarene college to prepare specifically for that.

"High school was sort of incidental to this future."

Ted liked sports and enjoyed recognition. "Sports were, as in most small towns, a big, big thing." By his senior year he had decided to concentrate on track and especially the mile. He wanted to win the mile in the state meet. Listen to the miler:

"The mile is always—it's a very individual thing, and it's longer, you know—the dashes, bing and they're over and you hardly know who's running.

"But the mile, you have long enough to concentrate on it, and there's more drama because one of the things, the way I ran, was always kind of to stay back in the pack and then get that final kick; and it's very exhilarating to—on that last lap, you run four laps of quarter mile, picking up steam—and then on the final turn to kick and pass everyone. And so it's more dramatic that way."

The state meet: "It was a rainy day . . . I came in seventh, eighth, something like that, and my father was there to watch, and I just remember it was a big disappointment."

And by college: "The mile is something that if you trained and conditioned yourself, up to a certain point you can win races on training; but beyond that it takes really some superior skill, which I didn't feel I had; and I think I began to recognize that and was interested in other things and didn't pursue it that far."

At the end of his senior year, Ted had a hernia operation and stayed out of school for a year. He was excited about college: "I was very idealistic and set in preparation for the ministry; I suppose I expected to choose a wife, which was very much a part of the ideal minister—to have the ideal wife. I can remember looking from the very start; instead of going with girls just to be going and having fun, I was always looking to see who would make the ideal parson's wife."

It is fairly easy to get an idea about the atmosphere of his chosen college: "In this particular school, you signed a pledge when you came to school that you would abide by the standards code, which included no movies, dancing, smoking, drinking, things like that. It was like one big family."

And more: "In a sense, as I look back on it, I think it was a very narrow education in many ways.

"This world is very, very temporary, of course; this world *is* very temporary I guess, but this was *emphasized*. For instance, one of the favorite songs was a gospel song; I don't know whether you've ever heard it: 'This world is not my home, I'm just a-passing through; my treasures are laid up somewhere beyond the blue.'

"To take too much stock in education was to make a man proud. And therefore this pride would be sinful. A great emphasis on humility . . . certainly a recognition that only God could give you wisdom.

". . . an extreme emphasis on self-denial and self-sacrifice, almost that it was *wrong* to be too ambitious . . . this all had to be subdued."

Ted was very involved in carrying out the principles of the school. He got good grades ("I mean, getting good grades would be pleasing to God") and always was trying to "be ready for the end of the earth, so to speak."

Interviewer: "At any moment?"
Ted: "At any moment, yes."
Interviewer: "That's a pretty heavy burden."
Ted: "Yes, yes."

Ted was "very gung-ho," "idealistic," "a class president or an officer nearly every semester I was in school." It was, in his word, a "high."

By his junior year he had been dating—and was engaged to—a woman a couple of years younger. But he simply could not deal with the idea of marriage, "or my urges, or something." He began to do excessive worrying over the approaching end of the semester tests and papers; and he was so overcome by his love life, his "relation to school," his being "leader in these organizations," and his "facing the ministry" that he became despondent.

He went to his room and took "antihistamine pills or something like this, ... very foolishly thinking I would end my life." The pills made him sleepy, but he was easily found before much had happened, as he had not locked his door.

They took him to a big hospital, one with a mental health ward; and for two weeks Ted had shock therapy. He stayed for a little while longer, depressed but with the urgency no longer there. Ted went home and did "heavy physical work" from January through the summer.

Ted did not go back to the Nazarene college that fall. He stayed out for a year. Being at home was an interesting experience for him. Since "it was the first time anything like that had happened in our family, they wondered if I was loony." He never really considered himself one of those "crazy folks."

He took some courses at a college near his home and did well. But "the key to becoming un-depressed was reading a book, amazingly Dale Carnegie's *How to Stop Worrying and Start Living*; and his frequent emphasis in that book—in fact, it's just illustration after illustration of his theory of living in day-tight compartments, what he calls doing one thing at a time, not borrowing tomorrow's trouble. That kind of helped me get unglued and back together."

Ted had broken the engagement, gotten himself together, and returned to college. Then he met Helen: "Suddenly I saw her and just fell in love, like that. I can remember, she'd walk across campus, my heart would just go pitter-patter, pitter-patter; and I really, really fell deeply in love."

They "started dating right away."

Ted worked hard, and courted Helen, and did well in school. In his senior year he wrote a paper for sociology class about coming "to the brink of despair, and the Lord had pulled me through. . . .

"At the end of the school year, we had a big assembly in the chapel. And the highlight of the year was the naming of the outstanding student of the year, and this was always a surprise. And I can remember, just all kinds of suspense buildup to this—I didn't think I had a chance because I'd been more of a student that year, not quite so active in all the organizations. And I can remember when they called my name, I was just floored. As I look back now, I felt guilty that I couldn't respond more fully . . . it was really a very great honor. Well, so this, I'm sure, only spurred on the idealism and all of the [desire of the] organization-loyalist man to achieve."

With degree and honor in hand, the organization-loyalist man went to a seminary.

DANNY

"In the eighth grade I was King Shit."

Danny was a star growing up. In a small town on an island in the Northwest, Danny did it all in school.

We talked with Danny when he was about thirty. He was almost six feet tall, with dark hair and eyes. He kept himself trim. He lived in a nice apartment with a view of the water. He had decorated in a casual/hippy/potted plant but very tidy kind of way.

Danny was an articulate and intelligent conversationalist. It seemed clear that he was working on personal matters in these talks. In order to try to get into the right mood, he would smoke dope before the talks; it relaxed him, he said, and there was no reason not to believe him.

He was a native of the Northwest:

"My mother's parents and grandparents were real pioneers in the true sense of the word. My grandfather was the first white child born [on that island] and my great-grandmother was a Mercer girl—she was a Mercer. Mercer girls were girls brought around by a guy named Asa Mercer, who brought a whole boatload of them from Boston to Seattle for the West Coast men.

"My father's parents were immigrants, and my mother's parents . . . were into farming the land, and my father's parents were into the theater or insurance or that kind of thing—so there was—I don't—I can't—like I find myself jumping back and forth.

"There are a lot of things about my folks' past history that have been kept a secret."

Interviewer: "On purpose?"
Danny: "I don't know; it just was not discussed, and it's hard for me to determine."

Of course there were memories and more:

"I thought he [his paternal grandfather] was a pretty nice guy—not real loose and comfortable, sort of domineering; had a temper and stuff. I remember a big scare and shock once—we went to see him one night, later in the evening, unannounced; and he came to the door and he had his teeth out and he had . . . his glass eye out, and here's this gaunt, tousled-white-haired, toothless, eyeless man answering the door, and I freaked out as a kid.

"The important thing to me was that he was a super-tyrant: He just ran his family like a dictator, and I think my father picked up a lot of his tendencies and how he lives from that man. My mother says she sees it all the time, and I do too—and I know I picked up all kinds of stuff from my father. It's just been passed on, generation to generation, and it's something that I want to stop in my generation."

Danny was "real sick as a child, had asthma and allergies, boils and all kinds of things. I was a kid who had to be taken care of all the time." His family lived in California until he was four, then moved to an island in the Northwest.

His growing up was not an uninterrupted treat. There was, for example, his family:

"We sure were not an intimate family—we were not a physically touching family—we still aren't. It's very uncomfortable for any of us. It's still funny when I shake hands with my father.

"My mother is a very fastidious woman—she would take three baths a day if it was possible; and if she thought it would get her more clean, the longer she takes. And the house was kept just spotless.

"I wanted to be in the house where my mom and sister were working—I didn't feel comfortable going and doing the outdoor kinds of work my father was doing.

"I was able to cry and I was in touch with my emotions and I was a very sensitive person and I was very shy . . . so I had a whole slew of things that I—made me feel like I didn't fit into the male role."

Danny said that he had "been raised by my parents, who had made me very dependent on them . . . by being subtly but extremely protective, and having strong, strong influence on my decisionmaking, and giving me very little responsibility."

And one last shot: "I think my father is a very, sort of, tyrannical person . . . determining of what's going to happen, short-tempered, extremely perfectionistic . . . and yet I think my mother just emasculated him so that in a sense basically his decisions were what she wanted. I think she wanted. I think she was very subtle about it and I think she had a *very* strong emasculating influence on me, to the point now where I think back on it—things were absolutely perverse."

Growing up on a sparsely populated island was an interesting experience. There were fourteen people in his school class—there were a few people who left and a few who moved in, but the core remained.

"It's really comfortable because you don't have to go about developing new friendships and figuring out new ways of relating to stuff because it's all been set down for years. When you come back the next year, it's all the same people.

"You get into patterns right away, and one of the problems of having the same group is that everyone gets their labels and their categories, and that's really hard to break out of, because it just builds each year.

"From as early as I can remember, I was always looked on as the kid who was going to do the best or knew the best in whatever we did in any academic situation, and I'm sure I felt then increasing pressure to keep that up after I got that label."

Interviewer: "By the second or third grade?"
Danny: "Oh sure."

And each year, there was increasing pressure and assuredness that he would do the best.

Danny's fourteen-person class was "exceptional," and had the same teacher for the fourth, fifth, and sixth grades. The teacher liked the students, and the students liked him.

An analysis: "I guess I really liked math for one thing because it was so cut and dried; it seemed more simple to have one single and exact right answer, and I could do it really well. But I basically liked it all, because I could do it all, really. I could get all of my accomplishment/gratification/ego strength from nearly any subject I did."

A social critique: "There were not enough girls of the kind that we felt acceptable. There were a certain few that we really dumped on in cruel ways—we found them ugly and dirty and unacceptable. In our class there were eight boys and six girls, and one of the girls was considered not acceptable . . . so there were really five girls, and it was just impossible."

A self-analysis: "I got a sense of winning out over the rest of the students, and I would really hate it if I didn't do it over everyone. I was the one who got all the gold stars."

Interviewer: "You thought of yourself as a person who was superior in many ways."
Danny: "Sure. I still don't think of myself as an average person."

A self-evaluation: "In the eighth grade I was King Shit."

In the ninth grade, Danny was a high school freshman and was with "people bigger than I was and older than I was and stronger than I was and smarter than I was; and so I started the whole climbing process: I was competing super-hard. When I was a freshman my entire high school took a test on English—vocabulary, grammar, and all that stuff—and I scored better than anybody in the high school."

In essence, Danny's reputation as the best stayed with him. His academic image was assured through high school, in part because of the test. He played varsity sports (125 pounds is light for football, but remember that the school was small), and in most sports he did well.

There were in his high school what seem to be the usual kinds of teachers: some good, some bad. Because it was an out-of-the-way place, there were many young teachers who apparently could not find other jobs and many older teachers who were getting ready to retire.

Danny liked and identified with a science teacher who "was just a different kind of guy. He wasn't a beatnik; he wasn't a bohemian . . . but he didn't dress like the rest of the people. He sort of wore . . . tweedy things and was a pipe smoker—he smoked a pipe and had fuzzy hair and he was interested, he was engaged in learning things himself, he was always reading things in interesting books and stuff, and always had new things to bring in to us that didn't always have to do with class. He was not married and, as I said, the community considered him really different; but I think he was a good enough teacher that they accepted him."

The social life seemed typical enough: "We would go a lot to school functions—sporting events or sock hops and dances. There were a couple of theaters on the island, but for some reason we didn't go to them. Drive-ins came around the last year or so, and we would do that to some extent, but, you know, it was mostly going to dances and sporting events and to the hamburger/malt shop and eating and then driving out to some lonely lane and groping around in the dark car."

During his last two years he was "paired up" with a younger woman. She—and her religion—were to have an effect on his college days.

Life at home remained tense: "I was not allowed to have my own car—they never specifically said I couldn't; it was done in a much more subtle manner. We had two cars in the family, and it was always considered such a great thing . . . because I could just use the other car, and I wouldn't have to make this investment in my own rattle-trap. So I don't think I felt psychologically as free, and they never quibbled about borrowing the car and there was never any problem as far as having money for gas. I wanted my own car and they didn't really want me to have it."

Danny graduated, "and it was neat, it was the final sense of accomplishment and victory; I did get to be valedictorian and had various honors and a high-point scholarship, and I was getting all kinds of praise and that was kind of high."

And college "seemed like a good thing. I don't know . . . it was another—you know, I wiped out all the other challenges, and it was time for a new one."

When we talked with Danny, we could not figure out whether or not that small island was a nice place to grow up on, so we asked. He told us: "It was nice in lots of ways, I think—but given the choice again, I'm not sure what I would do. I think I would—wow! I don't know. We've talked about some of the disadvantages . . . and yet . . . we had the woods and beaches and beautiful surroundings and basically friendly people, although nosy. I had a fairly strong sense of lifestyle and ways of acting and being from where I lived."

But that was over, and Danny came to the Big City and to Big State University and pledged a fraternity with more people in it than in his high school graduating class.

He got to school, and "I just felt very, very alone and very unable to develop close friendships and to feel comfortable socially; so I dived into the whole academic world where I knew I could perform." He joined a fraternity ("it was a comfortable place for me to some extent") and did new things.

Listen: "I got a haircut, too—I had it rather old-fashioned: slightly longish, probably fairly greased down, you know . . . with a weird part. I went to just one of the Avenue barbershops, and the guy cut my hair and gave me a—you know—very Ivy League modern-day type haircut, and that was a little freaky because my mother had always cut my hair before."

Also: "I was really in love with and wanted to spend the rest of my life with a girl who was a senior in high school when I was leaving to be a freshman in college, and she was also a Mormon and I got heavily involved in the whole religious thing with her."

It turned out that "I, you know, like I had three homes and they were all in conflict—my parents, and the fraternity, and the Church—and it was a really disruptive year for me—very uncomfortable time."

But in school (Danny majored in math and minored in physical education for the first couple of years), he did extraordinarily well. By the end of his second year, math did not seem "related to the world for me very much—just numbers and all that stuff"; and "I got into a calculus course that was proving very difficult for me, and it didn't look like I was going to be able to maintain my fairly high standards of academic achievement; and that was a signal for me to get out before I started failing."

Danny's girlfriend went to Brigham Young, and "we corresponded . . . we did that for two years." They saw each other summers. "We spent a lot of time together. It was very frustrating—you know, I had all normal physical-type urges, and yet because of the strictures of the Church where that was taboo, I just remember great frustrations during that whole experience, but with the urging on the inside as opposed to what my head said I was supposed to be doing—not too neat, really."

By his third year at the university, Danny had switched fields of study. He went into journalism: "It was kind of a more trade-oriented field; the people in journalism were kind of a clubby group; there was a more immediate prospect of some sort of real work and connection with the world; it was a kind of neat atmosphere that I enjoyed."

There were some conflicts with the Church—newspaper people apparently swear and drink beer—but he had not openly left the Church. He had, however, left his fraternity, as he "began to substitute the social atmosphere of the communications school...for the fraternity." Danny continued to do very well in his courses and worked for the school paper and a local paper. During the summer, he "fell into a really fine job" in which he learned a great deal of newspapering. Of his boss: "I don't think he was really very helpful. I think his theory was to throw you in the lake and let you learn to swim, or drown."

Danny spent time driving around eastern Washington State during the week and to his "Mormon girlfriend" during the weekends.

That fall Danny got an apartment "with a Mormon fellow who was several years older than I" who had just returned "from a two-year mission in New Zealand. . . . He was a very facile kind of guy; he was very glib and handsome and could just talk his way into anything . . . a real lady's man." So:

"I noticed he was getting all these letters from my girlfriend, and then eventually that fall quarter I got a letter from her saying that she had been seeing this guy and that they had fallen in love and she was very sorry and all this stuff [*short laugh*]. That was a bit weird . . . that he would live with me knowing that this had gone on that summer while I'd [been away] . . . no one bothered to tell me—neither of them or any of my friends in the Church or anybody, and they all knew that was going on, and I felt extremely used—a pretty painful situation."

Interviewer: "So did you move out then?"
Danny: "Well, the first thing I did was to stop talking to him."
Interviewer: "Did you leave the Mormon Church?"
Danny: "Well, yeah . . . I started to fall away fairly quickly after that."

Danny was very active on the school paper. He was the sports editor and then the managing editor and then the editor. He "didn't do a very good job—pretty disappointed in myself—basically because I just didn't know what to do. I was lucky enough that I knew some very talented people there and I hired them under me, and they basically carried the paper and me at times. I just wasn't very happy with what I'd done."

At the end of the year, "there are various awards from the school at a banquet." The big award "generally went to one of the two editors" but that year "it went to the person who was the managing editor underneath me, and he deserved it—he was the more talented person. I remember feeling that I was a failure, that I should have picked up that award—but it was something I hadn't been able to pull off."

That year Danny started working for a wire service, continued his journalism classes, and began dating. He even joined the army reserves, where he spent "four months and twenty days instead of six months—that was quite a relief."

In a very deliberate way, Danny ("I was twenty-two, I guess, and a virgin") went to see a woman friend in Salt Lake City. "I took a bus . . . this one thought in mind, and I was successful. It was traumatic and unsatisfying and weird in many ways, but you know—at least I lost my virginity."

The fall was uninteresting. He had a good job and "school couldn't teach me any more that would help me in my job." His undergraduate days just sort of ended; "I really rebelled against it."

To Now

Here, then, are four examples of what post-secondary education is like; of how it was experienced by four very different people. Essentially, we now have some insight into how each person grew up and how each one remembers college.

But these stories are only a part of what the book is about; they are stories that help form other stories. We need to know them both for themselves and in order to get to the next series of questions: What does college mean? How important is college to how these people live their lives? Years after college, does it make any difference if one did well or poorly, or if one loved or hated it? In terms of everyday life, does it matter which school an individual attended?

These are obvious questions to ask, and they suggest at least one more question: Are they the best and most helpful questions to ask?

When we learn more about how these people are doing now, some of these points will be more readily understood.

There are four more people to be introduced. They will be presented in the explicit context of being judged. In the following chapter a way to think about judging will be suggested, and the tone of the book will begin to change.

4 Judging

We don't start from certain words, but from certain occasions or activities.

—Ludwig Wittgenstein

Wisdom . . . is . . . a special sensitiveness to the contours of the circumstances in which we happen to be placed, it is living without falling foul of some permanent condition or factor which cannot be either altered, or even fully described or calculated. . . .

—Isaiah Berlin

There are two things that form the heart of this chapter; one has gone on in earlier chapters, one has not. The latter first: In this chapter, judgments will begin to be made about people's lives. They will not be simple kinds of pronouncements, such as "This is a good life" or "That is a bad life." Rather, the judgments are meant to reflect how an individual lives in his or her world.

To do that, naturally, we must deal with people. This chapter, like those before, will present stories of the lives of four people. These are the last people to be introduced; the following chapters will concentrate more on themes (work, politics, and large organizations) than on individuals' complete biographies.

The Crunch

The recent history of making judgments in the social sciences has been fairly straightforward: Judgments could be made most "scientifically" from quantifiable data.[1] A public policy could then be considered "best"—or could be "proven" most effective—if it was shown that resources were shifted around in a more equitable way. For example, we need public education so that more people can attend college, or a different tax structure so that more people can have more money, or a different housing policy so that more people can have better housing.

I am not against any of these policies. I believe college should be more accessible and that people should have both more money and better housing. But it is very, very wrong to stop there.

If not made by numbers, by quantities and statistics, then judgments are made on political grounds. There is some sense to this; it is not outrageous to judge what you like as good and what you dislike as bad. We get studies by liberal democratic scholars that show that liberal democrats make the best presidents. Certainly, given all of the assumptions that go into those studies, liberal democrats do make the best whatevers.

Built into these politics are one or many assumptions about human beings. There is an idealization about people that I am not willing to make. What I would like to suggest, and then try to show more fully, is that there are less obvious yet more revealing and informative ways to make judgments than by formula numbers or formula politics or formula idealizations. While not against numbers, politics, or idealizations in general, I am certainly not in favor of the particular formularization of any of them when it comes to human affairs.

There is, I admit, a certain amount of unfulfilled promise going on. In the way that I have constructed the book, this is no place for a full discussion of the philosophy and method on which the material is based. What we have are two "in orders": (1) In order for you to understand this chapter, I must present a few pages of theory; (2) in order for the book to be what I want it to be aesthetically, I must keep the interruption for this philosophical matter short.

Wisdom

The immodest topic of our judging is wisdom. It is a particular kind of wisdom that rests on how an individual lives his or her life. To be precise, it will be a judgment of wisdoms, for, as Max Weber writes: "If one proceeds from pure experience one arrives at polytheism." [2] It is a proceeding from pure experience that is the place to begin. It is, I might add, not an easy place either to think about or to begin from.

After deciding that phenomenology was something that might help us understand certain things better, and after studying several theorists, I got stuck on this problem: If, in the original phenomenological sense, everything simply is, if reality is, in Henri Bergson's words, "redundant and superabundant ... multiple and mobile," [3] then how do we sort things out? How, to put it more clearly, do we decide when to make those original conscious dips into the realm of pure experience?

I assumed that we could be taught certain responses that seemed to be almost "instinctive." For example, we can be taught to jump back automatically when we hear a car approaching—a trick some dogs never learn. While helpful, the idea was far from satisfactory.

There seems to be something that comes prior to those taught reactions. I believe we pick and choose much that will become conscious on the basis of what is beautiful. Or, in other words, our aesthetic sense. I want to argue that our deepest sense—the one that does the first sorting of experience—is the aesthetic one.

I am more and more convinced that one way to understand and make judgments about an individual's actions is to begin with that person's aesthetic sense of the world. Of the people I know best, either by interviewing or simply knowing, no one lacks this aesthetic sense. It is, as I am using it, a preconscious sense of the rightfittingness of the world.

It is, in part, social and political and economic and organizational. It is that sense of taste that accounts not only for what we wear or the kind of chair we would like to sit in, but also for the political or organizational or family form that seems most natural. The form that seems, in a word, best.

From what I have gathered, a person can consciously develop, in varying degrees, a sense of what his or her aesthetic is. [4] We can become articulate about some of it. For example, I can figure out many of the reasons—historical, technical, ideological, epistemological, political, sociological—why to dislike the bureaucratic form of organization. All of these ways of understanding are important. What

I am suggesting is not a know-nothing sense of taste. I have made an effort not only to know about organizations and their effects, but also to communicate what I have learned. I read books and write books about bureaucracies. All of that must be understood in conjunction with this fact: Aesthetically, bureaucracies repulse me. They violate my senses.

To carefully understand another person is to begin to see *who,* not *what,* a person is. The distinction comes from Hannah Arendt: *"Who* somebody is or was we can know only by knowing the story of which he himself is the hero—his biography, in other words; everything else we know of him, including the work he may have produced and left behind, tells us only *what* he is or was." [5] What is important, then, in terms of human meaning, are the stories of an individual's life. We must remember that the stories take place in the web of human relationships.

I want to add that to understand a person is to know what a "right-fitting" world would look like to that individual. It is empiricism that begins with a person and "certain activities" rooted in levels of experience and levels of chaos. It ends, I believe, with an anarchy of unifying tastes, definitions, and insights.

An attempt to understand wisdom, then, would be an attempt to understand a person. A wise person, I would like to argue, is one who does as little violence to his or her aesthetic sense as possible. That is, I believe, a very political definition, as any day is filled with all kinds of social and political and economic forms and facts not of any single person's creation.

I am arguing that for most people to adjust to their surroundings is a form of violence. Equally, for each social form, I can assume that it fits perfectly for some person's aesthetic sense. For most people to reject everything and adjust to nothing is a foolproof way to guarantee being shut off from most human contact. It is a constant struggle to construct a world that is beautiful if you assume that yours is the only definition of beauty. Equally, it is a struggle to live in a repressive world that is often ugly in your own eyes. Wisdom, in part, is to struggle without being too self-destructive.

Aesthetics

We therefore cannot *know* a self; we can only *betray* our self, and we do this, as the phrase indicates, fragmentarily and unconsciously. We betray ourselves in our gestures, in the accents of our speech, in our handwriting, and generally in all those forms or configurations which automatically register the track of the stream of consciousness.

—Herbert Read

It is important to be a little clearer about one's sense of rightfitting-ness; about what is being called one's aesthetic. First, to even write about an individual's aesthetic—not in the plastic arts (painting, pottery making, and so forth) sense but in a living of life sense—is clearly time- and culture-bound. Let me back into an explanation of what I mean.

Once, while in Africa, Carl Jung described his native guides. According to Herbert Read, the guides had a "darting restlessness of vision. . . . Such eye movement must be coordinated with mental alertness and a swiftly changing imagery that allowed little opportunity for discursive reasoning, for contemplation and comparison." [6] It is likely that the kind of aesthetics I am talking about becomes active after much of an environment has been stabilized—has, at least in part, been conquered and controlled—so that we are able to see and do patterns.

In what Herbert Read calls a "gestalt-free" setting, the setting of the native guides, we would not and probably could not see the kinds of patterns of beauty I am talking about. That is not to say that there is no beauty in a gestalt-free setting. We know for a fact that there is. And certainly people may do well or poorly in such a setting, but that is of no real importance to our study. What is important is to acknowledge that this work is time- and culture-bound and, for that reason alone, can never be value-free.

The second point to acknowledge is that *aesthetics* is a term generally tied to the arts—to painting and sculpting and those activities in which one can clearly control the shape of the final product. While it is not impossible to translate the word from the arts to people's lives, doing so is not without problems. To put it in a fairly simple way, I am not convinced that people's lives are works of art (in fact, I am against the idea), nor am I persuaded that works of art somehow have a monopoly on the use of the idea of aesthetics.

Enough warning.

It seems reasonable to begin with Ludwig Wittgenstein, who did much to open up the world for us. To quote: "In order to get clear about aesthetic words you have to describe ways of living . . . we find that if we have to talk about aesthetic judgments we don't find words at all, but a word used something like a gesture, accompanying a complicated activity." [7] A little later, he offers an example.

Suppose, Wittgenstein writes, that you meet someone on the street who has just lost his best friend. He tells you of the loss in "a voice extremely expressive of his emotion." It would be easy and natural to think he expressed himself in an "extraordinarily beautiful way." Curiously, one feels a sense of delight.

Suppose you then think, "What similarity has my admiring this person to my eating vanilla ice and liking it?" What, indeed? Wittgenstein says that, at least on the surface, "To compare the two seems almost disgusting." So it seems.

Finally, a third person suggests, "But this is a quite different kind of delight." Well, maybe. Wittgenstein challenges us: "But did you learn two meanings of delight? You use the same word on both occasions. There is some connection between these delights." [8]

What I would like to suggest is that the tie is an aesthetic one. It is the sense that can connect different kinds of beauty (delights); it is a sense that, when acted upon, may give shape to the who-we-are. Before I get away from Wittgenstein, it is important to repeat what was written earlier: "We don't start from certain words, but from certain occasions and activities." [9]

While it would be foolish to deny the specialized kind of aesthetics that begins with the activity of art, it would be equally foolish to limit aesthetics to that single sphere. We will soon see that aesthetics may begin with the occasions and activities of life.

In an extraordinary series of books, Herbert Read has traced the connections among art, culture, politics, economics, and human beings. He is able to show how changes in art are related to the way we think and conceptualize. I mention his work to suggest that you read some of his books and to share his sense of our aesthetic with you.

"We may therefore reaffirm a rational faith in human progress," writes Read. That is a thought that gets quickly modified; to be more precise, the thought gets radically changed: "[Man] has established a moral sense to guide him in his dealings with his fellow-men and *an aesthetic sense to enable him to modify the life of reason.* . . ." [10]

It is that aesthetic sense that becomes a key centering aspect of Read's thought. Listen: ". . . in the end the aesthetic sense is the vital sense, the sense without which we die." [11]

A Modest Summary

At the beginning of this chapter, the promise was that there would be judgments about people's lives. What I argued was that people live in a world that is chaotic and that is certainly not entirely of their making; further, that each person has a sense of the rightfittingness of that world, a rightfittingness that comes naturally from an aesthetic sense; finally, that wisdom meant somehow acting on that aesthetic sense more often than not.

What is clear is that wisdom, like aesthetics, is a daily, lived activity. It is never completed, never finished, just as the who-you-are is not completed until you die. When I write about the following four people, I am only writing a progress report. I assume that from the time we talked to now, they all have done things in and to the world, and the world, in turn, has done things to all of them.

It is necessary to clarify one last point: To isolate college and say that it is *the* critical factor in a person's life is an extreme (and very wrongheaded) claim. Any day in any life is the reflection of an enormous number of things that cannot be and probably should not be sorted out. Yet, by talking with and getting to know people as we did, and by concentrating on education, we found it both possible and beneficial to talk about the effect of education on the daily life of an individual.

What is important to remember is that education carries the force and power of society, and that this symbolic laying on of hands (or not) is full of meaning for the individual. Education (more to the point, a degree) has traditionally been the public passage into mainstream managerial America.

Of course, it is much more than that.

Education is one of those things that threads through the public and the private. It ties the person to his or her surroundings. Education, for those with it, frequently provides a sense of being in the world that helps shape and give meaning to a day. The sense of being is not necessarily a happy or healthy sense. Coming from the other side, the same kind of sloppy statement may be made about those without a college education.

Degrees of Education

"I'm scared . . . I can envision all the problems and a lot of things that I have no idea—don't really know anything about. And I'm going to learn them. It's really scary to do that."

BILL

Bill was a lovely man. He was tall and thin and walked with a certain grace. He was in his late thirties and had a weathered face with lines that seemed ready to smile. Bill was thoughtful, quiet-spoken, almost shy; and he took our conversations quite seriously.

He received an undergraduate degree later than most and moved to Seattle to do graduate work. He had a Master's degree and had done work toward his Ph.D. During the time we spoke with him he was unemployed and receiving unemployment compensation. He wanted to work but would not go to work for a huge organization. At that time he was repairing a friend's boat so that he could try commercial fishing.

To give his punch line first: It is fair to say that post-secondary education had much to do with each day this man lived. The "why" is what is interesting.

We can start close to the beginning—with his home, the town he lived in, and his growing up. "It was a small house, two bedrooms . . . small yard . . . all the houses on that street were just the same size." His town: "Dull . . . originally it was primarily a farming community. All the farmers that retired would move into town. The south end was primarily black and the east side was Polish and Irish."

About his childhood: "I don't think of myself as unusual, so I guess you could say I thought of myself as being average. And I suppose that meant doing whatever one had to do to get a decent job and earn a good wage and follow sort of. . . . You got married and had kids and bought a car and built a house with all sorts of things that you wanted."

Possibly one of the most remarkable elements of his growing up in that "dull" midwestern town was just how "average" it sounded. The American dream gets born again in a small house with a small yard in a small town. That is not to say everything was easy. There were hard times. Bill's father died when he was a junior in high school, and he was never really close to his mother. Yet, in a great many all-American ways, it was a normal growing up.

Bill chose to attend a Big State University for "normal" reasons: "There was one group in high school who obviously . . . sort of 'aimed' toward college. Everybody said that was expected of them." So he went.

He quickly flunked out: "I just *wasn't* interested in school, and I wasn't ready for it—it was the *wrong* thing to do, it was the *wrong* place to go. And, I can only see those things in hindsight." As he spoke, he wanted us to understand clearly that there was little right about his stay at Big State U. He shook his head a great deal.

He then went to work in a succession of jobs: "So I just went to work . . . not knowing what else to do, but knowing that I couldn't sit around; I had to do something. Strong Puritan work ethic." Bill was successful in his jobs. He went from working on road crews to white-collar employment but was not really satisfied. The solution was to return to college.

Instead of a Big State U., he enrolled in a (excuse the candor) not-very-highly-regarded-in-academic-circles school. It was not high-powered, but it *was* college and he *did* do well. There were interesting teachers, and some of the classes were enjoyable. He told us, "I felt good because I was doing well. And, of course, this was sort of reinforcement; you know, the better I did the better I felt. *It was satisfying to know that I could do it and I wasn't really as dumb as I thought I might be. . . . I saw that* [particular college] *only as a proving grounds for myself."*

I think that it is fair to take his words seriously. What he said was a reflection on much of what college is about. By the time he completed college, Bill's habits of mind and his confidence were pretty well set. At some preconscious level, as well as at the visible sign of reward, the society had bestowed its approval. He *was* intelligent, he *had* a degree, and by the kind of logic that helps run our society, he *was* all right. Society had confirmed him.

From a small town, an "average" existence, a small house, and parents who did not have college degrees, he had made it. Given this success and his ambition, Bill went west to do graduate work, not to a college but to a more prestigious Big State University. It was here that a second set of "normal" things happened to him.

Graduate school, which had begun as an intellectually stimulating place, soon began to reflect other parts of life. Professors, no matter how nice they were personally, were busy with their own professional businesses ("He [his advisor] was becoming more and more inaccessible; . . . you could go over to his house at night, but I felt somewhat wrong about dragging *my* business into his home"); and later, this person under whom he had studied was fired. The firing ("I was terribly, terribly upset about it . . . I really admired the man. He sort of became a model for me.") brought out the nature of academic politics: "I was becoming aware that it's no different than the sort of thing that goes on in the business world."

But of course it *is* different because we expect something more and something different from academics, academic life, and education. For someone who had so much tied up in the academic life, so much psychological motivation and energy, a bad experience in graduate school was more than just another disappointment. Bill told us, as a fact that he was sad about, "The idealism was being stripped away." That, and more.

"Things just sort of collapsed after that." His wife left him, he had quit school, and he lost his job. When we talked with Bill he was receiving unemployment compensation and living alone in a well-kept, comfortable apartment.

It seems important to note that experiences such as Bill's in graduate school are, regrettably, normal events for our part of the twentieth century in America. To a depressing extent, being divorced or watching a respected teacher and mentor/friend being fired is not an exceptional happening.

Normal is a deceiving category that frequently masks terrible experiences for those who are involved. For Bill the events of graduate school, not his graduate "studies," led him to seriously question just what was going on—just what kind of society would allow such events to be commonplace, what the prospects for that society might be, and just what he might be able to do about any of it.

In essence Bill found that the category of *normal* contained much that was personally hurtful. Part of being educated, for him, was to have the self-confidence to be non-normal, to pursue less socially accepted (and certainly less personally harmful) actions.

The question is this: What effect did education have on Bill's everyday life? That may be further reduced: *Which* education, and what did his life look like?

I want to argue that we must consider *both* educations. The first has to do with getting a degree, doing well academically, having confidence. The second focuses around the "realities" of American life. Just what kind of society could condone as "normal" so many terribly hurtful and seemingly perverse actions? Not having to doubt his own ability, Bill could face, and question, his surroundings. He could quit graduate school and not be personally damaged.

His average aspirations from his dull small-town background were gone. By looking at his work experience and his consuming, we can see examples of how his world had changed. "It struck me the other day that, outside of [one job], I've always worked for some federal or state or city government; I never worked for myself . . . and I guess I've always been sort of scared of it, you know." Bill was preparing to work for himself, and said, "I'm scared . . . I can envision all the problems and a lot of things that I have no idea—don't know anything about. And I'm going to have to learn them. It's really scary to do that. In a way, it's sort of a challenge, too. Whole new things to explore, and the mistakes I make are my own."

Consumption? The house and the new car? Bill was living what he called a "reduced lifestyle . . . I would like to be able to completely accept them [creature comforts] or to completely be without them. To me personally it's a goal that I'm shooting for. I was thinking about things like automobiles, and could I give away my automobile. And right now I find it extremely difficult to conceive of not having a car."

What is interesting is that Bill viewed the driving and owning of a car as both a personal and a political choice. He fully understood that "what's probably gonna happen is that it's gonna be one of those things where I don't make a decision: It's gonna be made for me." I think this is a way to see self-confidence mesh with reality as he understood it. That driving a car was *both* his choice and—he feared—ultimately the choice of society was a statement of a person making history within history. It can be understood as will acting in the context of the collective will.

We shall periodically return to Bill and fill out the texture of his day, but even with this outline we can say some things about his education and his aesthetic sense.

By most standard (socially acceptable middle-class) criteria of income, status, and the like, Bill's education had been "wasted." But his story is misshapen and misunderstood in the standard categories. He was—in traditional categories—overeducated for unemployment. He had no social mobility. He was of no great "use" to society. He didn't even consume much. It seems equally reasonable to argue that we should consider him a fine college product—quite in spite of college.

His education gave him a certain respect for thinking through problems, and for books and ideas, which helped him sort out seemingly unconnected phenomena. Socially and intellectually it gave him confidence to try and do what he considered right. Finally, by serving as an example of how a bureaucratic institution works in a bureaucratic society, college taught him how many things work around him. It is quite possible that without an education, he would have never been at peace about the myth.

That confidence was something beyond and different from rational thought. The confidence worked not only on a social and then rational level, but also on a more primary level. From his stories and his small apartment and even his appearance, one could tell he had a sense of himself and the world in which he lived. He had the time and the energy and the insight to make serious decisions about how he would best live. Decisions about how he could manage, given a number of objective conditions that he seemed to dislike a great deal, to live a life as "right" for him as it could be.

His carefulness in thought and action seemed to suit him well. It was beautiful for him. It would, I confess, make me crazy if I tried to live like that. But it is his life, his aesthetic sense, his wisdom we are concerned with.

It is possible to judge his actions in many political ways. In terms of energy or economics or ecology or almost any public issue, we could ask if we approved of his actions. We would then ask if *he* approved of them, and if we were good at our job, we could even try to understand whether he had put together his life in a way that seemed right according to his taste. From what I can tell, the man did make an effort to be wise.

The Drag of No Degree

"I said, 'What degree?'...And she said, 'Oh, I thought *everyone* had a degree.' When she hit me with that, I thought, wow, you *goon*."

SUE

The logical second idea of this section is that without post-secondary education—more exactly, without the blessings of society—we may expect a different set of problems or a different set of solutions. While this is not necessarily true, it is certainly true in the case of the woman about to be described.

First, higher education often seems to be more understandable as a personal experience, as a special setting for events, than as an intellectual undertaking. Second, what frequently distinguishes higher education from other experiences is the considerable mystery and status and symbolic importance given it in our culture. People may learn as much from other settings and experiences, but this simply does not count as much as college.

Sue was a striking-looking woman. She had dark hair and, for most of the time we saw her, was concerned and careful about how she looked. She dressed in jeans or in shorts but seemed always sure she looked right. Sue was quiet and did not often volunteer information. In some ways she seemed scared, but I cannot tell a story to explain why I had that sense.

She was always friendly and nice, and seemed to enjoy our talks.

Sue grew up in a small town in the Pacific Northwest. She had, in her own words, "an unusual home life . . . because my parents got along fantastic; I've never even heard them really have an argument, never have a fight, everything went along fine. It was a good way to grow up because I was just in this big silver cloud all the time; everything was good."

The family were German immigrants who kept close family and German community ties. The young taught the old English and American ways, and the old kept Sue and her sisters well protected and well provided for, in a loving environment.

Sue's public school experience was notable for its enjoyment.

"My social life and all that was important. Probably more important than school: I didn't pay that much attention to school. I was happy with a B, and if I could be a B I didn't push for an A. I was a real good one for not studying until finals and then cramming."

Both Sue and her parents expected that she would go to college. She applied to and was accepted at a private school in Seattle, and she and a friend went to look at it during the summer between high school and college. Seattle was a natural choice: "*I wanted to get away from home.* You know, I felt like I wanted to get out on my own and see what that was like. I'd been right under the wings for a long time."

So, she and her friend went to check out the possibility of going to Private University. She decided to enroll. Later that summer Sue returned to Seattle to visit an older friend. She helped the friend at work and "I thought that was really neat, so we decided to get an apartment and just—probably planned it in one night. I wasn't gonna go to school and was gonna work and be a millionaire."

So much for college, so much for "formal" education, but not so much for education. The decision, though a disappointing one for her parents, was in fact one that produced a collegelike education. Not a formal, diploma-giving, society-blessed education, but an education worthy of the word. If the argument is correct, and one of the values of education is the experience of it, then it makes sense to assume that the other kinds of experience can be equally educational.

In many ways Sue's was a classic small-town-to-big-city American education. Sue's new job was (symbolically, it would be difficult to do better) at an airport. Her stories were wonderful.

Of her new home—the Big City:

"Everyone was moving *so fast*. And I used to just laugh because it would take me maybe half an hour to get to work . . . if my father had to drive any more to work, he'd just crack up. I mean, people [back home] just think you were *insane* driving a half an hour to work, or fifteen or sixteen miles.

"I was, of course, very afraid of blacks 'cause they're—maybe still . . . only one family [at home]. I still am kind of frightened of them.

"Then there was a mixture of all different kinds of people, a lot of, you know, fast talkers, and you have to get used to that . . . just running into all these strangers all the time."

Of culture in the Big City: "You know, I remember the first opera I ever went to, the first ballet I ever went to; I pretended like I'd been there a hundred times, but I was just *amazed* inside. Just amazed."

The education meant, among other things, a break with her old friends. "I don't think I feel better than them: I just feel different, I just live different. They just can't imagine or don't understand how I could go out in the evening and have a few drinks and come home and get up and go to work in the morning. . . . They just can't *imagine* how you, a person, could do that."

Sue was married and had a child. She had worked, and worked successfully, at several jobs. Periodically she had attended classes at a community college or the state university. When we talked with her she had decided not to work for a while and was "just relaxing." By most common ways of judging, she was well off, and one could assume some level of happiness and fulfillment.

But something seemed lacking. Curiously, it had to do with a needless insecurity about education. One way to understand Sue's attitude about education is in her descriptions of her college-educated sister. Although she loved and got along with this sister, there was an edge to the relationship, and it was seen in terms of education. The story, fresh in her mind, was told both mockingly and a little sadly:

"We'll never be real close because she's very materialistic and doesn't want any children ever. She likes—you know, she was in a sorority in college ... and, you know, she's still into the sorority thing. She's very selfish.

"[My other sister is] easygoing, nothing bothers her; we laugh about my sister and her sorority when we're together. We had a big breakfast for my father at 'a fancy restaurant' for his retirement ... and my sister had to be an hour late because she had a sorority meeting. Do you know that she wouldn't give [that meeting] up—for fifteen people!"

The general demeaning of education and its odd social values are only half of it. Sue also had a respect for higher education that was reflected, in part, by the fears she had when she attended classes. Finally, there was the resentment that seems a natural part of our everyday environment:

Inarticulated:

"Education is pretty important to my parents. So I'm sure that they were really disappointed that I didn't go."

Articulated:

"A couple of my bosses' wives just *amazed* me. Like, instantly. I met this one lady, and she says, 'Oh, where did you get your degree?' I said, 'What degree?' 'Don't you have a degree?' 'No.' And she said, 'Oh, I thought *everyone* had a degree.' OH. You know, from then on, I couldn't stand listening to her. When she hit me with that, I thought, wow, you *goon.*"

It was a bind for Sue—she did not particularly need a formal education, but she could not escape the fact that she did not have a *degree* from a *college.* She lacked self-confidence—in part, the result of no degree. One could "see" a lack in her daily life.

Although she enjoyed working, she quit. The family was lower-middle/middle class, they had a neat, small home, they seemed comfortable in that environment. In many ways her day was "routine." She got up at 7:15 to fix breakfasts. Son and husband went to school and work, and she then tried to fill her day.

Her house was spotless, as was her son: "His teachers mentioned a couple of times at conference about [how], you know, he always comes to school neat and clean." She sews: "I made my husband pants; . . . he couldn't find anything he liked. I just decided that's it; . . . I made him, I think, eight pairs of pants."

But there was all that time: "[Things are] pretty comfortable, except I feel like I'm wasting a lot of time."

As she got further in time from work, she changed:

"I think my life has really changed, not working. I don't get a tenth of the things done that I did when I was working. Very unorganized. I was always extremely organized. Everyone's noticed it. Even the checker at the grocery store says, well, you're here every day. We used to see you, you know, once a week. And now I'm there every day, and I've always forgotten something and I run back.

"I'll just be sitting here and all of a sudden I'll think, [my son's] coming home in three hours; I should mop the kitchen and finish vacuuming the front room. And then all of a sudden, he's due here any minute and I haven't done a thing; maybe I've read through a magazine.

"I've gained a tremendous amount of weight since I quit work—twenty-eight pounds."

Her lived day, like all of ours, was much more complex than one can write about. But there were spaces in her day/life. Sue was competent, "independent," not afraid to support her child and herself if she had had to. But her imprint on her surroundings was not evident. Her tastes were not acted on, her energy was not activated by what she wanted the world to be like.

The question—in its most broad form—revolves around the society in which we live, and the political, institutional and socioeconomic setting for the alienation of this woman. We can narrow that question for the moment and ask: Has the lack of a college education contributed to Sue's life?

I believe so. In terms of learning helpful things I seriously doubt that the substance of a college education would have done much. She might possibly have learned a trade, but she could clearly have picked that up at a trade school. If not learning those things, what about learning how to live in the world? As we have seen, she learned that when she moved to the big city. She knew—in a realistic way—her choices in the world. She was independent and did not need formal education to help her understand that women may go outside of the home and have a career.

Since high school and her social success, she had had no recognition from her surroundings of those things she had accomplished.

She learned about the world, and did well in it, but there was no acknowledgment of that. There was, more exactly, no recognition that carried the formal blessings of our culture. Sue had, at best, only a limited amount of confidence to do the things she wanted to do.

It is here—in building confidence—that college may have been helpful. Or, more negatively but equally accurately, the lack of education was hurtful. Had Sue gone to college instead of to work, a certain amount of social approval would have been a result. It does not make me happy to reflect on the difference between her moving to Seattle, taking a job, and sharing an apartment with a friend and her then current life, which seemed full of calories and "empty" time.

All she learned by moving to the Big City somehow did not count, was uncertified, was lost. To indulge in a "what if" analysis becomes silly at some point. But it is fair to seriously consider the *What if she went to college?* question. One of the real possibilities is that she may have had enough self-faith to fill in the blanks in her day. Enough confidence to pursue her sense of the rightfittingness of the world.

College could have possibly provided her with a kind of reward and recognition she simply had not received from other places. She was trapped, not in a traditional way of having to be a servant to a houseful of children, but in a new, more subtle, less tangible, less accessible way. In a professional, status-conscious, degree-oriented environment, this woman felt (and this is a horrible word) obsolete.

It is possible to argue, rightly I think, that education has become a necessary ticket for most people to just be themselves. Generally, one must first come to terms with the cultural environment before being able to do anything about it. Maybe the easiest way to do that is just to get a degree—even if for no other reason than to reject it.

Being wise, the activity of pursuing wisdom, is difficult under the best of circumstances. It seems an unnecessary hardship for Sue to be insecure because she chose to do something other than go to college. Her amount of college education should have—at least in principle—had nothing to do with her pursuit of wisdom.

To judge the way she was acting in the world—to judge her world in terms of her aesthetic sense: She somehow was going through phases of "doing" the world, and then letting the world "do" her. When we talked with Sue, it was the world's turn.

There is a part of wisdom that connects a person with his or her past as well as future. Sue had spent periods of time creating a world right for her, beautiful to her. One could easily imagine that happening again.

To Contradict

With Bill and Sue we can see that a college degree is or may be helpful. In the lowest, least attractive formulation of the argument, we can say that not having an education is harmful. But it is necessary to remember that we are dealing with powerful myths and symbols. The next two examples will help us get another view of education: We will see education as harmful and the lack of education as beneficial.

It may seem curious that arguments can be made for four seemingly mutually exclusive positions. If one is to take individuals seriously, then it is not at all surprising to find a multitude of results and reactions to the same "event" or myth. Further, below the surface contradictions is the level of analyses that will help make some sense of what goes on.

The events of the world are not simply "relative" or "subjective." Those words demean us all. There are events held in common, "facts" that affect us all, conditions that we all must come to terms with. That different people are affected in different ways by post-secondary education may tell us something about ourselves and our common environment if we are able to find a way to study how that came to be.

While I do not want to suggest that the results of this study are unimportant, it is important to remember that the initial act involves *how* one decided to look at the world, that the first act is the statement of that fact.

Wisdom, it follows, is not only deciding and looking but also acting.

No Degree As Good

"I'll have to do something to make a name for myself, somewhere, some way. Maybe not in the world or the country . . . but to some people."

BETTY

If we are talking about college as a myth, then it makes sense that it may be a myth put to good use. I think it reasonable to say that not completing a college education was a good thing for the woman about to be discussed. Betty's year in college was wonderful—an experience that was magical—but there is little reason to assume that more schooling would have been beneficial. It seems that you can get some of the best parts of the myth without being certified.

That's the key insight; now for the stories.

Betty was what she appeared to be: an outgoing, friendly, attractive, and energetic person. Her conversations seemed a good reflection of her thoughts: direct, nice, and concerned.

It is, in certain ways, difficult to give an accurate picture of Betty. I could explain about her brown hair or her nice smile, tell you she was about 5'3" and was always fighting those extra five or ten pounds that seem a common problem when you are in your mid-thirties. But there was something more, and it had to do with competence.

Somehow Betty seemed able to take care of anything—not in a rough or pushy way, but in a much nicer way. There seemed no situation that she could not handle: a kind of super wife/mother/neighbor/community worker image. The further image was that she had the energy to do all those things well.

Betty was the oldest of a large (more than a dozen children) Catholic family. It is, at least for me, impossible to understand the implications of so many siblings. However, there are two stories that may help provide a glimpse of her growing up.

Listen:

"Mother to this day regrets that she gave me as much responsibility as she did. At age ten, I think I just couldn't take any more; . . . I broke out badly on my hands so I couldn't do dishes anymore; . . . I couldn't do this or couldn't do that; it was my psyche saying, 'No, I couldn't do any more.' But she desperately needed help and I was able to do it. She marveled that she gave me so much responsibility, say, to a five-year-old.

"Windows were always big for her [her mother]. And for some reason, that carried over to me—cleaning windows. And I think it was because she was inside too much and looking out and the world went by and she watched it go by and she wanted to see clearly." (As an aside, I am convinced that people who write good fiction fail to imagine much good "reality.")

She went to Catholic schools through high school. The nuns who taught her "had a stricter idea about discipline, and they had firmer control over us than teachers do now, so we did conform." She didn't mind wearing a uniform: "Our school was downtown . . . so we were in the public eye, and we were made to feel the importance of the uniform and not disgrace the uniform." Betty made good grades, was a class officer, was popular, followed the college prep program, had friends, and generally did well. Her recall in some instances was both detailed and revealing.

Her teachers:

"They made an impression on me at the time, and I admired them and I guess I wanted to be like them in many respects. You know I remember each one distinctly: Maybe that's why you think they made an impression. I don't think I modeled my life after any one particular one. I admired their dedication and their patience and their kindness and their wit, too. I'm just amazed, mainly at their dedication—to devote their lives to children and the teaching of the faith."

One can easily imagine that college was quite an event for her. The oldest child—oldest sister—leaving home for college. Everyone, it seemed, sewed and helped prepare. She went to a small Catholic college in a small town in the Northwest. After the appropriate warnings by the nuns from high school that college would be tough, Betty enjoyed a good summer following her senior year, and then was off.
It was fantastic.

"I was really very confident of myself, for some reason. Well, I was partly scared too, and when I get scared I guess I get real flippant and real smart-ass and I guess they like that. So I had a lot of dates, right from the start. I'll never forget the first day I was there. We were in one of [the] juniors' rooms, and looking down, here was this guy in a red convertible: I mean Mr. Smooth or Mr. Cool. Awe. He's really it. I dated him for six weeks.

"I'd only been at school, like, a month, before I met [my husband]. And that was it. I mean, that was it. I had a couple of dates after because I'd already made them, but it's been him ever since. But school, school was—I just loved every aspect of it. It was enjoyable and it opened my mind to different people and how they live. There were a lot of new decisions to make, and it was a very maturing year for me."

And that was the last year she would be a college student. Betty quit, married, and helped support her husband while he went to a professional school. College, in many ways, was all image for her. There was the excitement of Freshman Fun; of what "intellectual professors" were about; of meeting new people; of not living with so much family; of boys and men and finally the Right Man.

After beginning a family (they were to have five children in just a little over five years, and then to decide five were enough), they moved to Washington, D.C. Again, it was a fine experience. She learned to be around and to entertain bright, well-educated people-who-were-going-to-be-successful. She even developed a taste for the *Washington Post* and for being informed about world events. They moved to Seattle three years later.

Once settled, she became active in school and church affairs. Betty always seemed to be the representative on the block to collect money for various church charities. She also took care of her husband and children and house and entertainment. "During the summer, I'm the complete yard lady at our house: I mow and edge and take care of the flowers or whatever has to be taken care of outside."

There were at least two other important aspects of her day. The first was about privacy; the second, about change. First: "That's one thing I have to have is time to myself. For some part of every day there just has to be no people demanding my time at all. If I have to stay up late to get it, I do. My mother's that way, too. I guess when your time is demanded by other people, you feel this need more than others." It was a time for reading. If the time was in the morning, it was coffee and smoking and reading. Ah, privacy.

The second aspect, change, was centered around Women's Lib— a phrase she used. While we will come back to this when we discuss work and politics, it makes sense to mention it here, as it had had a great influence on her life. Betty read women's literature carefully, and did serious thinking as she worked through her day, and slowly introduced her husband to a new set of ideas. Her husband: "She never pushed it, but it was kind of a—her personality, her positions— she took on decisions, decisionmaking in the family; she became much more assertive than she had [been] in the past. It was nice."

Three examples:

1.

Betty: "I was working and he was working; we were both putting the money in the pot to keep our family going and our house going. To start with he didn't want my name on the checkbook: My name was nowhere on the check; he wrote the checks, all the bills, everything. Then it was 'both first names,' but he still wrote the checks, paid the bills every month. But then—"

Her Husband: "She seized power."

Betty: "Seized power so I not only had my name on it, I—"

Her Husband: "In the early seventies."

Betty: "And he has to ask me for money, which for me is quite a change."

2.

"I don't know if I'm a person that can work in my own little garden, keeping my own little house; I don't know if that'll be enough for me. I don't think it will be. I'll have to do something to make a name for myself, somewhere, some way. Maybe not in the world or the country or even in the city, but to some people; that I'll have accomplished something besides being a wife and a mother of five children."

3.

"I sometimes feel like the house is a reflection of me. I shouldn't identify with the way the house looks—I've come a long way 'cause I used to think—oh, I'd walk into someone's house and I'd say, look at hers."

Betty had a strong belief in God and was very active in church affairs. She had somewhat weaker beliefs that the general conditions of society and the economy, which were bad, would be better soon. In the early seventies Betty recycled things, was careful about money, and did not care what her children grew up to be as long as they were "reasonably happy." The center of her life was her family, but as she had more free time she became more and more active out of the house.

In many ways it would be impossible to even begin to understand her without understanding her basic attitude: Betty was optimistic. A way to see this is to hear how she felt about pessimists: "If they submerge themselves in self-pity and complain all the time about their plight in life and don't seem to be doing anything themselves about it, I have to say that I don't have much patience with them. I just get irritated with them."

If we look at Betty's surroundings it is clear that they were infused by her spirit, by her sense of herself and the world. She seemed happy and realistic; the present was a mix of both the past and the future. It seemed possible that she would return to college at some point, but I can think of no good reason to argue that she was somehow less than a self because she had no degree.

In fact, it appeared that she had got some of the best that the myth of education has to offer. That, combined with a self-confidence that let her see she was as bright as other people, and her interest in news and novels—and her hour a day to herself—had kept her well read and constantly considering new sets of ideas.

There was in Betty an interesting blend of intellectual curiosity and genuine modesty that is not generally found in those with college degrees. I can honestly admit that, as I understand it, not getting a degree was one of the good things that had happened to her.

To focus the judgment on a college degree is, in this case, easy enough. It is much more difficult to come to some conclusion about wisdom. Certainly, unlike Sue, Betty was not lost. In a sense, I believe she was working on the world to make it more beautiful. But to use the phrase "I believe" is to hedge a bit, and it seems fair to explain why I hedge.

If I am correct and each of us has an aesthetic sense that—at least in detail—is uniquely our own, then it will be difficult to appreciate a wide range of visions of beauty. Again, while Bill's carefulness was pleasing to him, I know it would be tiresome for me if I tried it.

Much of what truly appealed to Betty was straightforward, mainline, middle-class, American-Catholic-family virtues. Those virtues do have a beauty to them, and it does take an effort to live them. Betty made the effort. What makes it a little difficult to judge is that the life *seems* effortless because it *seems* normal and because there is strong institutional and ideological backing for it.

That should not blind us to the fact that even doing "normal" well is difficult—that even "normal" may be beautiful.

A Degree Isn't Necessarily So Good

"I'm bored. I think that's the biggest problem."

LIZ

Liz, who is the last person to present, like Betty had a quite comfortable life and status. She was in her early thirties, married, the mother of three children, and was—in socioeconomic terms—middle/upper-middle class.

Liz was blond, slim, and attractive. She was bright and had thoughts on many things. In a number of ways she was as self-conscious as anyone we talked with; but the self-consciousness did not appear to be helpful. Liz enjoyed shocking people by saying outrageous things or by appearing to be what she clearly was not—an empty-headed blond.

She was college-educated, appeared well read, was politically aware, and in conversation seemed intelligent and thoughtful. The other important detail is that Liz seemed lonely; and if one was to take what she said seriously, she was unhappy. While it would be unwise and simply wrong to blame her self-described unhappiness all on her education, it would be equally wrong to ignore the role that education had played in making her day what it was.

All of her growing up, through high school, took place in a small town in eastern Washington State. She had two brothers and one sister. Those first eighteen years were relatively uneventful; her life had revolved around home, school, friends, family, and religion. It is best to begin with her reflections on junior high school, for those days seemed a very natural lead into her then-current life.

First of all, we can get an insight into how Liz had seen herself as a younger person from the way she contrasted her sister with herself: "I remember that she used to get in trouble more than I did, all the time. She was, I remember, whatever was off limits; that was what she did. And I was the *perfect little angel*." In the context of the conversation, that last line was said half-jokingly. Half.

Listen to her school experiences:

"I always felt like I belonged, and by the seventh and eighth grade I guess I was a cheerleader, class president, and doing all those neat things; you know. Then I got to junior high and it didn't quite work that way, and that's when I decided that I was going to get straight A's. I spent all my lunch hours in the library: nobody else in the library but me.

"I thought that would mean success in life, I guess. . . .

"I don't know how I got that idea."

But there were problems: "If you spend your lunch hours in the library, you get ostracized pretty quick." And problems: "It started out—I think I had about three boyfriends by the first thing, but when I turned them all down for the first dance, when I told them I didn't believe in dancing (because of religion), that sort of screwed things up."

Her teachers were involved in her academic success: "Well, I do remember my geography teacher; he was the one that was so impressed with me. He used to tell me that my boyfriend was not on the A level and that I really should do better than that. He would say that frequently. I had another spurt of [religious reform] during the first few months of high school, and that managed to just screw me up socially for the rest of high school, it seems."

Things—at least socially—did not improve very much.

"And I didn't date my senior year hardly at all. I was really flirting with this one boy in my social studies class, but he never got around to asking me out until it was graduation night.

"It was hard. You know, I'd come home from school and I'd study and then I'd take a break and then I'd study after dinner; I'd study until midnight or something."

Finally, her intelligence, studying, and belief in God merged at the point of her decision of which college to attend. The story was told with a blush. The question was, *How did you decide on the college you were going to?*

"I really can't tell you: It's too embarrassing. I was still very religious at this point, and I was debating. I had a scholarship and I had been accepted into a special program at the [Big State U.]. It was just for people who were better than anybody else. And I had a scholarship for a [Small Religious College]. So, the beginning of the last semester, I started getting straight A's and I started being number three instead of number four in my class. So, being very religious, I prayed to God and said that if I got straight A's, I'll go to the religious school, and if I don't, I'll go to the [Big State U.]."

She made her A's and kept her part of the bargain; and, "I figured I was placing myself in a situation where I couldn't go very far astray." Before we get to college, one last shot at public schools: "And I'd come out of high school just hating people: They were the rottennest things in the whole world."

The bright, blond, soon-to-be slender, attractive young woman from the little town goes to college. A Small Religious College in a Big City. What did she want/expect from college? The usual:

To get away: "But no one wanted to say in [her home town]; . . . you didn't want to stay. It's a dead place. We wanted to go to college and probably get a teaching certificate and marry somebody who made a good living."

And more: "One thing is that I thought I would learn a whole bunch of exciting things . . . and I'd meet a lot more people I could talk to. And I thought I'd figure out . . . some fantastic career: It would suddenly become apparent that this was what I'd been looking for all my life, this neat career."

Her first year of college was the best. Somehow she felt that the world had finally caught up with her. Liz was popular, made pretty good grades, enjoyed talking to her roommate, and met the man she was to marry. So much for success.

Me: "And then it was fall again. Were you excited, were you ready to go back?"
Liz: "Yeah, I was. Except for the school part; I never did like school. I think I'd gotten sick of school by my freshman year."

She married in her junior year and moved off campus.

"I was so lonely I thought I was going to die. Because I was really isolated, I wasn't—I would go to my classes and then I would study. So I spent a lot of time in the library and in classes, and then I'd go home. [My husband's] sort of a quiet person, and I was very lonely.

"I hated it more and more. And cried a lot more than I studied.

"I would come home at four o'clock. I would just be doubled over with cramps every Friday afternoon."

Me: "Every Friday afternoon?"
Liz: "Yes."

By her senior year her neat, fantastic career had not become obvious; so Liz went into teaching. The time spent practice teaching was remarkable in the completeness of how bad it was:

"It was really awful . . . I wanted to quit after two weeks. I mean, it was really my first really huge failure, of trying to do something and really working at it. I don't feel like I was a good teacher, and it's not—it wasn't fun for me to do something that I didn't think I was doing well."

Bad. Remarkably so.
With great relief, she graduated. In retrospect, this seems to be the essence of what college was for her:

"You go to college, and all of a sudden you find out there aren't answers to things and you have to live the rest of your life without any answers.

"And I have a much more complicated idea of how a relationship should 'be.'

"I think I have a completely different set of friends than I would've if I hadn't gone to college . . . a completely different set of friends. It seems like the basic thing in one's life."

The couple moved so that her husband could get a professional degree. Liz supported them by working at the university. When they returned to Seattle, they settled down in a big house, with their three children and a dog. They went to church, and had bought a summer house in the country; but only in a limited number of ways was the world in order for Liz.

There was the world; there were the kids; there wasn't the job.

"I used to watch the 'Today' show; I watch it occasionally now. And then if I'm not going someplace, I don't know what to do with myself. And here it's just about nine o'clock in the morning.

"It's really easy to just sit back and feel sorry for yourself, because it's hard especially after you've been home for years to go out.

"I do get panicky sometimes. I sort of had thought, when I wasn't so tired, then I would just do all these things. Well, I just sort of walked around the house. Well, I made the mistake of drinking coffee, and that really wound me up."

In many ways, the world was simply painful for Liz during the time we were talking with her. One of her fantasies was to live in a commune. This was balanced by her husband's fantasy to be more alone and to become a cabinetmaker. An option for her, of course, was to get a job. After much debate, she had decided that "my occupation for the next two years is gonna be making friends. It sounds very—it sounds really very exciting to me." Also:

"I think I'm gonna take something . . . an assertiveness training program . . . through the women's institute; they offer the course. [One woman there] said, 'Have you taken that aggressive training yet [*laughing*]?'"

One way to better understand part of the dynamic is to think in terms of American individualism. Like education, individualism is one of those myths full of mixed blessings.

For her kids: "I think my number-one priority for them is to develop very strong egos . . . self-confidence, feeling independent—and that they can go out and do what they want to do."

For herself: "I think I thought it would be neat to have my own house and do what I wanted; I always thought it would be neat to be my own boss in my own house. Not having anybody telling me what to do at last. But then that's what I was, I was just lonely and I didn't like it."

For the power of myth: "I'm bored. I think that's the biggest problem. So I think if I were out there working, then I would be fulfilled; then I would be more of a person."

When we deal directly with work, we will explore Liz's feelings and realities in some depth. Now it is more appropriate to say that, at the time of our talks, Liz was seeing a counselor, staying at home, and working at being less depressed.

It seems to me that her ambivalence about "being boss" and living in a commune; about being able to do what she wants and being alone reflects attitudes about individualism. It is an American myth/tension that we can see played out daily. From the first-generation Puritans to their descendants who were interested in individualism, people have been confused about what is "best." What we are taught is right is rugged individualism, no matter what our instincts.

What we have is a dilemma: being boss or living communally.

If we add college, we find that there are more problems. Liz *completed* the myth. She *was* a good student. She did everything right. The promise of the myth is happiness—the reward is career and family and a good life. Education should produce the successful individual.

What this woman had found was that her reward was all surface: a big home, a summer house, free (empty) time. No career had found her. In many ways, the myth had paid in full . . . except for happiness.

Would she have been better off without college? A good question, but the wrong one. Had school been helpful? If we look at her day-to-day life, we can answer that school had probably not helped. Her being bored some mornings by nine o'clock did not speak of a full life. One thing we know is that to do all the "right" things, to be a "perfect little angel," to fill the requirements of the myth may simply lead to a lonely life of frustration.

On the brighter side, Liz at least did not have to worry about not having an education. But one has to admit that that wasn't as bright a situation as one might have hoped.

There are a number of ways to "analyze" this woman and the world in which she lives. Certainly her life seemed a powerful condemnation of many elements of our liberal society. There is no doubt but that there are parts of her past that have ongoing psychological effects on her. What I would like to argue is that she was not wise. What was missing was a sense of a way the world—her world—could fit together that would be aesthetically pleasing to her.

Wisdom is an active concept, not a static one that, once attained, can never be lost. While our blond woman might have been successful by family and community standards, the who-she-is was lost. The sense of rightfittingness of the world was buried deeply, and no one who had talked with her when we did could have mistaken her intelligence for wisdom.

Obvious Questions

Let me try to deal with some obvious questions, and see if I can make further sense of what I have been calling wisdom. The questions have to do with the relationship of wisdom to other ideas; and the first other idea is that of knowledge.

Clearly, wisdom and knowledge are not mutually exclusive. For many, I would argue that knowing things—that having knowledge—can only help one to be wise. But knowledge is basically an empty concept. You can, for example, get a lot of information and knowledge from college—you can be filled up with it—and not be wise. To be wise, you need that knowledge organized to fit your senses: It must be at the service of your aesthetic self.

To know the critique of society, to know its shortcomings and fallacies and injustices, is simply an intellectual exercise. To stop at that is to condemn yourself to a bitter and probably not very interesting or good life.

A tougher thing to sort out is the relationship between being wise and being psychologically healthy. What makes this so difficult is that there are many different psychologies and many kinds of health. It would be fairly silly to argue that to be wise is to be unhealthy, or that to be wise has nothing to do with understanding one's psychological self. I want to make neither of those arguments.

What I would like to argue is that the bias of most psychology seems to be toward adjustment. Good psychological health turns on the patient's understanding and overcoming the effects of his or her past, understanding the objective conditions in which he or she is living, and adjusting to them in one or another way. I do not particularly object to that in principle, and I would accept as true that for many people the process is a very helpful one.

With wisdom, the emphasis is different. We each have a sense that is different from—and, I would argue, more basic than—the sets of emotions dealt with in psychology. Oedipal feelings and anger and the like are things we are able to learn about and deal with. Psychologists are able to "cure" us. But we can never be "cured" of our aesthetic sense. Hopefully, the rages and the tensions and the joys and the quiet beauties will always be alive and active in us.

Clinically healthy people are not necessarily wise. Wise people, I would assume, are generally healthy. Maybe not well adjusted or remarkably successful socially, or even particularly normal, but at least healthy.

Using wisdom as a way of understanding people should help us appreciate and see more clearly the levels and dimensions of our times. It can be a help, even a great help; but to explore the mysteries of action is well beyond the sum of our knowledge.

Now That You've Met

This is the last chapter of "introductions." The remainder of the book will be concerned with these people. Some have been dealt with more fully than others, but none has been dealt with in anything close to completeness. As we now shift from biography in particular to biography in an American context, each person will be understood in more depth.

Before this, I would like to do selective summing up to end this chapter and introduce some topics of the next one.

All along I have made the argument that by doing research in a different way, by using different criteria and categories, we might find the consequences of post-secondary education to be not what we may have imagined. We can make good arguments that education may be harmful and not-education may even be helpful in a day in the life of a person.

We have seen education directly connected to high levels of false expectations and unnecessary guilt. Both of these affect the texture and the sense of a life.

We also know that there *is* a confidence one may get from formal education that may be useful. There is a curious dynamic at work in many of those with whom we spoke. In the cases in which education was "helpful," there was a cynical realism about the whole process. It was almost as if people were saying, "My education was meaningless, but no one can push me around."

In an important sense that attitude leads us to the topic of change. There is virtually nothing in our surroundings that argues for the opposite of change. But what we have come to understand is that most of the "change" that is suggested and that actually occurs is fairly lightweight surface stuff. Significant social and personal change is remarkably difficult to achieve and is rarely advocated in a serious way.

To write something like "there is inequality and injustice in our society" would be writing nothing new; equally, to find that people's lives may be empty and unhappy would be no surprise. What is pleasing is to find that some people are trying to be serious about change. Where they begin is with their work, their environments, or, put more simply, with a day in their lives. While this seems frustratingly small when compared to the problems of our society, it is a complex and difficult task for those who try.

An obvious question: Who might change, and what might education have to do with that? We will first look at education and non-change.

We saw well-educated people for whom change had been impossible. While knowing the arguments for change and knowing about the things lacking in their lives, we had a sense that there was too much to overcome. To change would be to turn their backs on the very society that had so richly rewarded them. Higher education had blessed them with the critique of what was wrong with the modern world—the cost of the critique seemed to be the will to act on it.

A garage full of cars, pots full of chicken, a store of good wines, and witty (but a little resigned and appropriately sad) conversation are difficult to resist. It is even more difficult to begin to create. What we get, after all, is a vision of the good life that lurks in most of us—wine and cars and chickens and good pot. It is not strange that those who have it—happy or not—will probably not want to part with it.

But if college does "give the critique," there are bound to be those who take it seriously but need some very strong and unhappy experience to act on what they know. Death, divorce, mentally retarded children have served as enormously difficult reasons for people to begin serious questioning and change. It is precisely at those points that education may be helpful.

To be more explicit, it is at those points that an individual seriously explores the world and how he or she wants to live in that world. To know the society and the critique of that society is important if one wishes to live his or her life more in tune with that deepest sense of what is beautiful. Education can supply facts and even help make whole social dynamics more visible for those who want to see. Those facts and dynamics help make sense of the world and help give the individual both a starting place and the confidence to make personal/political sense of the world he or she would like to live in.

One thing that seems so unnecessary, so cruel, is that it takes some *traumatic* experience to *reorganize* a "normal" wasted educational experience into a helpful one.

We know that education-like experiences may also serve the same kinds of ends. A new job in the Big City, a new life with high-powered people, a union hiring hall provided powerful experiences for some of the people interviewed, and the opportunities for people to rethink what was going on. It seems more difficult to accept the power of these experiences, because we are not taught to accept them. We can expect those without formal education to change, but in spite of our standard operating myths.

In order to even consider change, we must learn to see and talk about the sense and texture of people's lives, and the efforts they make to understand what makes up a day. Traditionally research has focused on creature comforts, social status, and an assortment of material and visual signs of class. The expectation has always been that up was better than down, and that happiness was one reward of social success. If that were true, it would be easy to understand change: We could say that people would change so that they could get more, have power and status, and be happy. Change would be a one-way process.

The problem is, it is not so. If the people we talked with are to be taken seriously, we cannot be nearly so clear about change. Education may lead to change in the sense that people with degrees might turn their backs on normally accepted values—in spite of their conventional educations. One ironic sign of a "good" education (in terms of change) appears when people turn their backs on the lessons of our educational system and on the powerful myths that surround it.

NOTES

1. Larry Spence has explored the many forms of hidden judgments in the social sciences. He has done so in a definitive way. He writes: "Sanity demands our allegiance to human survival at the highest possible level. Man, the species, is neither good nor evil, wonderful nor wicked, for men, the members of that species. The species is. We are members. . . . Men exist and their existence is the standard from which all evaluations on this earth are made. In short, men—their capacities and their needs—are the basic facts of social science." *The Politics of Social Knowledge* (University Park, Pa.: The Pennsylvania State University Press, 1978), p. 137.

2. H. Gerth and C. W. Mills, *From Max Weber* (New York: Oxford University Press, 1958), p. 147.

3. This is Bergson talking about William James, with whom he agrees. It is found in *The Creative Mind: An Introduction to Metaphysics* (New York: Citadel Press, 1946), pp. 210, 218.

4. Alfred Schutz believes that we do much thinking before we reflect on and consciously sort out phenomena. He writes that in the realm in which things are indistinguishable, we run "imaginatively . . . through a series of psychic states in each of which it expands, grows richer, and changes . . . until 'the free act detaches itself from it like an overripe fruit.' " *The Phenomenology of the Social World* (Chicago: Northwestern University Press, 1967), p. 67.

5. Hannah Arendt, *The Human Condition* (Chicago: The University of Chicago Press, 1958), p. 166.

6. Herbert Read, *Icon and Idea: The Function of Art in the Development of Human Consciousness* (New York: Schocken Books, 1965), p. 31.

7. Cyril Barrett, ed., *Wittgenstein: Lectures and Conversations on Aesthetics, Psychology, and Religious Belief* (Berkeley: University of California Press, 1972), p. 11.

8. Ibid., p. 12.

9. Ibid., p. 3.

10. Herbert Read, *To Hell With Culture* (New York: Schocken Books, 1964), pp. 174–175. Emphasis added.

11. Ibid., p. 177.

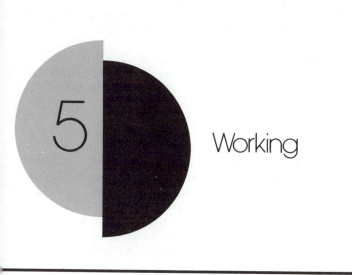

5 Working

The basic error of all materialism in politics ... is to overlook the inevitability with which men disclose themselves as subjects, as distinct and unique persons, even when they wholly concentrate upon reaching an altogether worldly, material object.

—Hannah Arendt

We are not just a developed country but somehow an overdeveloped one. No longer an industrial nation, we are more nearly a post-industrial one. Our economy is of a corporate capitalist kind and is fully capable of having inflation and stagnation get out of hand at the same time. None of the people we talked with are the rich and powerful who make critical decisions that have immediate, far-reaching effects.

There is another way to say that last line: The people we talked with were workers; in a blue collar or a white one, they worked for a living. They were not born rich and powerful, and none seemed destined to become either. So much for *that* American dream. I believe what remains will probably tell us a great deal about what it means to work for a living in our country.

Karl Marx, better than anyone else, wrote about the kinds of alienation that seem to characterize our times. There is no doubt that Marx was right and that alienation is a fact. I have no great desire to prove or disprove or revise what he and other sociologists and economists tell us.

What is more sensible is to see how people try to manage in a situation they did not create. Not only that, we can consider how people have been prepared—and how they prepare themselves—to make judgments and to do jobs in the United States.

LIZ

In the last chapter there was a section about Liz, a college-educated woman who seemed to be having a hard time in the world. She did not have a paying job ("I really do want to work, but not right now. Because I wouldn't be left with—[*pauses*]. I don't think I could come home and cope with the kids."), and yet work was surprisingly central to her. By understanding Liz and work, we can see several important personal and social themes that remain in constant tension.

Education is one of those themes. Listen to Liz: "... you've been educated to believe that there's something you can do about things, that you *don't* have to accept things as they are; then they've really got you in a double bind. Because you're not getting it, and you can sit around and blame yourself for not getting it instead of somebody else, and say, 'It's their fault: I'm not—I'm powerless.' I think we *are* to blame to some extent if we don't try to do—I mean, there are things that we *can* do."

The first bind: the promise and the power and the guilt. Liz was a full-time mother, yet "I'm not enjoying motherhood as much as I thought I would. . . ." She was trained for library work, so "the most obvious thing for me to do would be to try to find a job in the libraries. But—probably the job I could get would be sitting in a basement, filing. You know, its really not. . . ."

Liz did not "really want to go back to school. I know that." So she took up weaving: "It turned out to be *not* the kind of thing I can do; it was Navaho rug weaving—it's very, very slow, and I like something that happens a lot faster." She began playing squash and going to afternoon movies, but that was not enough. Liz enjoyed talking and ideas and that kind of activity; so squash and movies soon became tiring.

As we got more involved in the interview, another pressure became very clear: Liz was a woman dealing with the problem of work. In many ways, that was making things even more difficult. In the most simple terms, Liz grew up before the women's movement was strong, and was already out of school and had children when the movement began having a popular effect.

Her attitude toward money and her husband's employment was interesting:

> *Me:* "What if I posed the question, what happens if your husband would die? Would it—what would a job be then?"
> *Liz:* "It would be my sanity's salvation."
> *Me:* "It would be your income, too?"
> *Liz:* "Oh, yeah. But I'm not so worried about the income."
> *Me:* "If your husband dies, then . . ."
> *Liz:* "My parents will take care of me."

We talked about her husband, who had told us he wanted to be a cabinetmaker but who was doing other—and almost the opposite—kind of work. I asked Liz about that: [*Softly*] "Yeah . . . I think that's really—I guess that's where he's willing to compromise. I'd feel really bad if I were in his position, knowing that what I *really* wanted to do was be a cabinetmaker, but, I was gonna be a lawyer the rest of my life. That would really be a hard thing for me to say, that I was [*pause*], that I had to make that compromise."

My sense is that Liz was telling us a lot about sex-related stereotyping. In an old-fashioned way—one that both men and women may honestly resent—the underlying theme is that the man should support the family, and the woman does other things. Even if the woman works, it should be work for a reason other than money.

The attitudes are very real and, it seems, very destructive.

"All these pent-up feelings over the years and all the things that—and men still don't seem to want to admit that the role of men is not perfect: It's stereotyping and confining and too narrow. Roles that men have always been supposed to take aren't always comfortable for all men."

Liz, caught between promises and powerlessness and guilt, talked about work:

"I think there's been a lot of pressure for women—you have to go out and get a job no matter what, even if you don't need it, because that's just—that's the way you gain equality.

"My definition of a good job is some job where I feel really competent at what I'm doing and where I can be myself.

"If people were working at jobs that they liked more, that would be a real moral boost.

"I guess that I wanted to be recognized. I think what I want out of a job, as much as excitement, is identity. I don't feel like I have much of an identity, and I feel like a job—a job would do that for me."

> *Me:* "What kind of job? What would you like to call yourself? I mean, I hate to push—but I'm really pushy about this particular subject."
> *Liz:* "Oh, I'd like to be [*pauses*] Barbara Walters."

ALFRED

We did not ask Alfred if he wanted to be Barbara Walters. The truth is, I am not at all certain how he would have answered the question. As a high-school-educated longshoreman, Alfred, we can be sure, has a job with almost nothing in common with Ms. Walters's.

Alfred had had no great fantasies about going into the work his father did: "I didn't particularly want to longshore; . . . I definitely knew that I didn't want to longshore." There were union troubles: "There's a lot of politics, but it's terribly petty politics; . . . it's a very destructive—it's on a personal level and I really don't—I don't see that as being—it kind of turns me off. And as far as your meetings go—it's nothing but a drunk holocaust."

His fellow workers did discuss other kinds of politics, and Alfred talked a great deal about economics.

> *Interviewer:* "You know a heck of a lot about the financial system."
> *Alfred:* "I don't know if I really do."
> *Interviewer:* You think about it at least, as the center of something important."
> *Alfred:* "Yes. Oh yes. Well, you have to."
> *Interviewer:* "I think so, too."
> *Alfred:* "Yeah, because the bank deposit is your energy, you know, I mean . . . that greenback in your wallet represents your life."

While Alfred would never be rich from longshoring, he did have his card, he could work as much or as little as he wanted, and he accepted the "greenback" as important. Clearly he was willing to work for it. He had bought a houseboat, he had a car, and he had tried to make some sense of his work.

I assume that most people reading this have worked at one time or another. I also assume that most of you (like me) know very little about what it means to work at longshoring. We asked for, and got, a description of part of Alfred's day at work. Listen:

"A day? . . . Well, I get up in the morning about six—yeah, this would be about the easiest way of doing it. I get up about six-forty-five—not six-forty-five, but quarter after—I don't know—six-thirty, something like that. And I get up, and then I get down to the dispatch hall before seven o'clock, . . . and down by the Pike Place Market, and there are people walking around on the street, and I get out and I look at the street and I'm wondering when they're going to pick up the shit on the street—it's very disturbing. I kind of dig those old buildings and things, but not the way they're kept up—it's not too cool—and I say, 'Well, it's too bad that they have all these bums around here because this is their back yard.'

"And I go into the hall past some doors and things, and there's some fellows sitting around playing cards at the bar—in this hall that's about 50 X 150 or so. When you walk in on the right there's a dispatch office and it's got a board in there . . . and the board has everybody's name on it. To my right . . . they've got this master board, and they have all these different boards: bull boards, straddle board, bulldrive board, and stevedore board, and, well, and some other boards. And when the jobs come up they are read over a loudspeaker and everybody's smoking, and they've got these cans. . . .

"It's a cement floor, and about shoulder-high or neck-high around the interior of this room . . . it's painted brown, and then it's a dirty yellow with all this smoke and stuff. And there's a row of benches and chairs and things, and there's some oldtimers sitting there . . . and one of the things I look at—at a big glass board. Letters have been written . . . and I make sure—to see that my name is not on it."

Interviewer: "The letters are bad?"

Alfred: "Well, it's a complaint. . . ." [*A long discussion of complaints follows.*] "But anyway, getting back to the hall, it's a—it's really a dirty thing, and there's cans which people spit in, and Copenhagen flying all over the place; and these are grubby working fellows. There you are, you're standing looking at this board, talking to somebody or whoever happens to be there, and the dispatcher reads out what's going to be dispatched and there's grousing going on in the different jobs, and what's a good job and what's a bad job—for various reasons, what kind of job it is, you know, what the pay is, dirt pay and things like that."

The taking of a job—getting "pegged" on the board—is an interesting process. Depending on how you feel, how many people are on the board in front of you, how badly you need money, what jobs seem to be coming up next, you can either take the work or pass.

Depending on how many people are behind you on the board, passing takes you out of a job for that day; but it sets you up for a better choice for the next day.

So, in this dirty hall, Alfred "played" the pegs, got his job, and, I am convinced, labored hard for his pay.

Beyond the union hall, there was little said about the labor. But Alfred's description of the early morning seemed an odd mix of detail and disgust and removal. Alfred understood how to get what he wanted out of his job—he clearly played the boards well—yet there was seemingly no chance for that environment to be at all satisfying. Even if the labor he did during the day was tolerable, the union hall was, in his word, "shitty." I can think of few who would like to begin every day that way.

The world was changing some for his work: "Oh, I like Women's Lib. I think that—ah, that's a very . . . important thing. I see that as a very beautiful thing . . . what these women are doing: making men aware of their relationship to their job, to their employer, and just to their fellow worker; what they expect and what they should get in return and what they should put out and the kind—types of relationship—you know—that they can have a real relationship with their fellow workers as opposed to, 'Well, I'm down here and I have to work with you, [you] son-of-a-bitch.' "

On the other hand: "This one woman, who was on the Olympic peninsula someplace . . . longshored right there. *As a casual laborer.* There's lots of women who want to do checking; they want to check. But this would really irritate a lot of people down there."

Alfred was not so optimistic about race: "We have racial problems within our union; I don't know if it's really racial problems or not but it's racial activities of that sort. There's this one dude that's tellin' us how the workers are oppressed, you know—you know—the same thing day in and day out—or 'my black brothers' or this; and well, that's just so much. . . . Well, if you've heard it once, you know—big deal."

Interviewer: "You don't pay much attention to that kind of thing?"
Alfred: "No; well, not to people that repeat themselves—I repeat myself enough."

There are, for me, some interesting pulls when I think about what Alfred had to say about his job. It is certainly hard to make longshoring romantic: honest labor, yes; romantic, no. Yet, there was something about how Alfred had gone about it that had a certain style. Given some clearly ugly aspects of his work and his union; more, given an economic system that did little for those workers, Alfred had made much of what he did. That represents one of the definitions of alienation, and triumph.

Two additional things should be explored before any more final

judgments are made. First, there is the way longshoring was changing, and second, there is how Alfred saw himself.

First things first:

"Well, actually, if you really want to get right down to it, it was actually predicted that eventually machines would take over and do everything. They have to keep so many longshoremen because there are
some manual things. We are actually in business, selling our labor.
And if we can't compete, well, [someone else] will get it."

And himself and his work?

"I will probably—probably do it the rest of my life."

And his fellow workers?

"Well, the tradition of the longshoreman is a guy who could drink
a fifth of whiskey in a night, two fifths of whiskey a day; and believe
me, there were people like that and there are people that drink this
. . . and they're fighty and rousy and don't seem to have a brain in
their head, and they just sort of do what they want to do. . . . So I
can't really associate with this kind of thing . . . human beings. . . .

"It has changed because a lot of the old-timers are retiring and
dying out, and now there's a new caste—the drug addict—well, the
drug scene, I mean; that is the new longshoreman. You know—he's
with the times."

> *Me:* "If you don't consider yourself a longshoreman, what do you
> consider yourself?"
> *Alfred:* "Just a person."
> *Me:* "Just a person. O.K. Who makes instruments? Who lives in a
> houseboat, or just a person?"
> *Alfred:* "No, just a person—not a person that makes anything, or
> that does anything. Just a person."

At one point, there was school:

"Once I got out on my own, then there were some things that I
wanted to do; and the way of doing it was going to college to acquire
some skills, but—well, I knew I couldn't really read, and that I
couldn't write too good and I didn't have too good of a base on math
or anything like that, and I sort of—well, I had an idea that I would go
into business for myself."

Alfred still had that idea when we talked with him, but at the same
time he seemed to be preparing to longshore for the rest of his life.

TED

After undergraduate school, Ted entered a seminary in the Midwest. His first pastorate was in the Midwest, and after a year he and his wife moved to a small town in the Northwest, where he continued his preaching.

The full description of his dissatisfaction with the Church has been lost forever because of the cruelty of a small foreign-made tape recorder. Later, in another (and fully recorded) context, Ted talked about his job as a preacher:

"Well, the Nazarene Church wasn't really that big; you had to be friends with everyone, but there was a little bit of a sense in which I could see they were condescending toward us. There was also just plain psychic revulsion of what I was doing. I had some mental problems again—in that it was very frustrating for me to prepare these sermons which had to be right and pure and honest and all this business.

"You know, basically the answers that a minister was giving was, 'If you get your heart right with God, everything will be all right— that if you just pray enough things will be all right, if you study your bible every day, everything will be all right.' I began to have serious questions about that—I began to spend more time trying to achieve with myself. Some days I'd spend all day in the study, alternately trying to pray and read the bible and reach through to the heart of God.

"It was getting harder for me. I saw some of them needing some of the things that I needed—a little larger orientation. I got very disillusioned once, too. Our—one of our main members was the county auditor, and she was the pillar of the Church: a saint, supposedly. Her husband never came to church with her, and we were always trying to convert him. Well, they had an auditor come to review the auditor and found that she'd been dipping into the till, and this was a tremendous blow to her, to me, to the church; and I took it very personally. It was almost like a blow to me." (Ted likened the woman's reaction to being caught to Nixon's when he was caught.)

"I began to read some writings that the fundamentalist orientation is sort of a guilt-producing thing and . . . you're identified with . . . sorrow, with sainthood, with perfection. I was getting a preacher tone; I was believing it and yet not believing it."

Believe it or not, the job was doing horrible things to Ted's head. We saw how, when he was younger, Ted seemed to go into and out of religion. Its appeal was very strong for him, but somehow it was wrong. He became a preacher during a time of intense social and political action in the country. He entered the work world—an explicitly moral life—during the sixties. That his church was so insulated from such serious social issues as race was finally too much for Ted. In all good faith, he became a social worker.

"To work in social welfare was like a fountain of youth. Suddenly people were coming to me. They were asking for help, mainly financial help—I was able to give them help. Instead of asking for money, I was giving out money. This was such a dramatic change, I don't—I couldn't believe it, and I almost couldn't wait to get out of the ministry fast enough. It was just such a—an emotional load gone. We were living out in the country; . . . we called it Peaceful Acres.

"My mental health improved, my physical health improved, and it was kind of like being released from prison."

They even bought their first TV in the early sixties; ". . . and this opened up part of the world to us."

Ted went back to school, this time to the secular Big State University to get his master's degree in social work. His job as a social worker did put some pressure on him. He really "didn't buddy around with anyone" at work because "I was inwardly judgmental about the whole scene."

Interviewer: "Because they weren't working hard enough?"
Ted: "Yeah [*chuckling*]. . . ."

Finally Ted became friendly with the boss. As he stayed at his job longer, he began to "feel much more identified with some of those people."

Ted's wife, Helen, formerly a minister's wife and full-time homemaker, had found a job. While not the product of the women's movement ("the movement just made things easier for her"), Ted said that it "has admittedly been difficult for me at times. She does not cater to my wishes the way she used to—I mean, she certainly doesn't come and get my slippers ready, or try to do those little things sometimes that she used to do."

Helen loved her work and loved to talk about it. In fact, Ted made it a point *not* to bring his work home, but Helen felt no such restraint.

Ted had to work that out: "I just thought that was uncalled for." Later, he admitted his attitude was "... just, you know, my past orientation."

Because the interviews were open, not all the people dealt with the same topics. Or, if topics were brought up, they were likely to be in different contexts. For example, Ted said nothing about racism at his work. He did talk about his churches being insulated from the struggles of the sixties, and about how he admired Martin Luther King. Race was brought up in another context.

Helen and Ted's seventeen-year-old daughter was dating a black man at the time we talked with them. *Helen:* "I didn't mind the fact that he was black, but he was twenty-two and divorced; ... that *really* bothered me. Of course, she knew that that bothered me and seemed pleased to hear it." Helen went on to say that once she had gotten to know the man, she liked him and decided her daughter was better off with him than with "some of the other guys she's gone with." Ted said nothing.

At first, Ted could not have been more pleased with his job: "... it seemed to me that social work is pure religion—you accept people the way they are—you don't try to force them into a mold, you try to help them achieve this higher potential. I was suddenly really out on the front lines."

Ted called himself a "good" social worker and was beginning "to realize I'm pretty average," which was a change for him. Those at work were intensely interested in politics, and Ted was reading the newspapers and watching the TV news. After all, he said, Richard Nixon was his boss.

But there was something not wholly satisfying for him: "Another thing I've learned about myself is that, for some reason or another, I don't enjoy ... digging into other people's lives. I don't enjoy digging or prying, or maybe I didn't feel that comfortable learning how to make people open up."

There was more important stuff going on:

"I used to be very idealistic, ... so optimistic it was almost a denial of reality. I used to have a lot of goals and objectives, and you know ... I think I had always very—I had very grandiose ideas. I used to daydream a lot as a child about great exploits.

[*Later*] "... I went into all those social work meetings and organizations to try to change laws, to try to change the system or change the people. I think some of the disillusionment came not only from the fact that we were not all that successful—I think I was part of a whole group that kind of ran out of gas—there was sort of a sudden realization that people didn't want as much help as you want to give them, that people only change when they're asking for change. This is kind of a hard pill to swallow, I think, for me—to realize that a lot of people don't want my help, but more than that: that I don't have that much help to give them.

"But getting back to the change from idealism: I think, as I found, in one way that the world wasn't as bad off as I thought it was—that maybe the world didn't need saving; but at the same time I didn't think I then closed my eyes to all the ills of the world."

This is clearly the space for analyses. The question is, what kind? It would be appropriate to discuss how education had made so much available for Ted. First training for the ministry, then a professional degree that allowed him to be a social worker. Much could be made of how education opened up opportunities. Or, we could reconstruct how religion had been so powerful. A whole theme of Ted's life had been coming to terms with the issue of religion in general, and fundamentalist religion in particular. Much of his life was still dominated by those issues.

Or, we could do much with how his family had been so influential. How he saw his parents act and relate to each other and to the world clearly was an important image to him. The domination of his father over almost all of Ted's first thirty years counted for a great deal. Or, we could try to fully explore how the mood of the times—how social, political, and economic activity—changed and affected him. How the issues that finally made him change his work and really break with some of his past were quite time-specific in terms of their publicness. When that activity slowed down, Ted also slowed down.

All of these ways of understanding what went on are related and interrelated in complex and bizarre ways. In the end, they are all necessary to consider, though all incomplete in themselves: What finally went on with Ted was at least one-part mystery. We might use a phrase of Sartre and say that Ted was making history within history. He both acted and reflected; initiated and responded. To talk about his work is, in turn, to talk about most of the other things in his life.

What about now? How did we leave Ted?

"I . . . feel like I'm in a holding pattern. We have everything to be thankful for, and yet I still feel personally that something is missing in my life."

Ted had become "identified . . . with social welfare administration. I feel a little bit like a politician: The more you get into this thing of kind of high-level negotiations in social welfare policy, it sort of gets a little exciting."

And one more aspect of work for this forty-two-year-old man: "I don't feel the need quite so much for . . . escapism, but I keenly feel that I should start preparing for retirement now."

SARA

". . . but I sure miss that kind of unreality in people's lives in New York. People were just living for the moment, a lot of grasshoppers there. I strongly believe in the barter system, going back to barter as much as we can. We eat too much, we use too much, we eat too much meat."

One of the arguments of this chapter is simple enough: If one has the desire, it is easy to make the issues of work-life the issues of everyday living. The issues of work go far beyond the single fact of pay for many people. Work becomes part of life—and matters of style and value and politics and family are at least as important as money—maybe even more important. To repeat what was said earlier, we live in a post-industrial society. That means at least a couple of things.

First, what seemed to be "luxury" concerns in earlier times—concerns of style and politics, not money—have become very serious and important for some people. It is fair and accurate to say that for these people, the problems are critical, not just matters of luxury. Second, in our post-industrial society there has been a heavy emphasis on technical know-how. There have been no technicians in this chapter; in fact, I have avoided comment about both technicians and huge, complex organizations. That was done on purpose, as the next chapter will be filled with both.

Sara was a party-goer at Big State University. She did her sorority and her classes and her drinking like most people in the late fifties. When she graduated, she moved to New York City to look for a job. Sara, meet the Big Apple:

"So I went walking down to the Time/Life office and applied for a job, saying my mother worked here and my father worked here; and they said, 'Can you type?' 'Oh—and I have a B.A.—here it is. See—brand-new and shiny.' 'But can you type?' 'Of course not—I'm a bachelor of arts.' They said, 'Well we haven't any jobs unless you can type.' "

Sara went home, determined to learn to type. Before she could, Time/Life called her back and asked if she wanted a "short-term" job. They said it would be brief—maybe a two-week job. Sara accepted and worked there for seven years.

She had several different jobs. She assisted a chief researcher and did some very slow typing, and then became a "full-fledged researcher," which "at that time was as far as women generally went." She did some work on an American history series, and did a science series, and even produced a newsletter for schools.

During that time, she married "a banker; and he was really into that sort of money, social trip. . . . We knew a lot of other couples, more or less in the same situation. The men were bankers or lawyers, generally. The women usually worked, often in publishing or journalism. It was kind of the smart New York set. Oh, lots of entertainment, . . . and I got into a competitive cooking trip, which has taken me *years* to get over [*laughing*]."

At work, "My last project, which . . . just burned me out completely, was their cookbook series, and I was doing recipe research. I was working mainly on the Italian cookbook."

Interviewer: "Those are great cookbooks."
Sara: "Yeah. . . . I thought I was pregnant and I had hysterics because we had not really planned on having children at all. And I went to the doctor, and he said, 'Naw, you're not pregnant.' So we decided, 'Well, we really do want a baby, don't we?' So we had a baby."

It was "just a gas" for Sara. She worked part time and decided she could "sit back and see what I really wanted to do, which was really a relief, because I'd spent the years before just struggling to try to find something else I enjoyed."

If one were going to make a case for "typical," then Sara's life so far seems pretty typical. Of course, there is nothing in the outline of her activities to prepare us for what then happened.

While Sara was trying to find "something else I enjoyed," it became more and more clear that she wanted a life with her husband less and less. He was just being "sucked along" in a "very fancy" New York Bank, and Sara "wanted him to do something interesting so I could do something interesting too." It had not occurred to her to "do it on my own at that time."

In terms of time, we are now talking about the end of the sixties. It was a period of much social experimentation, much innocent but very earnest work. When a friend who "had taken an encounter group class at NYU" was going to take it again, Sara joined her.

The group changed her life: "These people were just really neat, and really supportive, and I suddenly began to get an inkling that I was somebody—and I hadn't—I hadn't really grasped that before. I sort of went along with what was happening, but it never occurred to me that it was within my power to control what was happening . . . the whole world was different. And also in that class was a man that

I fell *very* much in love with—which had a great deal to do with my marriage breaking up.''

In that little group of encounterers, three people got divorces, ''a couple of people changed jobs, a couple of people quit jobs—the whole tone of the group was—you know—change and we'll help you [*laughs*].'' Also in the class was a Jewish woman whose ''politics were radical—she'd been involved with all these radical groups, and I started smoking dope then with her, which changed my perception a lot.''

A world apart from exclusive Republican New York bankers.

With her husband, she ''. . . argued about politics *bitterly*—oohhh, bitterly—way into the night.'' She lost every argument.

Things were not working; so: ''. . . we both tried having affairs with other people and thought that maybe, you know, that would make things more interesting. It just made us more capable of hurting each other.''

They separated.

Her lover was married; so ''I couldn't really count on him for my future.''

Sara began making jewelry, and it ''really began to look like a possibility.'' She made a discovery: ''I . . . began to realize that you really didn't need a whole lot of money to live—that you could scratch by on very little.''

It seems that her encounter group class at NYU changed her a great deal. I have gone through two sets of thoughts about encounter groups. In the first set, I was of mixed emotions. Groups really did seem to help people like Sara make more sense of the world and determine how to act in it. The second set of emotions was much less mixed: I honestly believed their capacity for harm to be much greater than their capacity for good. Considerable research has been done on these groups, and there is one outstanding important finding: The people who are changed through encounter groups are the people who were predisposed to change.

In other words, those people who are ready to change and who want to change do change. During the sixties, many people went through these groups, got divorces and the like, received all kinds of group support for their actions, and at the end of the experience were stuck with decisions that left them less well off. Sara was lucky. She found good friends who helped her—and they would have helped her, group or no group.

Sara made her decisions, and they were good ones for her. During a trip to California, she decided to visit her former college roommate (the one with frizzy hair and black tights), who lived in Seattle. She visited, fell in love with a man, and decided to move there. Sara and her former husband arranged for their daughter to live with him in New York in the winter and with her in Seattle in the summer. For Sara guilt and trauma were associated with the decision, but when we talked with her, it seemed clear all was working out well.

From New York banker's wife to West Coast jewelry maker. From the publishing business to handcrafts. From fancy dinner parties to guild politics. Both working life and everyday life changed. Sara's life became centered on her work, and it is important to see how she understood that.

She learned this about herself and her craft early: "You can't construct a universal personality—make [your work] appeal to everyone. . . . What's important is to do what's meaningful to me, and what I enjoy, and what's important to me, and then there will be other people who like it."

Sara felt a "strong identification with the whole craft movement; . . . it's something that I—I sort of believe in philosophically as an alternative way of life . . . you know, making things, making things with your hands." She was attending the crafts fairs in the area and was being recognized more and more. That was important to her.

"My phone has been ringing too often—and somehow every time it rings, it's somebody wanting me to do something, either make something for them or come to this or come to that. People will come up and say, 'I saw your piece in the showing, . . . and I know somebody that has one, and I've heard all about you.' And it's neat, I love it. I found this need for applause a bottomless pit . . . and it's kind of overwhelming—you know, I feel like a star."

She also felt hassled by it and was beginning to believe that "a small town might be the answer." The question was, how to "go back into my quietness."

There was the involvement of her trade, the cooperativeness and the competition. Sara and a few others had started a crafts guild. She was the first leader of the group. She spent a great deal of time and energy with the guild. In it, she found friends, people with similar interests and attitudes; and a little security as well.

"Last winter I was more than happy to go to all those meetings, because I had nothing else to do . . . I had no other connections of my own. It certainly gave me a sense of identity; it bailed me out."

And now?

"Well, the guild is now becoming a pain in the ass, although I still really enjoy the people. I will stay involved with the guild."

If there was cooperation, there was also competition.

"I have to grit my teeth a little bit to cooperate, but I find it more rewarding, now that I'm good enough so that what I make is pretty much unique; and if someone copies, I—I'm sort of telling myself . . . if someone copies something of mine, it's probably someone who wouldn't do as good a job. Anyone who's going to be real competition isn't going to copy, anyway."

There seemed to be no issue for Sara about her current work and being a woman. She told us:

"I've never been politically involved in the woman's movement . . . but I'm solidly behind it. I feel my involvement in the movement is kind of—was settled as soon as I left my husband and made the commitment to be my own person.

"There seems to be a whole radical lesbian movement, which is maybe one of the noisest parts of the feminist movement, and that's just not my trip. I really think that those attitudes are personal and not political, and I just don't need their hang-ups coming down on my head. I really want to lead a private life, and it certainly will always include a man, preferably the one I'm with right now; . . . I'm monogamous and I'm family-oriented."

Her relationship with the movement? "I feel like my function is to be an example; you know, to live my life as a totally independent, self-reliant, self-sufficient person, and enjoy it."

Taking these statements as examples, was Sara a capitalist? Certainly. Was she an individualist? It seemed so. But, and here the questions come together in the form of a more inclusive one: Was she the prototypical American liberal? Was she alienated, alone, competitive, and all those familiar modern themes? Clearly, she was not that kind of normal American liberal. Was she a "good" capitalist? I assume there is that kind of capitalist—a small is beautiful kind —and Sara might have been one of them.

What I am arguing is that a list of her activities cannot be totaled and add up to a label.

Sara read *Craft Horizons* "religiously—every single word. I don't miss a page." And she was excited that there was a long list of "schools and universities that give degrees in crafts." Aha, education! What does it mean that colleges will give degrees in a certain subject? It means crafts are "recognized more and more as a legitimate art form."

Colleges annoint people as well as activities.

And about money and her work?

"If I want to get rich, I can crank out $5 rings and probably do it. I can also take time out and do really difficult, challenging, creative stuff, and I have that freedom to be me and it's something that I think is absolutely wonderful. And I think there are a lot of people who have the ability to do this—I don't think I'm particularly talented.

"I would say that I rank with better jewelers in Seattle, and I really don't—still don't believe that it's out of any, you know, magical talent—it's just from hard work and commitment, because I really enjoy doing it."

A nice way to end this first chapter on work: with enjoyment, commitment, and effort.

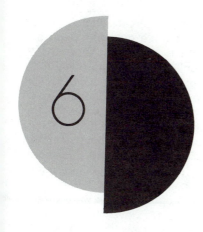

6

The Middle-Class Work World

> Gold knew that the most advanced and penultimate stage of civilization was attained when chaos masqueraded as order, and he knew we were already there.
>
> **—Joseph Heller**

While it was fun to end the last chapter with hard work, satisfaction, and stardom, that provides a less-than-whole understanding of work. Making jewelry is certainly work, but it makes sense to give attention to our more common context. This is, after all, an age of huge, complex organizations and technologies peopled by professionals.

In many ways, a college degree is the way to become a part of the professional work force. There are certain skills that are taught only in college, and it seems as if a certain style (how to dress and act and do "homework") can be most readily signified by a college degree. The degree is, in a sense, the sign of our times: the sign of a very specific kind of social approval.

Most of the people we talked with grew up in lower-middle-class homes. It was there, we thought, that col-

121

lege would most clearly represent a way to the middle class. In earlier chapters we saw that the assumption was of marginal truth but not harmful to our work. College seemed to be seen in about the same way by most people.

In this chapter there are questions of immediate importance: What is the work of the middle class? If most people deal with huge organizations and highly trained professionals, what does that mean? To put that more simply, just what is college getting us ready for?

Before we see how people work through these issues, I would like to offer a short review. We have become accustomed to technology—its presence and its products. While certain kinds of consumption seem to be retreating (we must become more comfortable in smaller cars, but we still get cars), technology is rapidly filling in more places. Computers are getting smaller and doing more and more little jobs; laser beams are great for eye surgery and sights for automatic weapons; and, at long last, we can record our favorite TV shows for our huge TV sets and see the programs when we want to.

Many things are much better than ever. We have technology to thank for that, and few are willing to deny themselves or others all of that better stuff.

Those technologies are often developed or managed or both by professionals. *Professionalism,* besides the name for a certain group of people and a certain status, is a word for a kind of quality of workmanship. If a person does a professional job, we at once assume it should be first-rate work. Professional work is the standard by which all work is measured, and we expect professional organizations to set standards for their members.

Naturally, degrees from professional schools become important in a society that values professionalization. The ordinary college degree is the important step before graduate school.

We are told, and it may be true, that our world has become so complex that it is necessary that only highly trained and highly skilled specialists do certain kinds of work. When we are sick, for example, most of us prefer to deal with doctors and surgeons who have been educated at medical schools. We want our lawyers to have graduated from law school, and our professors, from graduate school.

Of course professionalism is a very mixed blessing. It is the home of the middle-class success, but it is a hard place to live. We tire of the hold the professional organizations have on their members; we are outraged when a professional thinks he or she is really *that* special; we are degraded when a professional is more interested in status than in dealing with individuals.

There is an ever-growing literature about how huge organizations add to all of that.

It is time to see how people handle our modern work, but it might be helpful to repeat the centering questions: What is the work of the middle class? If most people deal with technology, professionals, and complex organizations, what does that mean?

CAROL

"... this incredible guilt, you know; here you're supposed to have a bright Jewish kid, and he's just not gonna be that."

It is necessary to catch up on Carol. She had decided to go to college "just because." Following the path of her mother and sisters, Carol went to the same university, pledged the same sorority, and graduated as they did. She got her certificate and became a school teacher.

Also, she married. The man was Jewish, and her family both disliked the religion and disapproved of the marriage. Her father died not long after the marriage, and the relationship between Carol and her mother was not a close one.

During the late sixties, she and her husband were politically active. For a while she taught in a poverty program, but, "... I wasn't comfortable teaching." Worse yet, the poverty program was a "gigantic rip-off, and that was *the* reason for my leaving." The program was full of "white, middle-class, college-graduated women," and when the director of the program visited, they would "go down to the Bowery and get all these winos in for the day ... so that everything really looked good."

Enough was enough. Carol "wanted to be a mommy ... and so I went home and proceeded to be a mommy."

White, with an upper-middle-class background, college-educated, with a profession; that was the social background of Carol's tie to the professional world. But the tie itself was this: Carol had two children, and they were both retarded. (Let me be more precise: At that time, they were diagnosed as retarded.)

Carol and her husband spoke of the children in different ways—spoke of them as exceptional or special children, for example—but the real feeling they had to deal with was that the kids were retarded.

I am certain that only those people with retarded children can truly understand the full impact on everyday life. It seems reasonable for us to try and learn as much as we can on two levels: the first, how people are affected, and the second, how that brushes up against the world of the medical profession.

Carol talked of guilt: "... this incredible guilt, you know; here you're supposed to have a bright Jewish kid, and he's just not gonna be that. It took a long time to work that out. The psychologist I did deal with was kind of off on his anti-Jewish thing, anyway, which didn't help at all." And anxiety: "Being a full-time mother has never been thrilling. . . . It was boredom, but it was also frustrations and anxiety about my particular role." And: "All the schlepping of kids to the doctor, and go[ing] through the whole doctor scene."

It gets down to this: "But before parents can even think of [integrating their special children into society], they've got to live with the idea that their kid's *not* going to play with the other kids on the block, that he's gonna *probably* go off to a special school, he's gonna be *transported* in a different manner, they're going to be *bombarded* with professionals for probably the first ten years of the kid's life; and it's not until they can deal with that, that they can love the kid. And if the kid's not gonna be loved, then you're gonna be in big trouble anyway."

Beginning with that reality, what about those professionals? "I'm getting worked over by stupid professionals all the time."

After a bad (no, *inadequate* and, regrettably, *inaccurate* are closer to the truth) diagnosis, Carol took her first child to another set of doctors. "In those two months we had twenty-six professional appointments. We're talking about piling the kids in the car, driving up, filtering through all the light-covered bodies—you know, doctors —with their egos wrapped around their chests. It's a degrading, self-denying sort of experience."

Of the best and brightest—of those who are hot-shot academic types—hear this song of praise: "I think all of these specialists who stick it out in the university setting probably hinge on being monsters."

Beyond monsters, there is professional courtesy. There is a not altogether funny joke about the relationship between sharks and lawyers; Carol, in a sense, told the same story:

"These specialists now that we're seeing say, 'Well, which pediatrician is watching these children?' And I tell them. And they say, 'Oh, yes, I know him—he's a good doctor.' And I can't be quiet about that! And I say, 'Yeah, except that—.' Yeah, he may be a good doctor; but he looks at my children, and their tongues are hanging out, and they're gasping for air, and their noses are dripping, and he says, 'Are they like this most of the time?' And I say, 'Yeah.' And he says, 'Well, then, we won't worry about it.'"

We colleagues respect our own.

Carol told us about how the doctors and nurses who were there to help her had "some pretty severe personal problems." Of the maybe fifteen physicians who had attended her children up to then, "There are probably two or three which I find as warm, sharing, giving people."

The nurses were little better. But Carol thought that because they were always in a subservient position in the medical profession, in some unconscious ways they "took it out" on the patients. There should be, if I understand the implications of several of Carol's stories, a special place in hell for nurses who "protect" their doctors from patients.

Part of the problem, to Carol, was the institutional setting. She spoke of "being hooked up to a bureaucracy like Public Medical Center," which can "be both helpful financially and devastating personally in such a situation." Carol believed they knew "nothing about special kids. They are a medical facility; they may have a mental health group, but I don't think they know anything anyway, and I think that—that the medical doctors can't deal with things that involve the soul. They're interested in the flesh."

In anger and frustration, Carol finally found help. She found a program, started by John Kennedy when he was President, that was partially funded by the federal government and partially paid for by the patients. Carol decided that she had to go "outside of those factories," away from the "freebies," and get what she could consider good help.

Each time I read her transcripts I want to call her and ask how things are. During the months we talked with her, there were more questions about her children's conditions than there were answers.

There is still more to understand. All of us know that there are some good professionals: that there can be good institutions and good doctors. I know people who have had positive experiences at the very same Public Medical Center Carol talked about. That qualification aside, how can we summarize Carol, her basic reactions, and her sense of what education might have to do with all of this?

"When I first started seeing a psychologist after [our son] had been 'labeled,' one of the things he said to me was that, as difficult as this experience is, you're going to learn from it. And I told him that that really made me angry. Why should I have this experience, this particular one, to learn from?"

The doctor was right: She did learn, and this was one of the lessons: ". . . people *do* help you, and when you call on them, they'll be there."

This was another one: "For every woman who feels she is stronger for the experience, there are ten who feel, you know, chronic sadness and inability to deal with the problem and inability to deal forthrightly with professionals."

We keep circling the relationship of professionals and education. Carol put them together like this:

"I think I'm a snob about medicine; I'll admit that. I like the type of people who really know their stuff—you know, have the right paper on the wall.

"My concern for other parents in our position is such that I'm always going to question the professionals and weight what they have to say, whereas other mothers without either my educational background or my financial background are just being raked over the coals and destroyed."

In our talks with each person, we would trade stories about what had gone on the preceding week. One day Carol told me a story that seems the best summary for introducing this chapter on professionals and middle-class work.

"I was sitting there, in his office, and I just couldn't believe how this doctor was treating me. I was a nervous wreck and just screamed at him, 'It's my children who are retarded, not me!'"

CARL

"Computers are very logical...."

Carl never got a college degree. As we will see, the way from his hard childhood to his current position as general manager of Big Universe Distributors had been characterized by a great deal of technical education. And an enormous will to succeed.

There are many ways in which Carl is an interesting example of professionalism. He was middle-level management striving for top level. He had gotten as far as he had—and I suspect he has gone farther still—because of technical know-how. The base of his competence was data processing and computers. In many ways he was the kind of person who keeps corporate America going—a bureaucrat who had mastered the electronic technology of complex organizations.

Of course he was more, and better, than that. He was certainly a personable, articulate man. In some ways, I felt sorry for him. He also scared me a little.

While interviewing people (there is much more of this in Chapter 10), we tried to get as rounded an impression as we could of each individual. We wanted to know about the person's past and present: about home life, social life, work life, relatives, friends, and the like. There were varying degrees of success. As I reread Carl's interviews, I found this: His work dominated his life.

Because everything seemed to revolve around work, it is difficult to settle on certain themes and pretend they are all-inclusive. As we see what Carl was seeing, it is important to remember that this man was truly professional. We can learn much about the white-collar worker from him.

Carl's career was closely tied to education. After high school he tried a community college: "I just wasn't ready for school. I didn't have good study habits; I really didn't know what the hell I was doing. All of a sudden you didn't know everybody . . . everything was much more advanced. . . . As I talk more about it, it was kind of a trauma."

He made "probably a lot of C's and maybe some D's" and quit college.

Young, a college drop-out, married with a baby: The prospects for Carl were not promising. He held a series of jobs, sometimes several at a time, and did a very important thing. Carl went to school and learned data processing. It was a six-month course in the Big City. He did well. He worked at a couple of other jobs—one with the government—before moving to the Big City and getting a job with a county agency. The agency worked with doctors.

Carl was hired to computerize the operations of the agency, which he did. He spent five years there, and when he left he was their business manager. He told stories you might expect to hear about any work situation. Some people (Carl) got promoted, while others (the business manager) got fired.

Also, and this gets back to what Carol said, there were doctors:

"They're all miniature gods. O.K.? And not as professional as you would believe, or as most people believe they are. You think, 'He's the most professional guy there is out there.' You know—and all of a sudden when you start working with them, you realize there's a lot of areas they really don't know very much. You go to the doctor: Everybody does exactly what the doctor says. That's it. It was a mistake, but that's the way it used to be; and when he said something, that was it. You didn't ask questions."

Enough about doctors. The collective problems with doctors as authorities—as tin gods—are probably as much ours as theirs. But Carl's five years at the county agency were spent doing much more than practicing office politics, computerizing the work, and understanding his own attitudes about doctors. Carl had a career to make.

Enter education.

While working at the county agency, Carl went to an IBM school. As his work went beyond technical matters, he began taking "accounting, management, and business law" courses at a local community college. When there was time, he would ride his motorcycle to relax: "It's a sport, a hobby; I ride some competition, but mostly just pleasure."

All the while he kept getting more responsibility in his job, continued to take courses, and kept moving up.

Finally, he took a six-month course at the Automation Institute. Carl loved it. The classes were small, the instructors stayed with the same group of people, there was "a lot of personal contact . . . it had something that college didn't have, you know, that maybe I personally needed more than a lot of people.

"We'd get together at night and study and work on projects together, you know. Really do things as a team. If you're together with the right team, by the time you're done, you've learned probably two-and-a-half times what you would've learned by yourself."

He did well at Automation and was ready to leave the county agency. Not only were the doctors difficult to work with, but "I'd been [there] for five years at this time, and the learning curve was starting to really dwindle off.

"First thing I did, I found a place to have a résumé professionally done. Which I would advise everybody to do. . . . They write it up and they put it in more the way it is, and when you try to do it yourself, most of us tend to grade ourselves down; most of us are not writers. They can put a lot on one page. A five-page résumé is no good."

Ambitious, outgoing, technically competent, with the right résumé in hand, Carl got a job at Big Universe Distributors. After the expected stories of some people (Carl) being promoted and some people (the general manager) being fired, we see Carl hard at work but still a little dissatisfied.

He was assuming more responsibilities in the tested way: "I'm not sure about the import and export programs: I'm a little over my head there. But I'm gonna take a class in import and export and I'm gonna find out about it."

And plans: "When I'm fifty-five, I hope I'm going to be—I will be the chairman of several boards and won't have to change jobs because I will already be involved in a lot of jobs."

Again, Carl had progressed from technician to manager. We can get a better idea of what that meant by listening to how he described management and how it felt to be a manager. For Carl, in particular, that also included schooling.

Carl was a self-described conservative:

"I tend to be very conservative. You know . . . I'm finding out everything I need to know. . . . Why spend more money on—? You know, you can spend a lot on magazines, articles, and newspapers, and never read it all. I don't tend to be a large spender.

"I'm kind of conservative; I have a conservative house. I should have a $50,000 home, and I have a $19,000 home. Sometimes my wife is upset about that, but the payments are right."

Carl had learned a fairly standard philosophy of modern management.

"Any time you get into a management position, if you're going to be successful, your success, I think, is really related to your communication.

"At one time I believe I was even weak in this area [*pausing*]. When I first went to work, it was pointed out that my grammar was very bad and some of my communications were weak. He [my boss] just says, you should work on this. And I had, you know, within a six-month period; I couldn't believe the comments I had—they just could not understand how somebody, without going to college and so forth, in a small period of time, could correct the problem.

"If you go out and say, look [*pounding hand on desk*], I want you to do this and I want it done by four o'clock. And I want you to do it this way, this way, and this way. Well, they know it won't work, but they aren't gonna tell you! The other approach would be to play on their sympathies and nice them to death. You know, and get them to do it because they wanted to do it."

Carl had learned much of this from a good teacher, a teacher with "real world" experience in business; and he believed teachers with experience were the best ones. Also, there was a book: "One course, management-minded supervision; I believe you would really enjoy the book. It's just great. . . . The book was really a story, a complete story. And you begin reading the book and they would give you a philosophy and they would apply it to this gentleman that we were reading about in the book. But you read a story about George working in a factory and going through the changes and going from a laborer to a supervisor to a manager, and the problems he ran into. But, by the time you'd completed the book, you had seen the entire cycle, and it was a story. The guy had just—the author—I can't think of who the author was—has done a beautiful job on it."

Beautiful, to go from laborer to manager. But there are insecurities and costs. One is being judged. Carl did not think grades were important. Only once did he mention that he liked getting A's, while he often told us how little he thought of grades. And there were worker evaluations: "I very definitely have employees [come in] and ask them direct questions about myself. But I try and pick the individual, I try and pick the time. You know, you have to be very careful when you do it, to get a good evaluation."

And friends:

"I don't have a whole lot of what I'd call really close friends; . . . maybe that's why I'm in management. Every once in a while, I catch myself wondering why I don't have some really close friends. Well, you can't become that close to people working for you, or you'll have a hard time managing. You know, friendship gets in the way.

"I'm not a very avid sports fan, so I'm never up on sporting events. This is something you'll find people are.

"I'm not really an extremely outgoing individual. I tend to be involved in my work, and if I'm going to lunch, I'm going to lunch because I want to take care of this problem. And when the problem's over, I'm done with lunch and ready to get on to something else. . . . [*More emphatically*] I do not enjoy a two-hour lunch. I'm not a social individual.

"So something in that respect. I'm starting to go to movies more—you know, so I have something to talk about."

It is somehow right to end this section with a statement about the relationship of technology to bad moods:

"Computers are very logical and everything, and you have to go through a very logical sequence so that it makes you—you learn to sit down and think about a problem from beginning to end and define that problem."

Later, this exchange:

Me: "What do you do when you come to work and you know you're out of sorts, moody?"

Carl: "To a degree I will try to avoid people. But I do have regular meetings set up each morning: I try to meet with all the department heads individually. And, you know, *you can learn to have control over yourself. Extreme control.* And I just try to exercise that control. Generate the kind of conversation that gets you out of a mood. You can take somebody else and generate a conversation and try to bring his spirits up; why can you not do that to yourself?"

WILLY

"Well, actually, I think I'm not an engineer type since I'm not an engineer that other engineers would normally converse with. . . . Very seldom are engineers introspective."

If Carl seemed totally involved with work, Willy first appeared to be at the other end of the scale. Willy in fact was an engineer, an inventor, a man who was truly curious about how the physical world works. His profession, in his mind, was a highly skilled tinkering with nature.

At the time we talked with Willy, his life was not a happy one. The real world of people had overtaken the real world of science in him, and there was a lot of sorting out to be done. There is much to be learned from that sorting-out process.

Science has produced wondrous things for us. Science fiction is no longer as interesting or as inventive as what our scientists are producing. We are, of course, more and more aware of the costs of scientific invention and the resulting technological developments, as we pollute and radiate and poison ourselves on what seems to be a daily basis.

With Willy, we get a closer look at the professional scientists in the social world.

After World War II, Willy went to college in California. He lived in San Francisco and seemed to spend more time with people in the performing arts than with those in his engineering program. The years between his graduation and the time of our talks were filled with many jobs and several moves. It is reasonable to review Willy's professional life. After all, it is argued that a college education will help make an individual more mobile.

Just a little background on a technical mind:

"Going backwards one step, in high school I had always been very skilled in physical sciences, chemistry, physics, mathematics. My own feeling was that I was a writer and a literary critic or social critic. The process of learning to teach shipfitting—very, very simple: It's very simple geometry. *Anybody can build a ship.*"

Anybody, indeed. The point is not whether Willy was right or wrong; it is rather that we have here a good example of the mind-set of a competent professional.

After graduation Willy went to work for a big manufacturing firm.

"I went from San Francisco to Philadelphia to Florida. I was sent there to a school to learn the details of certain particular radar sets. And I arrived on X day, and something like nine days later I was teaching class to the same type of students that I was hired to be one of. And I taught there until perhaps as late as December. At which time school stopped, and I was transferred to Fort Bliss in El Paso, Texas, where I again taught electronics, electricity, radar, to army personnel until sometime in the summer of that year, when my brother suffered a mental breakdown and I zoomed into San Francisco to take care of him."

He changed jobs and finally worked at "one of the biggest construction companies in the world." He described the business as "the god-damnedest hobby shop that you have ever seen in your life [*laughs*]! A seventeen- to twenty-man hobby shop . . . we made money for them hand over fist."

Willy was also involved in theater work at the same time.

After a couple of years in the hobby shop, he went "over to the shipyard, an old Kaiser-built shipyard in Richmond. I lasted for a year as a God-only-knows-what. And they had a mixup and I got laid off, which was quite reasonable, and found a job working for a high-vacuum pump manufacturer, a manufacturer of iron pumps."

Although the job lasted only a year, it must have been fascinating for him. Willy, for one of the few times in our conversations, talked about his work. For someone like me, the description of the way a vacuum pump works ("There's no such thing as suction, for instance") was truly interesting.

When we talked with Willy, he had been at Big Airplane Business in Seattle for many years.

In our first conversation he said this: "[My wife] spent more and more time at her art and less and less time at home with me and the children. And the conflicts that are natural in life became greater, and so we are getting a divorce as of a week from today, at 9:30 in the morning."

After almost twenty years of marriage, with two fairly independent children, Willy was a lonely man in his mid-fifties.

It seems important to have a sense of how Willy saw himself in his hard times. We will then turn to his work, the split he saw in his work and himself, and the role of education. But first, some views of himself.

"From time to time in my life, I have done periods of a year or a year and a half of dull, pointless living and then. . . . But I have no bother in telling you them. It bothers *me!* I'm very forthright myself, and I have, oh, jokingly, insulted people who really—years later said, you know, you hurt me badly. I didn't know that! To me, it would have been nothing.

"I'm in the throes of beginning to try to develop a new life. Centered around *me* rather than a family—never in my life have I been a high-importance character. That is to say, my work has never been of penultimate importance to me. I've never wanted money particularly . . . I've never been goal-oriented. I never wanted to have something in particular.

"I've always been quite self-protected."

Willy: "I am—created myself in many different ways. At the same time. . . ."
Me: "How did you create yourself?"
Willy: "I didn't; it was an accident."
Me: "In the beginning there was an accident [*laughing*]."

Finally: "I—I've been going through a very difficult period with the divorce from my wife. It was very, very painful [*pausing*]. In fact, more painful than I realized intellectually. I can only realize emotionally."

And his work, his profession? There was this underlying attitude: "I have a curious nature: If I didn't know, it would bother me. I ask questions a lot.

"The generation and transmission of electric power is a mystery to almost everyone. The operation of the most common thing that we have, the gasoline engine, is a mystery to 95 percent of the people who drive them. I still find it amazing.

"What I was speaking out about the delight of the technical qualities is that it's delightful to know so much. In—in that I can *really* do something I like to do, that is enjoyable, and that will be agreeable in all aspects of society and living. Knowledge of machinery, knowledge of physical properties—I feel physically and socially competent."

In order to keep up with his job as an electrical engineer, Willy read an electronics journal regularly. "And I spend most of my time—I'm in the laboratory [*pauses*]. *Inventing* things! It's great.

"I do not go and work at random. I am supposed to be working and my hours accounted for under a plan that has been written and approved by supervision, and accomplishment is expected; target dates are supposed to be met, and you run into the same organization schmeer that your contract is connected with. But in general, nobody knows what I do from day to day. Unless I tell 'em. [*Pauses.*] And then it's difficult to get their attention.

"What they really want is a well-written report, which doesn't have to say anything as long as it's thick enough. You can't say in those reports, this is *great!* This is real *good!* You have to say, this seems to show promise.

"My everyday is mostly working with instruments and devices, constructing or designing. And in that sense it's pleasant for me. I work in the laboratory 90 percent of my time.

"[They] get more work out of me at home than they get at work itself. The random nature of my thoughts is entirely beyond my control. Perhaps for only a five-minute span—or I may be eating dinner and say, 'Oh shit, that's the way to go, obviously.' Not knowing why it impinged itself on my mind at the time. And can barely wait to get to work in the morning to *do* it."

From what I know, that description of how an engineer/inventor works is not unusual. But, Willy contended that he was "not an engineer type since I'm not an engineer that other engineers would normally converse with."

Listen to what an engineer is: "Oh, engineer types in general tend to be conservative politically. Totally unaware of the art and culture world. Perhaps devoted to a hobby or two. PTA types. And, in general, conservative politically.

"Very seldom are engineers introspective. [*Pauses.*] They have a degree of intelligence . . . they are very disciplined . . . even the poor engineers know about these disciplines and . . . are physical scientists; they have, in general, reference to very solid background information. It doesn't change from year to year. For instance, there are no engineers who argue engineering—either it's correct or it's incorrect. By demonstrable experiment. The cases of difference of opinion may come as to what is the best economic way to go about it.

"But in one sense, I am an engineer, in that I do this sort of disciplined work daily. I am happy to be in the best hobby shop I could imagine. And I hobby at it. Other engineers write reports. I make little machines."

An engineer but not an engineer type? Here's more:

"I'm not religious about God; I'm religious about sunlight and the smell of grass in the morning. It's very nice; it makes me feel good. The warm sun makes me feel religious. Not in the sense of the God-oriented religious person, only it's kind of exalting; it's nice. But—a—the technical qualities of how things fit together, I guess they satisfy my mind more than anything else. There is some machinery up there whirling around—like tungsten. I'd like to know it; it's very difficult to find and very difficult to refine and smelt and make into something. Very useful. [*Pauses*]."

Tungsten and God? And what about this:

"[Indians have] an awesome reverence for the place that they live. It's—we don't break rocks; we go down and find little ones. And we don't chop down trees, because there's plenty of deadfall.

The almost mystical way of living with, together, and merged in the land and the natural habitat.

"And joy and delight of living as animals, which is—which can be delightful. The animals make poetry and dance in the meadows. This delightful love of living in a land, our technical society *ruined*."

At that point, the split between his art life and his engineering life seemed wide; so I asked him about it:

"I don't think I can really put them together. I find the combination rather odd. The only other combination that I know of that is in common existence is that musicians are people who could be mathematicians.

"Well, in my case [*pauses*] they aren't separate, actually. I—I can't tell you how they're intermingled and co-related, but they are. I find it difficult of expression to. . . . As I said before, I'm contradicting myself, which is perfectly all right."

Finally he said: "My engineering is an art thing. It may not seem to be, but it is."

And education. What did education have to do with making little machines, and God, and big rocks, and contradictions? There are two answers.

"Well, certainly in my case, the education didn't impinge that heavily, to begin with or while it was happening or since. With the one exception of the fact that I do have a degree and I can walk into an employment office and say 'I have a degree.' "

And ". . . education changed my life. It actually did."

DANNY

"I just feel that I need more privacy and freedom. . . ."

After some notable successes and equally notable problems in the same school, Danny graduated. He was a good journalist and had a great deal of training and experience by the time he got his degree. To write that Danny was a skilled and reliable professional would truly miss the point. He was those things, he was intelligent, he did do his work well; but equally important is how he was structuring his life.

Danny was a son of the sixties. The social forces of that time were still at work in him ten years later, when we had our talks. There were many things at work in him, as in all of us; but here it makes sense to focus in depth on the way a profession comes up against a lifestyle. It is best to begin with his early—pre-Italy—career.

"I'd started working for [Big Universal Press] in the early sixties. They asked me would I like to work for them—an incredible job, and it fell into my lap. So when I graduated, I went full-time at [Big Universal]. There was that opportunity, and I did that. As I said, I got married . . . and my wife . . . had a Woodrow Wilson Fellowship.

"So . . . we moved east. I asked for a transfer and they hemmed and hawed about it a long time—basically what they didn't want to do was pay for my moving expenses. So I went to my boss here and said, 'O.K., look. I'm going to [Big Town] whether you people transfer me or not. My wife is going to school there, and I'm going to live there. Now, is there a job for me or not? I will pay my way.' And so they then said, 'Yes—you have a job there.' [He laughs softly.] Wonderful business. So we moved there."

After having been there for only a few months, the political editor of Big Universal quit, and no one seemed to want his job.

"I was like the last person left—I'd only been there a few months. Here I had this really *highly* responsible position that required actually a basic amount of knowledge that I just didn't have—I had never been in the area before—and, well, I accepted it. It was scary. . . it was a big-time job. I got lots of by-lines and met all kinds of famous people and did interesting stuff.

"The East Coast was just a lot different. The pace of life was a lot more intense, and I found the people a lot more abrasive; and also there was the culture shock. I had an incredible amount to learn so I could even function as a newsman; . . . it was a struggle."

Covering politics in a particularly corrupt state was tough for a newcomer: "Each day I would go to work hoping to come home alive. I felt an intense amount of pressure, and I started chain-smoking cigars. The one thing that saved me to some extent was the [rival] newsman and I became best friends . . . and we would look out for each other. I think I'm not competitive . . . and also he was a nice guy, basically calm and honest and sincere and a quiet person. He had many of the qualities that I had."

To end this pre-Italy phase, we can follow Danny home: "I would just be in a knot when I got home and would jump all over my wife—it was a bad situation. I was playing the role of husband as learned at the feet of my father—and that was middle-America, middle-class, male chauvinist pig—dominated the relationship: short-tempered person who in reality was emasculated by his wife."

Enough hard times in the East. Danny and his wife went to Italy to teach.

"At the school they introduced a whole group of teachers to smoking marijuana. [My wife] didn't want to smoke grass again ... you know, it just seemed to emphasize the kinds of differences that we already had and the splits we were already feeling. And so I started smoking grass fairly frequently then. I think [it] was the beginning of a loosening up for me, the beginning of breaking away from sorts of uptight, conservative and constrictive, narrow ways of how I considered life and how I was going to lead it.

"I guess ... maybe people who smoke dope have ... a broader outlook on life and the possibilities of what one can do and what one can experience ... whether it's only working part-time instead of working full-time, or whether it's living together instead of getting married, or being comfortable around nudity, or maybe having some idea of intensity of experience, of fairly deep sensual, emotional involvement with the world around you; and I see that kind of trait as something that people who smoke dope have.

"I'm not comfortable sometimes when I'm around someone that I know doesn't smoke dope and doesn't seem to at least be tolerant."

They moved back to Seattle and, after some hard times, divorced. Once when we talked with Danny, he had just come home from work. Before the tape recorder was turned on, he turned himself on. Later, he described himself: "I walked around nervously—and that's what [Big Universal] can do to me if I'm there very long—for very many days, and that's basically how I'm not very comfortable. I was—I mean my muscles were just tightened up and my mind was all screwed up tight, and you know ... I probably was frowning a little bit."

Danny was working part-time at the time of the interviews, generally only a couple of days a week. When others went on vacation, he often worked full-time, saving the extra money for special things. He was at the top of the pay scale and could earn about seven thousand dollars a year working the way he did.

No doubt, the job was demanding. His description:

"[Big Universal] is an interesting job—there's no question about that compared to all the jobs in the world; it's high on the list of interesting things to do. I feel lucky that I can go to work and not feel bummed out about it. I don't like the hours: I just don't like getting up at 4:30 in the morning to go to work, or going to work at 4:00 in the afternoon and getting off at midnight, or going to work at 10:00 at night and getting off at 6:00 in the morning. Now I'm working two days a week: That's just great.

"Another thing that I dislike is that it's—it's done on a rather skeleton basis; there's never—there are never enough people around to properly do what I consider a proper standard. It's sloppy, and I would prefer to do it under different conditions, but it's something that I've learned to adjust to; it used to drive me crazy. I would just get upset and angry, and now I am more accepting of what I can do under the conditions.

"Several of the shifts down there, you're the only person there, and that's all right; but I just find it pretty dull with myself knocking around that room doing all that work for eight hours—it's really boring. It's an easy job for me now: I can do it in my sleep. I've done it for many years and I've got it down pat.

"It's nearly impossible—it is impossible for me to write outside of [Big Universal]. I write so much each day at work that I'm burnt out.

"I really need a place where I can lay back and relax because, you know, my job and other things and various harassments and requirements and responsibilities take up a fair amount of energy and concentration."

Danny's job, background, and the times led him to serious reflection on how he lived. It was clear from our talks that there was little about his life that he was unwilling to talk about. First, what he would rather be doing.

"I'd love to be a photographer professionally; I'd love to make a living being a photographer." His self-assessment: "I'm the only person I know who would carry a camera around once in a while just to take pictures of flowers or grass. I came back [from a trip] with just an incredibly commercial quality pictures, and everybody just had the pants impressed off them when they saw them; and they said, you know, 'Far out! You ought to do something about these!' And I got to thinking—'Yeah?'"

And, there was this bonus: "Being a photographer is the only thing that demanding technically and creatively demanding that I feel I could smoke dope and do a better job at."

In the end: "Journalism is not my main interest at all: It's fairly boring to me."

The change came in the mid-sixties.

"Physically I've altered myself completely. I've grown my hair, and now it's shoulder length; I guess it's shoulder length. . . . I've grown a beard, and the kinds of clothes that I wear has changed. How I dressed when I was going more informally or casually, in say '65, is not how I dress all the time.

"Instead of wing tips, I wear a Wallaby-type desert boot . . . it just makes a great difference in how I physically feel every day. So I wear those shoes all the time, and they're not—they're certainly not very dressy.

"I enjoy going to establishment, conservatively-dressed-appearing-type news conferences or functions or groups, looking as I do."

Although Danny did not "put as much energy into developing and maintaining friendships and relationships as a lot of other people I know," he did have "a quite narrow group of people I do find very comfortable.

"Sports is a strong source of interest to me . . . my brain cells have taken up storing vast amounts of sports trivia; but at the same time I do enjoy it.

"I fight against all this sort of middle-class conservative kind of drive that I'm sure I was raised with—that I ought to make myself more secure, that I ought to invest in a home. . . . I feel sometimes like I've really got to look into investing in a home. Sure, it takes an incredible amount of time and money to pay that off, but at least you're paying it to yourself. When I figure how many thousands of dollars I've paid in rent in this particular apartment, it's depressing sometimes. No, it isn't either—I don't feel depressed about it.

"I fight against that and I wonder sometimes if it's wise to fight against it, but you know—who is gonna take care of me when I'm sixty-four?"

Danny and his friends "talk about life or our potential lives—fairly detailed assessments of our lives. I've been more concerned with my own goddamn problems and those of my friends, and I don't know if we've gotten into a broader discussion. . . . The ills of this country causing all this tension—I wouldn't be surprised if that's true.

"It's very hard, I think, sharing a living environment—I just feel that I need more privacy and freedom than that would allow me."

And school? Our topic:

"I can remember people telling me in . . . maybe college, 'These are the best years of your life.' And I always think, 'Man, who needs it! It was awful.' I certainly would never call those the best.

"I think each year gets better—like each year I understand a little more about how to deal with me, and know more about my needs and what is realistically satisfying, and I learn more about dealing with the outer world and arranging my life so that I can get the basic comforts and yet the maximum amount of involvement and satisfaction and things like that. I know that I haven't perfected it, but each year I make progress toward that."

Progress toward perfection. In a strange but understandable way, that seems to be the most suitable way to mark where we are in our professional society. It is the overlay of technique on human beings.

The demands of our work world seem to be as great on the worker as on the client or consumer. While exact professional standards are respected, and rightfully so, we have somehow gotten to the place where everyone involved pays a prohibitive price. Even those who do what they do with mastery—those who are productive and efficient and effective—appear to be more and more troubled. To many, the world seems out of control precisely because of its productivity and efficiency and effectiveness—or, more exactly, because of the way those qualities are defined and pursued.

This, it appears, is what college is getting people ready for: jobs that pay well, carry respect, and, possibly, make people sick.

Later, in the last chapter to be exact, we will explore college more fully. While it can be argued that the world must change before anything else can, and that college is of only marginal importance, I believe that college can do a better job than it does in helping the individual in the work world.

It seems appropriate to turn next to the context of jobs, to our public business. In the following chapter we will see how people think about and do politics.

Politics

As a perspective on life or a prerequisite of scientific research, value neutrality, like skepticism, is humbug.

—**Larry Spence**

Every political system I know of operates on a series of comonsense, culturally biased truisms. They are the justifications for any action; they form the basis of public slides and ascents. In this, the "home of the brave" and the "land of the free," where "the government which governs least governs best," and there is "liberty and justice for all," we have no shortage of patriotic truisms.

There is fierce competition for the title of Tritist Political Phrase. We judge the winner every fourth year, during presidential elections.

It is easy enough to make fun of our public shorthand, but the fact is I do not really mind our common sayings. Most of them are potentially ennobling. This chapter may be understood, in part, as centering around a particular article of faith. The article of faith is this: It takes an educated population to make democracy work.

The truism has been a strong argument for more schooling. Before going on, let me register an objection. This article of faith rests on two assumptions about our current condition: (1) that we have a democracy, and (2) that what we have works. Those are two extraordinarily weak assumptions with which to begin an argument. It is possible that in order that we have a democracy, the citizens do need to be educated. My objection is that we cannot tell either way from the American example.

This chapter, however, is not about my objections, but rather about people and politics and education.

It is necessary to offer a definition of what politics is—well, if not a definition by standard terms, at least a way to think about politics. In most empirical works, definitions become critical to the task of measuring. The more exactly you know what you are looking for, the more exact you can be. But, if you begin empirically, with people in the world, it is not at all helpful to sharpen those sharp definitions and then insist on them. They will only cut into your work.

In a later chapter we will return to politics, and I will offer what I think is a sensible way to think about it. Now, however, it makes sense to simply offer two broad categories of politics.

The first has to do, basically, with government and the governmental process. People involved in political parties, pressure groups, voting, and the like are involved in politics. This definition has to do with what most of us were taught in civics, or what is taught in a regular introductory American government course. This is a "how-a-bill-becomes-a-law" view of politics.

The other category of politics has more to do with the ties that bind personal and social actions. As I write this, for example, I know people who have accepted the fact of waiting in line for gasoline, of a coming recession, and of what appears to be muddleheaded government policy about everything. These people seem less concerned about power on a large scale and more concerned about what it takes to lead a sane existence. In this view, the series of decisions in any single day is more important than working for a presidential candidate every fourth year.

There is a line, and a thin one at that, between the thinking-through of the "political" implications of an act, and the plain selfishness of an egotistical person. Hopefully, the two will not be confused in what follows.

If there is an equation between education and democracy, which of these categories would be most democratic? Equally important, which would the well-educated person practice?

There is nothing rigid about the categories. It would be silly to suggest that any single individual would be strictly in one or the other category. For example, during the time of our talks, Nixon was big news. He was on his way to becoming, and finally became a "former" president. Everyone we talked with knew something about what was going on, whether they had voted or not.

The media is simply too big and too inclusive to have allowed us to find people ignorant of at least the broadest topics of current events. One thing we did find, however, was that a person could be both informed about and uninterested in the events of the moment. That, somehow, goes against our conventional wisdom.

Part of what is implied here (and this will be argued later) is that the normal definition of politics is quite limiting. If people choose to withdraw from the standard ways of politics, it does not follow that they are apathetic. Nor does it follow that democracy is doomed. It may mean just the opposite.

One last note about politics and America and education. We seem to be firmly committed to a pragmatic way of dealing with the world. It should come as no surprise that any single person should have—and be comfortable with—ideas that purists would see as mutually exclusive. This pragmatism, the theory goes, makes for a tolerant and stable political realm. Later we will review this theory and, using what we have learned, be able to see the strengths and problems that are involved.

CHUCK

"Wouldn't you guys hate to see me in control?" [*I laugh.*]

The last time we saw Chuck, he had decided to go to college to escape the hassles of being degree-less. College was tough for him. His learning problems had made (and were continuing to make) many common situations into big problems. Reading, for Chuck, was not easy.

His college grades were low and he cheated now and then; but he got his degree, and it looked like everyone else's. He went to law school and flunked out after the first year.

When we talked with Chuck, he was very involved in real estate deals. He had been employed by the city government but had not enjoyed the work. He was on his own, and much of our talk revolved around real estate. In that context a great deal was said about how the country was and might have been run.

Chuck, college-educated Chuck, was not at all pleased with the world. In order to convey the full idea of his politics, I should give some background on the critical themes of productivity, population, and power. These were, of course, *his* critical themes. I can do that by beginning with Nixon.

During the course of our talks, Nixon was Watergated and resigned. But to Chuck, he was "poor old Nixon. He was wrong, but I still feel sorry for him. I think Nixon was guilty. But it was so minor compared to his responsibilities in his whole job."

Chuck sensed something unfair:

"Well, I don't know, when you see—the other day in the headlines for Nixon, they started out with a handwriting expert. Nixon is defeated because of handwriting. Well, how would you like to have *everybody* in this country picking on you, including your own signatures, and somebody get up and say, well, Nixon is insecure. Well, now, to me that's a bunch of bull.

"Now, I'm still for Nixon—now, sure he was wrong, there's no question about that, but I—then I do find, naturally we all relate everything to our—our own feelings."

And just what were Chuck's "own feelings"? Have a look: "The city—a—I feel the city—they spend all of their time trying to stop people from producing something." When he worked for the city, he would "cut corners. . . . I take lots of shortcuts—for instance, if I came up to you, you were living in this house and I had to get permission to trim trees out in front—if you weren't home, I'd sign your name. And then call my boss. All right, now, some people can't do that." Chuck could do that, and he did.

We talked about many of his business dealings. He said that, according to the city, much of what he was doing was "illegal. It's illegal. It's absolutely illegal—everything's illegal. Anything you want to do is illegal, practically."

Yet Chuck was very serious when he said, *"I don't wanna control anyone."* Just as he wanted no one to control him.

For example, the city had put nets around the Space Needle so that people would not commit suicide. But Chuck would "take the rails down. If a person wants to go, that's their choice. I mean, I wouldn't push them, but I wouldn't push anybody—or I wouldn't stop 'em. It seems to me putting nets up—I think everyone should do something or do what they want to do and then we should all pay our—pay our price."

There was sympathy—for Nixon and his small mistakes, for people who wanted to kill themselves and were not allowed to; but there was also the idea that we should all "pay our price." To understand what that meant to Chuck is, in an important sense, to understand the end of sympathy.

The sympathy ended with unproductive people and minorities, especially black people. While Chuck would occasionally qualify what he said about blacks, more often he would stereotype them as the enemy. This was Chuck at his most optimistic: "If you take one hundred blacks—I think even statistics—you will prove that you are asking for trouble, for destruction, for not paying [rent], and *trouble!* I'll be glad when five hundred years has gone by and when society has accepted it, and they no longer have my attitude."

Five hundred years of what? Listen:

"I lost one job . . . a black man got it. And there was no 'he's better qualified and you're not'—they didn't say that. They said, 'He's black, he's got it.' They sent out something for whether I was white, black, Indian, Spanish, or Spanish surname or something; I put down I was half Indian! Well, why not? If I put down white, would I be worse off? I *know* I would be worse off!"

It was not only blacks. In the case of renting, "Had someone come up to me ten years ago, it was easier. Long hair—automatically no! And I think basically, at that time, I think that *was* true."

What Chuck in part was really talking about was "non-producers."

"In a sense we have people who are not producing. One-quarter *cannot* produce if the other three-quarters are so destructive; . . . you know, *you can't have* a cancerous or destructive segment growing and growing and growing and growing; eventually it's going to eat up the good.

"As far as I'm concerned, the ones that are controlling the government, the ones that are getting more and more *in control* are the people that produce the *least.* As you know, and I'm sure this is true, there are cases where some people on welfare eat better than people not on welfare.

"I think of—society as a whole is like one person's body. If you have a small cancerous cell and you can say, well, maybe your littlest finger has cancer, that's the only part and it does not spread anywhere else. You can say—but a person really should, is entitled to having five fingers. I mean, after all, everyone born is entitled to five fingers. This is a God-given right. The only trouble is, if you say that's fine and we must protect that one finger, what will happen?"

Cancer is no fun, and Chuck had thought about cures. The following exchange got to the point:

Chuck: "Well, again, I wouldn't want to be the dictator to decide, but there are still basic low-on-the-rung that I think should be eliminated. And as long as they're not eliminated, they're going to grow."

Me: "Eliminated, meaning? . . ."

Chuck: "Um . . . how would you, if a dog ran down the street mad, biting people, killing them, making people afraid to go out—they could not go out and enjoy, they couldn't go out visiting because they're afraid—what would you do to that dog? Would you torture it?"

Me: "It's clear that people—"

Chuck: "You wouldn't torture it."

Me: ". . . shoot mad dogs."

Chuck: "Right . . . If a man had been committed to an institution for killing—let's say, three women in separate instances . . . three complete separate incidents, where it obviously is a pattern. All right, now I am—I feel that society does not have the facilities to rehabilitate all of those. Therefore, *unfortunately*—and I think it is unfortunate—I think he should be put to sleep for his *own* sake and for society's sake."

There was no bias when it came to the unproductive:

"Let's say—even a physically handicapped person, which we all feel sorry for—I still think that they're—if I knew we could save you, yourself, from a heart condition, and it's gonna take ten billion dollars, I would calculate, and I would say, hum, as society is—values things; but I hate to say it: 'You're not worth ten billion.' I wouldn't save myself. I'd say, well, it's too bad, but you're not worth it."

A last word about blacks: "As a matter of fact, I would even give power to—well, it's gonna happen anyway. If the blacks, for instance, do keep increasing in number and even if they are the biggest in crime, the biggest destroyers—well, if they succeed, if the destroyers —or what I consider the destroyers, which are the people who do not build—if they do succeed, then they have the most power, and therefore I guess they're entitled to it. I'm for the strong, not necessarily—well, even the physically strong, if that's what it takes. If our intellectual society breaks down and the other does not, . . . if they take over, then blacks it'll be."

The rule of the powerful. For what? Why did we need it? According to Chuck, we had too much control and were heading straight for trouble.

"We've got a USSR/United States." He believed that it was wrong to be controlled; that we should all be allowed to "do our own thing."

"Well, basically, the first wish I would wish for would be, in a sense, for myself, 'cause the best way to wish for yourself is to wish that everyone could be happy."

An example may be helpful. Chuck wanted to tear down a big old house on a hill in Seattle and build a high-rise apartment. His way, more people could have a good view. Of course, he was right. People who wanted to preserve old houses were horrified. Those people were saying and doing ugly things to Chuck.

His belief:

"Anybody says there's not gonna be problems worldwide, they're in a dream world. Where our government has been relatively stable, . . . any logic will tell us that it can't go the way it is currently going.

"I don't know, but if we had a complete breakdown of the food chain, many people would have to die off fairly quickly . . . because there would not be enough fish, game, and, you know, wilderness to absorb all the people running around with guns—you know, for hunting—and each other, too.

"*If* we're gonna fall, we're gonna fall. I can't be concerned with it. I have to go forward. Now you could build or I could take this house here, for instance, and this is a substantially built house, and I could stock up with lots and lots of foods, with ammunition, with guns; that's not gonna be sufficient."

To add a fact: Chuck had a year's worth of canned food stored in his home.

And what about that minimum act of citizenship, the vote: "Normally, I don't vote, I do not vote. It's not gonna make any difference . . . my vote against ten that all they can do is get to the polls—they're not working anyway, so they go to the polls—my vote is becoming less and less and less. And besides, again, if we're looking at it from a selfish standpoint, I can live with anybody." Anyway, "the American public is looking for maybe a saint, and there is no such thing."

This is a fair representation of Chuck. I have left out many stories, as well as his theory of sterilizing people at birth so that they would have to "make a positive move" in order to have children. There are some parts of what he said that may easily anger a reader; there is the great temptation in other parts to dismiss him altogether. That would be too easy.

This is what he said in the early seventies: "I've heard predictions that, coming close to four or five years from now, all the money will be practically out of the country. I mean, not this country, [nor] all the Western countries; and it'll be into the Arab countries."

Here it is, 1981, and I have heard the same thing from more official sources.

BETTY

"You feel a great deal of strength—at least I feel a great deal of strength—being with people and sharing experiences."

Earlier, we made judgments about Betty and how she worked out her aesthetic sense. We traced the outline of her life: from her experiences with her many siblings to her one year of college to her happy marriage, five children, and very active days.

There were stories of how she finally had taken over the checkbook, why her mother had kept the windows clean, and how Betty was a serious yard-person and an optimistic human being.

It was also mentioned that Betty was active in community affairs. Very active. Now, as we get more involved with her politics, we can see certain political themes more clearly. The fact seems to be that there was a mix of motives alive in Betty at any one time. The base of much of who Betty was may be gotten at by understanding a little about her nature and her church.

"I'm an optimist anyway. I'm practical, but I think I try to look for the better aspects of things. And I've never really ever suffered anything horrible or experienced any great difficulties in life in a certain way, but I just feel very favorable about life and what's to come. That's very general, isn't it [*laughing*]?

"I guess I'm not a person to mull over things very long after I've done them. I—I make a decision to do something, and I don't look back that often.

"I just didn't have that much contact with the outside world. And I—I felt like I was turning into some kind of drudge, you know. Well, I maybe dwelled too much or thought too much about myself, and I don't like to do that. You feel a great deal of strength—at least I feel a great deal of strength—being with people and sharing experiences."

And church: "I have a great faith in God, and trust him as far as living my everyday life and helping me with raising my children in the right way, and maybe wrongly depend on him to help protect my children and my husband in their daily lives. And not only my immediate family but my parents and my sisters. I'm turned off by some of these Jesus people or charismatic people or those kind of things.

"I've—I've never missed mass on purpose, ever. I—there is a thing that makes me—that I have to go, that obligates me."

There was a problem, once: "I don't think I came close to losing my faith or leaving it entirely, . . . but it was—it was hard to be enthusiastic about it." The reason was birth control. One Sunday, Betty,

Don (her husband), and their three children, then all under three years old, went into church.

"I was walking into the church and this priest came up, and he said [*lowering voice*], 'You know, there's something you can do about this. And, OH! Don was *so mad*. Don said, 'we—we're aware of that, and don't worry about us,' and all this sort of thing.... You know, there are clods everywhere.

"That he, without my asking, my going to him—he offered, he butted into my life—and, you know, as if, as if we couldn't help, we didn't know what we were doing, and I knew every time; and it was a conscious decision and I knew every time, when we got pregnant except for once. And I won't say which one. But I—I resented his thinking that we were this 'breeding' [*I laugh*] couple here, popping out children without...."

Later Betty said this: "I think a turning point in my life . . . was when I started taking birth control devices, birth control pills. I—I just suddenly felt free, that I didn't have to worry anymore, that this nagging fear of pregnancy was—it wasn't a burden."

With faith in God, regular church attendance, a deeply rooted optimism, and the pill, Betty did her share of work in the world.

"I just feel that being part of the community is to help, if I have the time and energy. I've never thought of it in the aspect of religion or faith or anything like that. It's just a job that needs to be done, and I try to help do it. I guess it ultimately helps the religious aspect, but I don't look at it as a matter of Christian duty. It's just me."

Betty is "service-oriented, [a] volunteer . . . there would be no reason for me to take a job with pay when there are other people who need them and I don't basically need a job as far as earning a living."

When we talked with Betty, she was very involved on a church council. She went to meetings a couple of times a week and was working to bring changes to the church. She was also the neighborhood volunteer for several local charities and sometimes worked in political campaigns. Betty voted.

But, for all of that, Betty was "a dependent person; and security means a great deal to me. I'm afraid to do anything new, not as much as before; but any big things for fear of making a fool of myself. I guess to make mistakes or flub up or whatever is hard for me to do, although it's getting less and less hard for me."

For example, she did not learn to drive a car and did not travel in an airplane until she was in her thirties. She enjoyed the independence that came with the car. She was now taking advantage of the planes.

Her fear had another side: "I just very much admired brave people, people who think of something they want to do and go ahead and do it. I just think they're great people, and it doesn't matter what it is, if it's writing a cookbook or . . . climbing a mountain."

There were other kinds of fear and bravery: "I think I felt . . . a big turning point; I guess I attribute it to the age thirty. I think the worst time was the year before . . . like six months before thirty—fashion magazines and everything else—after thirty, it's just downhill for women. You know, the wrinkles start, and the gray hair and the flabby body and the—all this kind of thing, and it's a depressing thought."

Also, you will recall, during those times a person over thirty could not even be trusted. In spite of all of that, thirty "was just a super year, it really was! All in all."

The tie of age and politics:

"I think that the community and the country or whatever looks more toward this age group, say thirty to fifty, for making decisions, doing what has to be done than say the younger age groups, because they are inexperienced: They still have more to learn. And then the older ones have done this, and it's time for them to be able to rest and enjoy . . . and not feel that they really have to hustle."

Although Betty said that she "can't deal with a large system," she had ideas and opinions about national events.

"Well, I just feel like it's getting worse and worse for everybody, all over the world. And I think we're in fact realizing how bad a lot of people have had it for a long time.

"I think there's a different kind of feeling of troubled, and uneasiness and uncertainty . . . where people are, even more, trying to find themselves and who they are and what they want to do."

Immediately post-Watergate for this enthusiastic citizen:

"Of some of the ideals that were taught us to be important as far as what leadership means, as far as how government operates: Of course, I've learned, you know, gradually over the years, you know, the [pausing] the bureaucracy and the whole thing. Just more cynical about politics: What you'd call the establishment or institutions or that sort of thing, there's a cynicism there. There is a little bit of fear as far as what's gonna happen and will there be somebody to take over and grab hold.

"I find some satisfaction in seeing some of those big honchos and know-it-alls get caught up and have to pay."

And the radicals? Patty Hearst and the SLA? A view from this churchgoing woman:

"I was angered at them for their tactics. I could sympathize with their—what I thought was what they wanted to accomplish. I could sympathize with that, but I was turned off by the way they operated. And I could see how Patty was very much influenced by the people that she was with for that long. I think she was, you know, a nice girl but didn't have that much in her head about the world and what was going on in the world.

"You know, she was a little Catholic girl in school, and she was picking out her china and getting married and all this."

We returned to the subject several months later.

Me: "In one of the transcripts we asked you about the SLA and Patty Hearst, and I was thinking how extraordinarily far away that seems."

Betty: "Um . . . hmmm. Doesn't it, though. Well, it's funny: It's of paramount importance for a day or two, and people write— everybody has to write about it, and in a very short time it just —it doesn't mean anything. I don't know."

It all seemed a little unmanageable.

"I know that we're looking for some great person that we can look up to, but I don't know if there's anybody like that around. I think that we need someone inspired to get to work and do things . . . cutting through the crap and getting something done. Cutting out a lot of unnecessary things: We've got to do something about all this unnecessary waste. It's just awful; it really is."

But this was Betty, this was the optimist:

"I think people are thinking more of recycling, reusing, rather than just throwing away. I think that a lot of people show a great deal of strength and imagination and creativity when things are bad. It proves itself in incidents all around you all the time. I'm not very hopeful in some of our leaders that we have, and I don't think that we should depend on them to make it easier for us . . . I think we have to find our own ways.

"That sounds very idealistic and quite general, actually, but I just think that we've got to, you know, get tough. That tells you a lot, doesn't it [*laughing*]?"

Of course it does. What tells us almost as much is the fact that Betty's analyses seem as appropriate now as they did five years ago.

Even with the rush of momentary good news, the basic uneasiness does not seem to go away.

ALFRED

"I don't think a lot of people are very politically educated that they would know exactly what they would want. They know one thing—that they don't want to pay high prices."

Alfred is the longshoreman with the delicate hands. As we saw, he had some trouble reading and spelling; his formal education had not been successful by any useful measure. His day at work was not wholly attractive, yet it was clear (at least to me) that he was doing the best he could.

In the work chapter, we found that he was nervous about automation but pleased with the prospect of women working with him. His periodic desires to go into his own business were cut short by the self-realization that he would probably work on the docks all of his life.

There are a few key lines that help form an important backdrop to Alfred's view of the world. For example: "Trade—trade—well, that's my picture of the world—the trading world. It's not [the] theoretical political world that is the world, and it doesn't matter what these other countries are doing; but the interaction between the countries will be trade."

And: "But as far as politics—no, I'm not political."

And finally: "I took a course—I think it was political—American history or something like that. And there's a teacher, and he—he had a book and he wrote a lot about a lot of different documents and the theories on, well, American government and how it worked and some of the understanding. Because I can see the—a pattern of why different people react the way they do, and then I find out where a specific object or bit of news or something that comes into my life . . . "

> Interviewer: "So for the most part, you're fitting what you hear into that framework."
> Alfred: "Yeah. . . . I try to."
> Interviewer: "Well, what are the basic things that are happening in the world and in the United States?"
> Alfred: "In the world as far as the United States goes? Well, that's a toughy. I could lie a lot—or a little bit—or fib."

Trade and economics, Alfred's entry into the world, seem a sensible place for us to begin. It should be of no great surprise that a discussion of politics became a discussion of money in America. The two have been confused for some time, and whether one approves or not, there is simply a "factness" about the ties between government and money that cannot be denied. For Alfred, as for others, the topics were hopelessly entwined, and to mention one was to imply the other. Politics has become a big money-pie, and government, the slicer.

"That greenback in your wallet represents your life.

"If I understand the question to be, 'Does the rest of the world affect me,' yes, sure it does—as far as economics, like the price of copper or anything, raw materials—it affects me just as the coffee I'm drinking right now. The political overtones of different countries affects on what I can purchase or buy.

"There seems to be a—there's some overall planners, financial people who are trying to—well, the pattern seems to be is that there's a breakup. A group is trying to break up the basic pattern—financial pattern—of the United States. There will be more money for a lot of different projects and things, and there will be a cheap labor—labor market in the United States.

"But there's gonna be a rich class and a poor class. That's what people tell me.

"There seems to be like a conglomerate or the term *multinational* type warfare between these big blocks—many blocks. That's just an idea I have. I think business will look for new avenues of money. New markets, maybe, new avenues of trade. I have an idea that some of the underdeveloped countries will be—there'll be trade with the United States. Well, that's just an idea I have.

"Well, I read a coin book one time, and they were very up on monetary—on the value of different currencies. They were talking about the control board ... the Federal Reserve ... and how they print up all this money; and I started putting two and two together, and ... they're printing too damn much money."

Too much money. Could be.

Interviewer: "What about some of the campaigns that you hear around here, like you shouldn't put fertilizer on your lawns so that fertilizer can be sent to the Third World and used there so they can grow food."
Alfred: "I never heard that."
Interviewer: "... we should eat less meat, for example, so that the grain will be saved from feeding our cattle to be sent overseas, and those kinds of things—they seem really far-fetched to me."

Alfred: "I wouldn't want to comment on that—I really wouldn't take it seriously."

And America? What will become of the United States? Many things, if Alfred is right.

"Well, I think in the next ten years, things will get better, because there's a lot of things that aren't being done—a lot of services and things. And I believe that will keep people busy, as opposed to not-busy people on the streets with really nothing to do.

"It could either be a very loose thing, or it could be a very controlled thing. And the controls on, and who's doing the controls, it might matter, see, if it did happen—that's what I was kind of thinking, that the country could kind of break, break into geographical blocks. It could be states in the truest sense, or it could be complete anarchy, but I'm not sure. It could be complete anarchy for a number of years, because there's a lot of foreign governments, I believe, that would put money, well, into the country, and there would be different blocks.

"As a country, I think we're going to be polarized—in different geographical sections of, you know, of the country—unless there's a mass poverty." In that case, according to Alfred, we would have the kind of migrations that went on during the 1930s.

"You might have some kind of a revolution in this country, but I think the effect will be—it will be a second republic. It—a—because —because people are becoming politically aware, and as far as their rights go, and a second republic sort of would fulfill these things; and it would do away with a lot of hate towards the United States government."

And there is hate: "I think they all hate somebody. I don't believe the Chicanos are particularly interested in blacks, and I don't think blacks are particularly interested in Chicanos. I think eventually the Chicanos will eat the blacks as for a long range; but the United States will be a black country within not too many—let's say a hundred—couple of hundred years."

Interviewer: "Well, would you be more comfortable or less comfortable to see general mixing of the races?"
Alfred: "A little spice in your life doesn't hurt anyone. No, that's a terrible way of putting it. Well, I would hope that—that there would be a separatism . . . not for the sake of being separated but for the sake of blending all the spices into one bowl. I mean, like a goulash is fine for a while—for a meal but not everyday."

Alfred got his information from newspapers ("At the very best you get an occasional news item, and sometimes, probably, you can read between the lines"); and, "Sometimes I talk to sailors on ships. For right now, I've been kind of barraged by people who are very political.

"I—I'm very depressed by looking at Walter Cronkite. Oh, I don't know, and those people—it's more like a mortuary. But it's kind of depressing—but well, they bring on the news and it's very incomplete, and it's all the same."

In concrete terms, Alfred "was more or less against a bunch of students sort of rioting. It was kind of like a good thing because it was opening up a lot of people: It seemed to be a way of expressing some kind of political thing. Chicago—that something like that could happen, and well, in a way, the whole—elections of, well, McGovern —I wasn't for McGovern—but anyway, it was a mess.

"The only thing I've heard about Ford is that he's kind of like a do-nothing; he just sits and does nothing. And he's kind of like a do-nothing President. There's a rumor . . . that once Rockefeller gets in there, he'll get away with—he'll do away with, physically do away with Ford. Well, I think it's kind of scaring people, because people didn't know that much about Rockefeller . . . they can't figure out why he wants to become Vice-President. Because he's—he's old."

Alfred was asked if he had any heroes. "One of the Presidents, probably, Pick or Pickett or Pi—he acquired a little bit of land for us; like the Southwest, I believe it was."

Interviewer: "I'm blanking too."
Alfred. "Well, I think he was a great President."
Interviewer: "Has to be in the 1840s; now who am I trying to think of? You're right, it begins with 'P.' "
Alfred: "Pollk, or Polk?"
Interviewer: "Polk, yeah. On the basis that he acquired the Southwest?"
Alfred: "Yeah, probably, yeah."

He went on to say that there was an ancient Egyptian king whom he admired. No one came close to figuring out that person's name. So much for personal heroes; the last time I checked, Polk showed up on few top ten charts of great American Presidents.

Alfred just did not have much respect for what we think of as normal politics, and he had even less respect and trust for politicians. He thought that his union's politics were petty and corrupt; as we saw earlier, he hated to go to meetings.

All of this had helped develop in Alfred a keen sense of American individualism:

"San Francisco, a very lovely city . . . I felt you can do anything you wanted to in that town, . . . say from walking around in cutoffs and bare feet to a tux/tie. I suppose they do have barriers—I suppose. . . .

"I'd always lived with my folks; and then when I wasn't dependent on my folks for a lot of things, I developed my own way of being with the world."

But the world seemed so messy and uncertain and unclear. Too many facts from too many places about too many things. Alfred's "own way of being" kept running right into a hard world. What about change? Would there be help?

"A lot of people are talking about a revolution, how there's going to be a revolt revolution. Well, people are tired of working so much for so little, and this is the agitation, what I hear."

In 1981, there is still a lot of talk about too much hard work for too little pay; but the language of revolution seems to have faded with Nixon and Vietnam. This college-aged generation is going to business school; maybe the next one will go back into the streets.

BILL

". . . if you have some values and principles, you've got to stick to them. Unless you've reasoned out a valid reason for changing them. . . . To espouse one thing and do just the opposite: . . . I can't do it."

In an earlier chapter, we learned about Bill. There were his "normal" growing up, his final success in college, his great disappointments in graduate school. Bill, a well-educated and very careful man living on unemployment, had done much thinking about the world in which he lived.

With Bill, we have a person who had had the time and the inclination to think about the world and his place in it. If one were to make the education-equals-a-strong-democracy argument, Bill's thoughts and actions would have to be considered. As with much of what we have already seen, Bill's example may raise more questions than provide answers.

The world, according to Bill, was in trouble.

"I see many, many problems of crisis proportion which are not being dealt with—for instance, population. The population problem seems to almost be a key to all the other problems. Closely related to this population problem is food supply.

"This energy crisis has been known—the minute the TV started calling it the energy crisis, it was all over the country, you know. Suddenly everybody woke up and there was an energy crisis. I can remember reading stuff clear back in '67, '68, '69, predicting these sorts of things. I anticipate another fuel crisis again.

"Well, we're heading for some sort of crisis. But I'm not sure what the crisis is going to be. I would be sort of—well, what I'm thinking about is in terms of famine. Serious world famine. And certainly that's going to be a major problem. It may even erupt into more— more Vietnams.

"Another thing that strikes me: More and more of these people, such as the Symbionese Liberation Army people, were not uneducated people. They were all college graduates."

Bill then mused about "how easy it is for anyone with a good physics background to build a bomb in their basement. A bomb big enough, say, that it would destroy one of the skyscrapers in New York. And how relatively easy it would be to steal the materials."

These are fairly serious problems, and they may never be solved. Here are Bill's assessments: "The people in this country don't seem to be aware of what's happening in the rest of the world. Or—and I guess it's only because it's so far away and it doesn't—it doesn't hit them in the pocket. If a problem isn't forced on most people, they tend not to think about it."

And this: "I see man as being such a—in a sense, a fool, and tampering so much with natural processes ... man, at the end, is gonna be erased."

> *Me:* "You don't have a whole lot of good things to say about your fellow citizens."
> *Bill:* "Yeah. I'll stand by that."

In serious and careful ways, Bill got information.

"Lots of people rely on TV for the news; and, well, TV, radios, newspapers all get their information from the AP or UP, so it's just a variation. And television is even worse: It seems to me to be very superficial, very sort of glossy and quick; and one of the things that I have against television is that it's sort of 'instant knowledge' but it's very superficial. And so I think—and I do it, too—I just ignore it, and I think that's what a whole lot of people do.

"I *do* watch [public television] once a week. Because it is good."

He read no newspapers but listened to public radio: "Their correspondents ... are people who apparently have been around Washington for some time. They know people and they can be somewhat more insightful into some of these things than, say the five o'clock news. Now I—that's my sole source of information. But there are sources of—if you're really seriously interested, you can read the *Congressional Quarterly*."

How did he handle the massive amounts of information? "At times I find it very important and at other times I could care less. I can't imagine being ignorant of it, although I may temporarily be unconcerned about it; I can't imagine not being—just being able to turn myself off and not even know what's going on."

In the end, the media conquered Bill: "It would require an awful lot of effort on the private citizen's part to keep track of what's going on. And I know I don't do it as I should and, so, how can I ask someone else to do what I'm not doing?"

The fact is that of all the people we talked with, Bill was probably the most well informed about public events. That he felt inadequate had several sources. One was certainly the complexity of the world in which we live; another was our inability to sort out what we do know in any sensible way; and a final reason was that the media, while making a business of reporting events, by definition, ignored the more basic ties binding those events together.

One result is that we, as citizens, almost routinely concede that we do not know enough to make an informed judgment about anything.

What did Bill feel about politics—normal politics that has to do with political parties and the like?

"It strikes me that there's not that much difference between the Democrats and Republicans. The Republicans do liberal things and the Democrats do conservative things. Because one can't afford to do the other. Kennedy invades Cuba and Nixon has detente with China.

"But, sort of the irritating thing is, maybe—and then maybe I'm just not smart enough to see it—is that there doesn't seem to be an ongoing basic philosophy which both Democrats and Republicans operate on. Or if there is one, it's more of a crisis: We'll meet the crisis when it comes.

"Platforms are written and somebody reads them, but nobody really pays attention to them; the average voter doesn't pay any attention to them. But on the other hand, it's extremely difficult to find out about elections: You have to go to a lot of work. I applaud very definitely the League of Women Voters because they *do* make an effort to find out about issues and be aware of them and understand them.

"This may sound very idealistic, but it seems to me that you would have to have a lot better people running for office than there are now. It's not true, I know, but it seems almost to be true that if you can't do anything else, you can run for political office."

What about seemingly serious political activity, such as the Watergate hearings?

"The debate seemed almost high-schoolish: not really substantial things being said. It was commented on several times before the hearings were gotten underway that the frantic, all-night sessions working out compromises—obviously these sorts of things can't be in front of anybody. So these sorts of dealings can't be made public, I guess. And so I sort of take these public displays that Congress makes with a grain of salt. You know, it's *all* going on somewhere else. To a large degree.

"And, you know, it may seem very egotistical or [*pauses*] . . . but I can't help but feeling if more people had the same sort of [*begins to laugh*]—if more people behaved like I did!" [*Lots of laughter and comments.*]

Most of us feel like that about ourselves, Bill.

Bill admired the Environmental Defense Fund and groups like it. "And they're primarily lawyers and scientists. And they work almost entirely in court. They're not interested in stirring up public outcries, but to take it on issues; and they have a staff of maybe a few scientists paid, but most of them are on a retainer basis. They have a very high record of success. The thing is, they're not just sitting back waiting for a problem to happen."

There are, of course, other ways of "not just sitting back and waiting." For Bill, those other ways were not very appealing:

"At first I was really enthusiastic about the antiwar protest; and the more and more I watched and listened, the less and less effective they seemed to be. And, although I didn't pursue it, it crossed my mind as a worthwhile thing to try and figure out what really *did* stop the war. I have a feeling that it wasn't the demonstrations and the riots—it was something else. As a guess I would say it was economic pressures and the economic problems resulting from the war that finally brought it to a halt.

"I think it just sort of reinforces what we were talking about a few minutes ago: that the government sort of *does* what it wants to do regardless—the will of the people is only a reflection of the government and what they're told by their government. I just don't get that feeling that people spend enough time being concerned about what's going on . . . [they] accept what's given them and then bitch about it."

The future holds little promise if you begin with Bill's premises. This was the best he could see: "Evolve rather, as opposed to, say, a revolution—massive change or overnight change. I think it's gonna be sl-o-o-w, painful—hopefully—I guess I'm optimistic to say I hope the change won't be too far behind the problem 'cause the problem is always gonna be out ahead. There's always gonna be a crisis."

Optimistic? Sure, if you compare it to his longer-range analyses.

"Well, I would see the government takeover as being sort of insidious and happening—it *is* happening, I think, over time. And I think the majority of people would accept it as being what's good for them. They would be told well enough in advance that what we're doing is for your own benefit. And you're told that enough times, you begin to believe it. And so, I would see maybe—I don't know what sort of time period it would take—maybe thirty years, forty years, a fascist state in this country. And accepted by the majority of the people as being necessary and worthwhile and achieving the ends."

Later, he got depressed enough to tell us about a psychic who predicted that Rockefeller would have concentration camps. He quickly changed the subject, but the fact is that he brought it up.

And where did Bill fit into this national set of ongoing events? "I used to think that I could have that much personal power. But I don't think so anymore, except on a very small, tiny scale. The government ... strikes me as a bureaucratic structure whose orientation is or whose purpose is to perpetuate itself."

A "very small, tiny" amount of power, a self-perpetuating bureaucracy: Those can be rather imposing limitations. Interestingly, those limitations seemed to drive Bill to consider almost every aspect of his life. In a sense, it is fair to think about most of his actions as having had a political element.

In Chapter 4, Bill's "normal" background was noted. He said, "I have never wanted to be normal! I've consciously gone about doing things just the opposite of what was considered the *in* thing to do. Now I never even consciously think about it. I'm not normal because I see the majority of the population being swayed by whatever happens to be current."

But when pushed he admitted, "Yeah. Yeah, I suppose if I had to choose, I would say I'm normal. I'm certainly not radical. It gets back to the old problem of how you define normal."

Definitions. It seems to me that they have always been a problem. Like self-definition. For example, after being away from the Midwest for several years, Bill returned home for a visit:

"At the time I had a moustache, and everywhere I went I was conscious of being stared at. Nearly all my friends I talked to were very conservative: They were very much in support of the war, thought Nixon was doing the best job possible, [and], you know, McGovern was next to being a Communist. It was really a shock to realize I'd changed."

Me: "Do you consider yourself a true person of the twentieth century, a modern man?"
Bill: "No."
Me: "What, how do you—"
Bill: "I suspect that I would be much happier in the nineteenth century . . . I think, because I'm interested in so many things. And I think in the nineteenth century you were able to do that. Now you're almost forced to have lines and credentials. Maybe I'm exaggerating . . . and there are certain things you couldn't possibly have done in the nineteenth century that you could do today. There's a lot more freedom today."

A man born a hundred years too late, but a man who liked much of what he was born into.

Just as Bill was broad in his interests, he was thorough in his life:

"I jog in the morning for two miles—every other morning. A physiologist friend of mine told me that was all that was necessary. If you exercise vigorously, one mile or two miles, it was good for about forty hours.

"I don't eat junk food: candy bars, potato chips, stuff like that. Three meals a day, three good solid meals a day. [*Long pause.*] I *try* to eat a balanced meal. . . ."

At that point, Bill talked about the relative nutritional values of many different foods, as numerically scored by a group called Science for Concerned Citizens: "And McDonald's hamburger ranked, I think, about two steps above two tablespoons of peanut butter . . . ice cream had a score of about −80." In the end, it gave him a basis for judging: "I want to feel what I'm buying, what I'm paying for, is gonna be worthwhile."

He gave several reasons why he enjoyed his new vocation, which was fishing. Here are two: "I really enjoy—like being outside, being on the water . . . and . . . I feel that fishing is important in the sense that it's helping add to the food supply."

And his intellectual roots? Very American: "Probably one strong influence was Thoreau. There was one strong influence in high school: my English teacher. She was just a really dynamic person. I know she had us read Thoreau and Emerson. And the—finally then when I came here to go to school, the man who most interested me in the geography department was very strongly interested in conservation . . . and all these things started reinforcing each other."

What they reinforced were his beliefs, which he took very seriously.

"Many people in this country, I suppose, hold in principle many of the things that Thoreau and Whitman and these people say, but [*emphasis on next part*] what they do is entirely different. And I guess that bothers me. I was impressed, I'm sure, by my parents and especially my father, of being honest . . . if you have some values and principles, you've got to stick to them. Unless you've reasoned out a valid reason for changing them, adjusting them. To espouse one thing and do just the opposite is—it's foreign to me: I can't do it. Maybe that's just me being a snob.

"Too much of the time the end justifies the means. I cannot agree with that at all. I think that's totally wrong."

And a further belief: ". . . so I feel a certain, over a long period of time, that I should, in any small way that I can, leave the world a better place. I feel a social responsibility. But I've not been able to figure out how exactly to do it."

There was some self-evaluation: "I tend to be somewhat of a perfectionist, and if what I'm doing—if I can't make it come out to be just perfect, you know, I get upset."

It makes some sense to want to do a perfect job on a small fishing boat that will take you to sea. But later, Bill began talking about social scientists who advised the government. He was particularly interested in the bad advice (the plans that did not work) given to the government.

Bill: "And this seems to be almost the problem of the social sciences, that they don't have theories to work with that seem to fit, that seem to work."

Me: "From my point of view, not only do I not find that a problem, I find it very, very encouraging."

A perfectionist, it seems to me, is bound to have some trouble in this world:

Bill: "But when you start thinking about what's going on around you, in the total world, then I think this idea of despair comes in . . . it gets depressing . . . the chaos we're living in. You certainly can't—you certainly can't as an individual do anything about it.

"Well, it must always be there. It's just that I'm able—it's sort of covered up. Put into the background. Sublimate, is that what you do?"

Me: "Or repress."

Bill: "Repress—that's it. 'Cause that strikes me that everyone has a certain amount of responsibility for what they do, and you repress this too much and you're abrogating your responsibilities."

He was "pessimistic enough that when I was married I didn't want any children . . . and now I'm even more glad than ever; it strikes me as a frightening place to bring people up."

Yet, he said, "I think I'm a lot less pessimistic now than I was. I guess the only thing I can say is my pessimism didn't accomplish anything, so why stick around it, why not a brighter look on—just try something, try something else. Why stick with the old if it doesn't work anyway! The thing—I think being less pessimistic—is that you tend not to enjoy things when they do come along."

One of the undeniable facts of doing this kind of research is that every person's story is incomplete. While it is fair to say that what has been said about Bill—what he has said about himself—gives an accurate accounting of his life up to the time we talked, we have no way of knowing how he is doing today.

The best we can do is hope that the fish are biting and that he is finding less pessimistic better than more pessimistic.

Later, in the chapter on method, we will look into the problem of incomplete stories in some detail.

Politics, Democracy, and Education

I think it is right to remember the conditions that existed at the time of these talks. The United States had just finished with the war in Vietnam; the President had been thrown out of office; the presidency was under attack; there was a fuel crisis; what the media called the "mood of the country" was unhappy; and the future seemed uncertain. Some of what was said in the talks may have been influenced by those hard times. It makes sense that some of it was, but *only* some.

The fact is that what was said is as applicable today as it was in the mid-seventies. Certainly government still seems very, very big, and each of us very, very tiny. The bureaus in the bureaucracy appear just as intent on surviving now as they did then, and they continue to enforce a particular set of rules to that end. The actual social usefulness of those rules is an issue.

The perceptions of those in politics remains unchanged. The public has little confidence in the ability of most politicians to be effective.

For a variety of reasons, it appears that participating in normal politics made little or no sense to the people we talked with. The people were concerned about the world and the country and their community; but there were only limited ways to make those concerns felt politically. The political system itself seemed overwhelming, and offered no—or only a very small—way to be active.

Writing letters or voting was seen as doing next to nothing. Active protest was considered ineffective.

Concerned citizens seemed cut out of most political activity. Simply to be informed was a more than full-time job. The common estimation of the media was this: The media chose currency over depth; and that a person knew about many events was of no particular help in understanding the world. The amount of misinformation and mistrust was impressive. The amount of time it took to come to terms with what was happening was great.

To relate money directly to politics simply complicated things. Job issues and governmental policy tie personal ability to social responsibility in frustrating ways.

There is much to suggest that it is all a mess.

What about education, the backbone of a democratic state? The despair felt by those with college degrees seemed no more profound or of no higher a quality than the despair of those without degrees. Even the quality of misinformation and speculation appeared to be about the same.

Certainly authoritarianism could be found as easily in one group as the other. Also, the mistrust of others' authority and power seemed to be a shared trait. Finally, the idea that most Americans are gullible seemed to cut through educational lines.

It is exactly at this point where this chapter on politics turns for me. I am not at all convinced that we are all gullible. What seems a more righteaded argument is that we are stubborn individualists, and that, as we are pushed further and further away from politics, we mistrust not only our government but also the individuals around us.

Education, as it is now carried out, will not save—or even produce —a democratic state. On the other hand, isolation will surely destroy much of the freedom we have left.

In the final chapter it will be important to return to this theme.

I find these conclusions full of ambivalence about higher education. The heart of the myth of college, which was discussed in Chapter 2, can certainly be seen. Yet, the people we talked with were adults who had lived in the world long enough to know the limitations—and the false promises—of college. Their conclusions clearly reflected that knowledge.

While no one advocated abolishing higher education and everyone acknowledged that there were forces much more powerful than college, there seemed to be agreement that *something* was wrong. Something was wrong both with the world and with higher education.

In the last chapter, the concluding concluding chapter, we will return to that thought.

8

The First Concluding Chapter

New power was disintegrating society, and setting independent centres of force to work, until money had all it could do to hold the machine together. No one could represent it faithfully as a whole.

—Henry Adams

This is the first of two concluding chapters. While that seems a fairly irreponsible use of the language, there is an explanation—hopefully, a good one.

In important ways, this is the end of the middle part of the book. The middle section, Chapters 5, 6, and 7, has dealt with real people in the world—in particular, the work world, the professional world, and the political world.

Also, to here, the book has centered on twelve people: their words about their lives. This is the last chapter in which individuals supply the words. This is *their* last chapter.

Almost a year after we began the talks, we gathered people together for one last summary session. We divided the people into groups and met the groups at different times. It was the first time people in the project met others in the project. These were the only group interviews we had.

The aim of the talk was to provide some kind of overview: some self-assessment in terms of both higher education and the research project itself. The groups were formed on the basis of formal educational experience: We reasoned that those with virtually no college education might possibly be uncomfortable talking about college with those who had college degrees.

In one group, people had some college but no degree; in another they all had a degree, or almost; and in the final group all had graduate degrees. Not everyone was able to attend this last talk.

On the whole the sessions were fun and interesting. Some people did not come across any differently than in the individual talks; others seemed entirely different. Prior to the group talks, we had given each person a list of four questions to consider. These questions were never explicitly addressed in any of the groups. While they did help focus on education and the research itself, they were of little specific use.

This chapter differs from the others in two ways. First, Ken Dolbeare and I appear as ourselves in this chapter. We were interviewees as well as interviewers during the project, and this was our last interview, too. In the context of the discussions, these were our conclusions to that point.

Second, you will find dots (. . . . . .) separating sets of conclusions. These are to separate either different conversations within the same group, or one group's conversations from another's.

In the last three chapters another kind of work will be done. In Chapters 9 and 10 there will be a discussion of methodological concerns and a description of the project. Chapter 11 will be my conclusions.

But, this is Chapter 8: the first concluding chapter, the one in which the people interviewed offer *their* conclusions.

Advice

We can begin concluding in the form of a question: What advice would you give a person about whether that person should attend college?

Alfred: "Young people have asked me more than once, and the only advice I ever gave them was to—don't stick around where you're at now. Go somewhere else, out of town. Get away from your parents, see the country, and to go to school. Like, I definitely am for going to school. And the way to do it is to go out of town. For an education, you would get a different—a fresh look on what you're doing and how to go about it. You would have a much broader base of deciding for yourself. And just another aspect of —try to give a person advice on how to make up their own mind, on how to reach a decision with the most information that they could gather."

Betty: "I would encourage someone in high school to go to college. If nothing else, to broaden their horizons, to give them the opportunity to meet people very different from themselves. A college education could offer courses and give them a chance to decide what they want to do later on. I think mainly it's the experience of meeting and interacting with people very different from yourself."

. . . . . .

Ted: "It seems to me if I asked my sixteen-year-old boy, 'Why would you want to go to college?' And this is one of the things that he mentioned: 'Well, there's a status that college people have.' "

Danny: "That's one of the words I wrote down for why I went . . . for status."

Me: "What do you think now?"

Danny: "It's probably a bunch of bullshit, really. I don't see where it makes any difference."

Ted: "But could you have gotten your job? . . ."

Danny: "The job that a person is doing is not status to me anymore. . . . It [the job's status] didn't change my life and it didn't make me a better person."

Ted: "I've got four kids . . . the thought occurred to me, do I really want my kids . . . to go through the whole college experience and to—to go through it? When I look back, I'm not sure; but it seems like most of the important things happen outside the formal structure. You know, on the job, the people I met in life experiences or whatever. You know, most jobs, you have to learn what you're gonna do on the job. And you don't ever look back through college notes."

[*A short time later in the same part of the conversation, Ted continued.*] "But I keep wondering if—if your formal education doesn't need to be fused back in close to the marketplace. And on the one hand, there's this thought that you know you have to separate— there's a certain value in separation from the marketplace to study and do research and so on. Well, as a parent, the biggest motivation for me encouraging my children and for them wanting to go on to college is really a job opening or a motivation. My daughter's working as a clerk at [Big Discount Chain]—she doesn't, you know —she's worked there long enough now: The excitement's over, she doesn't want to work as a clerk at [Big Discount] the rest of her life. But the ease of moving into more exciting or more remunerative fields is, you know, very limited unless you have degrees.

Danny: "Oh, I just met a guy yesterday who was a bookbinder, and I don't think he learned it going to college. And he did beautiful work, and he and his wife lived in an A-frame over on an island, out in the woods. There are a lot of aspects of their life that I appreciate and would seek myself."

• • • • • •

Carl: "When it was time for me to go to school, I didn't know what in the hell I wanted to do, or, you know, where I wanted to go. The thing I wanted was a fast car and somebody to buy me a case of beer, and, you know, right out of high school. Let's take the case of my daughters. Hell, if they hate school, don't send them to more of it. Life is so damn short. And I think you have to look at the individual. I have one daughter; I would say . . . she's a little bit domestic. One's gonna be a little bit domestic—I would like to see her finish high school and go out and be a secretary, just to get some exposure before she settles down and has a family. I don't think she's gonna be the type to go to school. On the other hand, the other, she just reads all the time and everything; she may be a good candidate for school."

Willy: "But the thing that you're saying is that you don't necessarily require that your children complete your life. Well, for so long this has been the condition with America, that the child will satisfy the ambitions of the parents. But, my congratulations to you."

Carl: "Well, you see, when I originally got out of high school, I went to college because that was expected of me—to go to college. It had been pounded in my head from day one. And all of a sudden I said, what the hell am I doing? Who am I trying to impress? I don't want to go anymore. . . . You know, four years of college isn't the right thing for everybody."

• • • • • •

Sue: "I, for sure, think that education is important. I don't want to leave that out. Our son knows he has to go to college [*laughs*]!"

Ken: "You're gonna make him go?"

Sue: "No. Certainly not if he doesn't want to. He doesn't do anything that he doesn't want to. But I try and, you know, would like to encourage him in that field. And I think it's—I mean, college is definitely important for so many reasons. And a good education is important. I mean, there are a lot of very, very intelligent people that are self-taught. But I think it's a lot harder, a lot harder in the long run."

• • • • • •

Me: "I was surely forced to go to college; it was never an option in my home, and, of course, the way it turned out was exactly perfect. I was lucky. I was one of those coincidences of a person who has never thought about it for himself and didn't have a choice and went, and it turned out he loved it. And I, you know—it's scary to think that I wouldn't have been forced to go to college. And yet being forced to do anything seems so bad. Except it's not some-time."

Danny: "Well, what about those people who hate it and don't participate in it as they're supposed to and flunk out and get a sense of failure—'cause they were forced to.'"

Me: "I agree."

Danny: "It's a hard thing to just—"

Me: "Sure—all I was trying to say is that it's hard to reject out of hand some kinds of pressures and some kinds of being forced."

Images

Earlier we talked about the myth of a college degree. Certainly parts of that myth were seen in the above discussions, and other parts will follow. In this section, I would like to concentrate on some of the images that people have of college. While it is an arbitrary topic (images of college run through the whole chapter), it does help divide the chapter into more understandable parts.

Ted: "I really feel like—that somehow the educational system has departed so far from what it was really intended to set up. . . ."

· · · · · ·

Danny: "You can view college as a place to go for training or a place to go for learning. And most people, I think, view it—and probably the people you're talking about—see it as a training ground or a union card."

Ted: "Well, college would [now] be very different from college for me twenty years ago, too. I mean, colleges are different in some of their expectations. . . . Even here on the campus, the School of Social Work is radically different than what it was in '63 or '65 and what it is now. In the expectations of students. In some ways, there's a lot more freedom, but I hear the students now saying, . . . the profs don't give you anything; you know, it's so free and easy that—that a lot of students get the feeling—well, they don't give a damn. They hardly even come around and see what I'm doing, you know; it's—so education is a lot different. I'm not saying it's better or worse now necessarily, but it's a lot different than it was when I started out."

· · · · · ·

Betty: "Do you think there was a mystique about the value of a college education that has dissipated now that more and more people go—that it isn't held up as the awesome thing that I think it was thought of at one time? Especially for the depression parents who didn't have a chance to go and wanted their children to go, and this was the ultimate and the summit of life; and now people are achieving success, so-called success, earning a good living very often without going to college or in spite of going to college, so that it doesn't have the. . . ."

. . . . . .

Chuck: "Every generation up to now has always—we have consumed more, invented more, done more than our previous generations. Now we are getting to where people cannot consume more or do more. Education, as you know—right now education, the educational field is just overflowing with an excess of people."

. . . . . .

Bill: "Well, I mean, education in general I think tends to be very conservative. At least, that's my feeling about it."

Ken: "You mean, the School of Education?"

Bill: "Yes. Regardless of whether it's here . . . or wherever. Well, I guess my real criticism of the School of Education is that they seem to be very practically oriented—as opposed to being theoretical."

. . . . . .

Willy: "You mean, after college you went to a commercial trade school?"

Carl: "I never graduated from college."

Willy: "Well, I mean, after your college experience, you went to a commercial trade school—such as are advertised in the newspapers, learn this—"

Carl: "Yeah."

Willy: "Oh."

Carl: "Computer programming to be exact."

Willy: "I'll be damned. And it actually helped you?"

Carl: "Very definitely."

Willy: "Wow! I've always had a great suspicion of these commercial schools."

. . . . . .

Willy: "You can probably get just as much from any textbook as you get from any professor. Most courses are taught from a textbook."

Me: "Is that right?"

Willy: "Yes!"

Me: "God."

Willy: "Or multiple textbooks. Or multiple textbooks, paper, and the personality of the teacher."

Me: "Oh, come on." [*Ken laughs.*]

Differences

While there were differences among the groups, there was one noteworthy difference. In the course of the conversation in the group of people without degrees, someone said that there was a difference between college-educated people and others. Not only that, but a person could actually pick out college people in the crowd. Later, we asked the other two groups about that idea. First, we will see the responses; when we begin the discussion with Alfred, we can see how those without degrees saw those with degrees.

Danny: "I don't think I could [tell the difference]. The line between is getting more and more vague all the time."

· · · · · ·

Chuck "I don't think I could [tell the difference]."

Willy: "I don't think I can."

Carl: "If you take a group of people, let's say a group of successful people, I don't think you could go to that group of people . . . I don't think you'd be able to tell who had what education. I don't think you'd be able to tell what degree of education they had."

· · · · · ·

Alfred: "There is a difference between people who go to college and people who don't go to college."

Ken: "Is that really true?"

Alfred: "Sure, definitely."

Sue: "Oh, sure—there's definitely a difference."

Me: "Oh [*skeptically*]. Is that right?"

Ken: "Describe it."

Me: "Yeah."

Sue: "Don't you think so? Just, like, people who have gone to college and people who haven't. They have a lot of confidence in themselves."

Ken: "Would you know the difference by talking to them?"

Sue: "I would know probably *at least* 70 percent of the time. Sure."

Ken: "How??? What would be the clues?"

Betty: "The way they talk—"

Sue: "Vocabulary."

Sue's husband: "I would say their reasonableness, basically."

Sue: "Oh, I think so, for sure."

Ken: "Vocabulary?"

Sue: "That has a lot to do with it."

Betty: "Their interests. I might—can't speak for everybody, but the spectrum of their interests in reading, arts, history, beyond the survival standpoint—I think more well rounded, shall we say, in their knowledge and their interests. Not everybody is. But, I think that, for the most part. . . ."

The discussion continued until we got to the point of asking about the importance of a degree in the differences among individuals.

Betty: "You don't have to have a degree; it's just if you spend time in higher education—yes."

Ken: "You mean, it's exposure . . ."

Betty: "Oh, no, just the exposure. I consider one year exposure. My own personal experience—sure."

Sue: " 'Cause what you put into it. You can get a lot out of a year; you get a lot out of six months if you put yourself right there."

Worth

The next set of conclusions concern the "worth" of a college education. While clearly much like the "image" conclusions and the "advice" conclusions, these are a little different. In some ways, these conclusions are more personal than the preceding ones.

Sue: "And I do think that some of my first college education was . . . definitely a waste of money. Because I went there for the social life, which I could have gotten anywhere else. Not the same type of social life, but equal, equal to me in value. If I would've just looked at the people I was working with—the right type of people —I could've met the same caliber, the same type of people, and probably learned the same thing from them that I learned going to college."

· · · · · ·

Chuck: "Years ago, a college degree was more of a guarantee."

Carl: "I don't think you're ever gonna find the economy again that you found in the early sixties. . . . As far as I can see, there's not just—it's not going to matter what kind of an education you have unless you're right at the top."

Willy: "I wonder if the emphasis has not gone back to living your life rather than getting a job."

· · · · · ·

Alfred: "Maybe we need a new frontier. A place to—a place to put all these people who are going to college. Maybe we need a colonized place to send . . ."

· · · · · ·

Chuck: "Education to me has always been a negative. Education did not, as far as I'm concerned, succeed—because, first of all, education, what you're looking for in education was certain things. For one thing, they failed, anyway. I never did learn—like you guys could sit down and write a book. As you know, I do everything non-written. I've been successful in doing everything non-written, but minimal. College did not teach me English; if I'd live to be a thousand years old, they'd fail."

Willy: "What about high school? Did high school do anything for you?"

Chuck: "No. No. All the way through. I was on probation four times as an undergraduate. On probation once, I had to lie, I cheated on tests; I finally made it. Some people have hang-ups and I had a block—basically it would be an English block."

· · · · · ·

Sue: "Yeah, you know. For sure, if you can afford to, go on to college—so many advantages."

Betty: "Yes. I do think there is a lot of wasted time."

Sue: "Particularly at a university if you're going into an office job. I mean, I really see a lot of girls going to the "U" because their parents have the money, because they don't want to really look for a job right now; and so they go to the "U" and they're taking typing! At [the Big State University]! What a waste! Why not go to [Smaller Community College], you know. And they're not meeting that many people, either. I really see that. They're just—they're getting up ten minutes before they have to be to class; they're going to class and they're going to class and they're going straight home. Really."

Ken: "Is there prestige to go to the university?"

Sue: "Yes. I'm sure of that. A lot."

· · · · · ·

Alfred: ". . . like a lot of academics that say they're teaching about a certain field when they haven't—academics haven't actually gone out and actually worked in a certain field and have [not] gone through the field. Because there is firsthand knowledge and secondhand knowledge, and there's too much secondhand knowledge. And I think the way to break this thing and to really have a well-educated person, [one] that wants to be well-educated, [is that he or she] has to move around."

· · · · · ·

Betty: "Well, people have to learn how to use their leisure time . . . to extend what's going to seem to be more and more leisure time in a satisfying and enjoyable way."

Alfred: "Maybe we should all be educated and trained to be a monarchist. To lead a life of royalty."

Me: "That's right."

Alfred: "A few very smart people could—"

Betty: "Push the buttons and—"

Alfred: "Right."

Sue: "The processed food coming in and wastes going out and the—"

Alfred: ". . . automatically done so that—"

Ken: ". . . one of the easier tasks."

Alfred: "And then when, you know—'cause then you might run into a situation where human beings might not be worth very much. And if you tell them—a garbage disposal—well, a shredder—that's, you know, . . . when people aren't valuable you can just shred them up."

· · · · · ·

Chuck: "I mean, I've gotten my college degree. All I'm saying is it was a struggle, and I really don't think that a college education helps that much."

· · · · · ·

Chuck: "Do you resent not having a—or not resent—do you feel bad by not having an actual college certificate?"

Carl: "Less and less all the time."

Chuck: "I feel this way, too. I told you I went to law school and I flunked out. But I would have liked to have had a law degree."

Willy: "So would I."

Chuck: "I would have liked to have had it—and I will always feel bad that I did not get it. I always will."

Good Things

There were, in the course of the discussions, several times when the experience of college came up. In the whole of three evenings, only one person talked, in a pointed way, about just what might be good about actually attending college. As we have seen, people have some respect for the idea of being educated, having a degree, or simply having the experience of a year or even six months in college. We have seen that a degree might do you some good in employment. But what about college as an activity? Here are the thoughts of one person (speaking at two different times).

Bill: "Because even though it is compartmentalized and departmentalized, even though it's not the best system, and maybe it's just luck—but if you go there and just sample—and maybe if you were forced; for example, the distribution requirements: You're forced into these sorts of things. And sometimes, you know, something will click. And maybe . . . just one course is enough to get your thinking going and to reorient you and give you a whole new view on things. Somehow, . . . maybe there is too much freedom. A certain amount of force is necessary, I think, somewhere along the line. And I don't know how you determine those points, but after that point then you can go anywhere you want to go."

• • • • • •

Bill: "In sort of a curious way it goes back—at least for me it does—goes back to university experience. Before I went to the university, I know, in reflecting, that I was somewhat narrow and limited and very opinionated. And that's why I really value the university experience. . . . I was forced into situations where I had to learn; read something whether I got anything out of it or not . . . a germ of an idea here and a germ of an idea here. And maybe . . . it took three or four years, but finally these things are sort of slowly rolling into place. Giving me an entirely different perspective . . . on what we expect in life and what our roles in life can be."

Bad Things

If those are the good points, what are the bad? What follows is an interesting assortment of complaints about higher education and its effects on the individual.

Alfred: "And this, I think, is what—what education is kinda lacking, is how you become responsible."

• • • • • •

Bill: "Well, I know many people who are my age and older who are just as narrow and bigoted and uneducated as they were before they went to college."

• • • • • •

Me: "But I suspect education, the end of education, the end of formal education is a clearly definable stopping point for a lot of people."

Danny: "Yes. Something to—an accomplishment of a particular goal or things that you felt were expected of you, that you reached a point where you'd accomplished something in some way the—"

Me: "Or, the last institutionalized place where change is even an issue."

• • • • • •

Willy: "Well, actually, I've decided the society does not deal with its own individuals in a group fashion. We are sort of forced in individuality rather than group action. Group action today comes, as far as I'm concerned, only by—well, it's sort of hardship."

· · · · · ·

Bill: "Curiosity has always been a big factor in my life.... I think that's one thing that has sort of helped me to sort of get through the sort of bureaucratic bullshit that goes on at a university. My curiosity. And I guess, coupled with the fact that I'm able to say 'This is bullshit' and put up with it—for the sake of satisfying my curiosity."

· · · · · ·

Willy: "The electronics industry has burgeoned in the past, well, three years and then ten years and then twenty years. But as an electrical engineer, I cannot keep abreast—it's totally impossible for me to understand my own technology. Twenty years ago [*snaps fingers*] I knew most of what was going on, and my percentage of knowledge of my own field in that period of time has gone down steadily."

Chuck: "That's not gonna be just you, that's gonna be everybody."

Carl: "Things are changing so rapidly that it's, as you said, in fact impossible to stay abreast. Yet we have to be able to intelligently communicate with people. At your work, you know there's new new technology around; you might not know about it but you have to be aware that it does exist. O.K. So somehow, you have to stay abreast of these things." Later: "I do have to know individuals that know—then, when I do need to use that new—or whatever it may be, then I know who to go to." And: "I run up a lot of time reading, and I find I like to listen to the news on television. I find it a very frustrating thing to keep abreast, and you're always really fighting to keep abreast."

· · · · · ·

Danny: "It's just like a fancy form of the military. Really [that's what being a professor is like]. I mean, the people who remain in the army as career noncoms: They aren't officers; [but they] wanted that same kind of security, and anything that threatens it, puts them in any sort of risk position, is eliminated. Until they know all the rules and they could just roll along...."

The "Real World"

There were some conclusions about the relationship between the academic world and the "outside" world—a relationship that, at best, always seems tense.

Chuck: "And I've always felt that academics and what things are in the real world are two quite different worlds at times."

• • • • • •

Alfred: "I think the outside contributes more to the school situation than school contributes to the child. Maybe there is—there's where the failure is."

Betty: "I would have to agree that, or I would like to think or I believe that parents' interest or parents' enthusiasm makes a big difference in how a child learns and what a child does in school."

• • • • • •

When credentials were discussed, Willy said that he really did not believe they were terribly important. When pushed, he also admitted that no one would be hired where he worked without the proper papers.

Willy: "I know two guys in my life who had quality engineering jobs with no academic credentials."

Chuck: "On credentials. It's possible to fake credentials. On paper. And as much as I almost dislike having to have credentials and think it's . . . not a waste but a hindrance in some ways, I would look at credentials of other people. In a world where you still have to go by statistics, why should you chance it?"

• • • • • •

Carl: "I find myself watching people that have a good command of the English language. They can just whitewash you so fast!!! [*Ken laughs.*] And I have gotten burned a couple of times this way. Somebody comes in with a *good* command of the English language and really has a line: I take about five looks."

Willy: "You're saying, society contains con men."

Ken: "And maybe that college helps create a kind of PR mentality among people—or a capability at least, among people who can go out and talk you—"

Carl: "It's any line you want to go in, there is a jargon. Once you master that jargon—"

Willy: "You can pass as an expert."

Carl: "Right. You come in and just sit there and just bullshit with somebody, you know, and you just have to have a little idea what the words mean: bang, bang, bang."

The Project

There was curiosity about the research project itself. Not only were Ken and I interested in their perceptions, but most of the people wanted to sort out their thoughts about the talks.

Sue: "I think you probably understand each of us, but I'm not sure myself what you've gotten out of it."

Betty: "I feel that way, too."

Sue: "I mean, I wonder if you think that—I mean, how do you feel and how do you base education and do you think it is that important, from talking to all the different people that you've talked to? Is it hard—I mean, it's got to be difficult after talking to all these people! How can they even expect you, in this program, to decide if education is still that important?"

Betty: "Well, I felt at the time of the interviews that I was saying what I thought I was at the time and what I was really thinking at the time, but then reading the transcripts afterwards, I thought—oh, did that come across like that? Just, oh—"

Alfred: "Well, what you're talking about there is a written language and a spoken language . . . they're two different things."

Ken: "Do you think David and I could answer a long questionnaire about your lives and your likes? . . . "

Betty: "I think from that standpoint that you would know mine."

Sue: "Oh, sure. I wouldn't have any doubt."

· · · · · ·

Willy: "Well, I have said to a number of my friends that I have been interviewed for six times with two intelligent men—not just one, but two—and I get to talk about myself. And to get that from a psychiatrist would have cost me a fantastic sum of money. [*Ken laughs.*] And probably been less profitable."

· · · · · ·

Willy: "Do you have any dummies?"

Ken: "Dummies?"

Willy: "Yeah."

Ken: "What do you mean, dummies?"

Willy: "Well, let's say a person who went to college and—average in—"

Chuck: "I must be the average!" [*Ken and David laugh.*]

Willy: "I've known some pretty dull college graduates, who went through college and didn't have—"

Chuck: "Probation four times, flunked out of law school."

Willy: "Um, you are not a dummy. You are—"

Chuck: "You said—"

Willy: "Not a dummy, by my definition."

Chuck: "You said, somebody who went through college—average—you couldn't get closer!"

Willy: "Yes, I could."

Chuck: "Well, not closer—"

· · · · · ·

Danny: "See, they [academics who did quantitative work] made themselves seem practical because they measured everything and they put it all in behavioral objectives, and that supposedly is concrete and usable. And we became known as the how-do-you-measure-a-rainbow crowd because we claimed there are some things about teaching which are an art and are not easily definable and are not easily, if at all, able to be taught."

• • • • • •

Me: "It is striking how people are just enormously decent and trying very hard."

Danny: "And you see this as representative?"

Me: "Yes, I do."

Ken: "I do, too. Although we can't show it."

Me: "It would be impossible to show. There's no way: The way we've looked at the world, there would be no reason to believe we could show it. If we look at the world—a Catch-22—if we looked at the world another way, we couldn't see it but we could show it. If we do it this way—"

Ken: "But the question of whether it's representative or not lies in the future. It lies in whether or not a whole lot of people can find something [in what is written] that they can identify with and say, 'That's it, right.' "

Goals

Goals and the good life seemed a logical extension of some of our conversations. After all, part of the promise of the myth of a college education is the good life.

Carl: "But so many [college students] are forced, very early, to choose a track, to maintain an identity. If they could have a series of courses on self-reflection and in how to become a more enlarged person, not necessarily always related to what I'm going to do in a job. . . . I wish my kids could go to a school where, say the first six months or the first year, they took self-reflective courses and had exposure to various disciplines and, you know, tried to form—to match up their life goals which they think they have with the discipline of the ages."

• • • • • •

Danny: "I'd like to escape the control that they have—not seeking the secure, comfortable position to the detriment of a lot of things that I think are more important. It's really deadening and frightening to me. If I could escape it somehow, but I don't know how."

Bill: "Maybe I'm going out of my way to escape. But as I think now, the approach is to know when you're being manipulated and be able to say no, and accept the good points and be able to reject what's bad ... because you spend all your time trying to escape, and you end up nowhere. So, you can't escape organizations, anywhere in this country, or in the world, as far as I can see. Only, you've got to be able to deal with them."

• • • • • •

Carl: "The good life does seem to be being happy. And what does it take to make me happy? I'm not always sure. I do get very involved in my work.... I think you'll find that most people, especially in America, have the basics: a roof over your head, a reasonable amount of food to eat, a reasonable medical care, these are the basics. O.K. So compared to fifty years ago we probably have a good life."

Willy: "Well, I think my answer to that would be that I don't know."

Chuck: "Well, I found mine. Just—in my house. What's the good life? As far as I'm concerned, I've got the good life today. I have achieved my personal good life, I have achieved that. As far as the good life—I got it."

• • • • • •

Willy: "Did you set out, some time ago in your life, the goal?"

Chuck: "[To live] high on the hill."

Willy: "To achieve something?"

Chuck: "High on a hill."

Willy: "And get it?"

Ken: "He's got the best view in the city."

Me: "And that's what he's always wanted."

Willy: "I never did want anything of any particular quality. Did you?"

Carl: "Yeah, I had a goal. I wanted to be successful."

Willy: "I did never, in my entire life, have any definite objectives. I had very vague objectives, and they were almost daily."

Trust

The last topic of conclusions was trust: Who, and/or why, do you trust? Part of the issue, of course, is, just how do you go about making sense of the world? Does having a college education make any difference?

Betty: "Do any of you make decisions depending upon what people respect—say friends—or respect what they think about a situation? How they assess what's happening? I think I sometimes do, and maybe it's an easy way out."

Sue: "We always discuss this kind of thing in the office ... and I just kinda sit between and just listen to 'em. I sort of have this checklist, and, you know, I have my favorite. You know, I kind of fall into their category too easily. But I find myself doing that. There are definitely people that I associate with in the office that I think are a little more intelligent . . . so I really tend to listen to them more."

Alfred: "Well, I find it fascinating to find out where that person got his ideas from. If it comes off the top of their head, it's nice—you know, it's really nice, it's refreshing: I smile and don't care whether I completely disagree with it or not. I don't place too much store on what they said unless they say, 'Well, I got it from such and such.' You know, they say this and this. But what I kind of find kinda hard is people who will—who predict what's gonna happen. Those are the people I like to listen to. See if they're gonna make a prediction, Oh, well."

· · · · · ·

Bill: "Immediately you can come up with certain groups of people who, without even reflecting a second, you automatically distrust. Obvious example is used car salesmen, insurance salesmen. Or, even in a broader sense, anyone who's trying to sell something. I'm immediately defensive toward anyone who's trying to sell something. But then you try to turn it around and look at the other side, and who . . . what sort of people do you trust, sort of, on the first go; and it's really, really difficult to define those sorts of people. And the only way is to listen to what the people had to say. And if it struck me as being honest and they weren't playing games or role playing or trying to put me on—you gain from experience . . . in being able to identify what those people were doing."

Danny: "I think I listen to people and see, how do they relate to other people, and how do they relate to me, and how do they describe the world or their experiences? And if it matches up to what I think is honest and sincere and not using things or people in some dishonest way, then I begin to accept them."

· · · · · ·

Carl: "Well, I personally trust—I have to develop a trust over a period of time. Partly the way I trust is, number one, knowing a little bit about the subject myself—not a lot but seeing how people answer questions. Then you can check over an individual's track record, you can check back and know what they've done for other people that you've associated with. So you build your trust, and this guy builds his trust by getting you to trust him, and I grow to trust even more; and I think it happens in this sense."

Chuck: "Track record, I go by track record. Up to a point."

Willy: "I go by feelings."

Chuck: "Up to a point. Well, I go by feelings, too. But it's still—you're still talking about track record in a sense."

Willy: "Well—I don't know. I think I trust people because I want to."

Chuck: "Yeah, but I was just gonna say, you could be a softy, too."

Willy: "I trust people because I want to: my own desire."

Chuck: "You know you're gonna lose, but you're not gambling on much."

. . . . . .

Carl: "Well, you go to an individual specialist who—"

Willy: ". . . will tell you what your need is."

Chuck: "I can't trust a specialist. Because I've gone to—oh, O.K.—the tax accountant who makes his own résumé, who makes his own, literally, his own degree. So you're looking for the specialist: My problem with the specialist is that I won't trust the specialist."

Willy: "How do you determine who to trust?"

Chuck: "Well, unfortunately, I trust everyone to begin with."

9 Back to the Basics

> ... the sequence of men led to nothing and ... the sequence
> of their society led no further, while the mere sequence of
> time was artificial, and the sequence of thought was chaos.
> **—Henry Adams**

> Thus a truth, if it is to endure, should have its roots in reali-
> ties; but these realities are only the ground in which that
> truth grows, and other flowers could just as well have grown
> there if the wind had brought other seeds.
> **—Henri Bergson**

> ... ordinary men and women whose lives are the actual stuff
> of history.
> **—Isaiah Berlin**

Reading and studying epistemology is, for me, in many
ways wonderful and fun. The underlying issue of truth—
or at least its close approximation—is always in the
background of most of the better works. And even in the
less interesting works, it is fun to see smart people pick
at other smart people.

And, of course, curious things are always going on.
For example, while issues may be settled by philoso-

phers, their findings are then ignored by researchers. Theories, or schools of thought, may be triumphant in terms of technical accuracy but silly in terms of inclusion or exclusion of facts. What seems most clear is that to ask what the truth is, is to guarantee failure.

What is most interesting to me is that epistemology is, in large measure, a social question. It involves nothing less than or more than the sum of what we can know.

Given such sentiments, it follows almost logically that it is somewhere between foolish and masochistic to do empirical research. Sometimes, as I was doing this study, that seemed the case. But once I got comfortable with the messiness and grandeur of the world, and once I enjoyed the empirical fact of multiple truths, the feelings of foolishness and self-destructiveness almost vanished.

The central task of Chapter 9 is to address this: Why did I do what I did? What follows is something less than a formal epistemological statement but something much more than my personal musings about research. It is a kind of intellectual mapping out of issues I understand to be of primary importance in the context of how a great deal of social science research is currently carried out.

Let me give the order of the chapter, so that you will know what to expect. First come a brief description and critique of positivistic science—brief, in part, because this has been done so often and so well. A more lengthy description of some ideas of Jean-Paul Sartre and William James follows. This will help provide a different perspective on our world. Finally, there is a discussion of Hannah Arendt's work, so that we can more easily understand the relationship of the individual to his or her environment.

Rejecting the Rejected

For some time now, for generations in fact, philosophers have explained the shortcomings of positivist social science. It is not difficult to find an enormous number of correct reasons why much of what we call empirical social science is wrong epistemologically and morally.[1] Interestingly, none of those reasons has stopped the use of those "scientific" methods. What philosophy and science have rejected, we studiers of our own species have accepted. It is wrongheaded equal opportunity.

In this section I would like to make one thing clear and outline something else. The clear thing is this: Quantitative methods can, in fact, provide data for many questions of secondary importance. It is necessary that these questions be understood as secondary and that the biases involved in the method be acknowledged. To say that a little differently: I am not arguing that no one should ever use quantitative methods again; I am simply in favor of being serious about their many limitations.

I would like to present an outline of some of the problems of positivist science. The urge to do a full critique is small: It has been done and redone, and repeated. What follows is simply a short review of certain problems. It seems more important to try to work out what might be closer to right than to endlessly repeat what we know is wrong.

There are three ways in which I would like to divide the problems of positivist science. The first has to do with its foundations of rationality, the second with its ties to society, and the third with the role of the person doing the study. The division is arbitrary and is made in order to simplify the critique.

The bias of positivistic rationality is, in part, built on a wonderful coincidence: After assuming that we can discover the basic laws of the universe—or even of human behavior—we are blessed with the method to make the discovery. What we know as rationality, with its roots reaching back to Descartes and Newton, corresponds exactly to the fundamental laws of nature.

The scientific method [2] itself is built on these assumptions:

1. Basic laws of nature are discoverable.
2. Human behavior can be fully understood.
3. We are able to understand interactions in terms of cause and effect.
4. This implies that time is linear.
5. In order to carry out investigations, we must ask questions in a special way.
6. These questions are aimed at "measuring reality" in order to standardize and compare success, growth, failure, progress, and the like.
7. It must be assumed that the world is material in order to do this.
8. Relationships must be as standardized as possible if the investigations are to provide as much quantifiable information as possible.

Two things seem indisputable. First, the use of positivist rationality and the scientific method has provided the world with remarkable technical achievements. On any scale, we have more things than any other past society; on some scales, many of these things are better. And if we have yet to discover the basic laws of nature, we have certainly developed the capacity to destroy our planet. Much of science simply works, and many of those workings are useful. The second point beyond dispute is that philosophically and empirically it has been demonstrated that the above eight points are inaccurate. To be rigorous in the use of that rationality and that science is to systematically misunderstand and misrepresent our world.

As Larry Spence writes: "... an erroneous epistemology results in a proliferation of verbalisms or an extremely narrow focus if consistency is attempted. The social disciplines show just these characteristics—theoretical profundity and meticulously irrelevant investigation.... These methodologies all share the false assumption that the central problem in knowing is the avoidance of error." [3]

The phrase *meticulously irrelevant investigation* suggests the second division of concern. That concern, the tie between social science and its social context, is an important one when we consider positivism and our post-industrial society.

Let me stop for a moment and clarify what has been only implied. I know that the above points describing the scientific method are not a true reflection of the way scientists research the world. What those points represent is how we are *taught* to understand science. Basically, I am in favor of the mucking around many of the scientists do and am against the kind of narrowing of the world represented by the above description.

The study of society is value-infused. Max Weber argued correctly that "the significance of cultural events presupposes a *value-orientation* towards these events. The concept of culture is a *value-concept*. Empirical reality becomes 'culture' to us because and insofar as we relate it to value ideas." [4] He makes the point more specifically: "All knowledge of cultural reality ... is always knowledge from *particular points of view* ... the notion that those standpoints can be derived from the 'facts themselves' ... is due to the naive self-deception of the specialist who is unaware that it is due to the evaluative ideas with which he unconsciously approaches his subject matter, that he has selected from an absolute infinity a tiny portion with the study which he *concerns* himself." [5]

What we have, then, is a social science loaded with values that are seldom mentioned but that when mentioned are often denied. We have a method that requires that only certain things be studied. We have a researcher who is full of values that are taken into the research. It is possible, and I think necessary, to briefly show how the research begins with the myths and biases of the investigator's social/psychological context, and how the results of the research routinely reflect those myths and biases.

In our setting, which is ideologically committed to materialism and individualism—to take two obvious examples—we find that positivist social science is the near-perfect way for one to do research without being intellectually or politically disruptive. The method mirrors the ideology. Or, we can see that positivism works best by studying masses of data from the perspective of the top. The researcher positions himself or herself in order to look down at the many. The view of the masses from the top reflects the bias of insiders; it reflects the bias of the policymakers.

The values that are inherent in the very nature of quantitative empirical science are the values of bureaucracy.[6] It should be no great surprise that a society filled with the latter is obsessed with the former. Permanence, regularity, and "the avoidance of error" seem to be prime virtues of our organizations and our empiricism. It is the status quo, with a vengeance.

But why? To argue that our society needs change comes very close to being wrong because of understatement. Given the problems of our society, why do people study it in a way that supports injustice? The reason may be very unpleasant: "While ancient despots ... could always hire an astrologer or soothsayer to advise them to do as they wished and add the approval of the heavens to their whims, modern officials can always find a political scientist, sociologist, or psychologist to confirm their impulses and lend to their fancies the authority of computers and abstruse formulas. ... Political scientists [are] more interested in finding a mantle of respectable authority than a rigorous method of investigation that would lead to the challenge of many cherished political and social myths."[7]

One suspects that an important and strong tie between our social science research and our social/psychological context is the researcher's desire for power and respectability. I am less troubled by those desires than by the masks of neutrality and disinterested search for truth worn by many social scientists.

In one sense, we have touched on the role of the researcher in any research. Earlier I made the statement that all research is infused with the values of the researcher; the researcher is present even in the "hard" sciences. We reviewed the idea that values come from the social/psychological context as well as the particular researcher. There was even some fairly harsh speculation about the motives of those people doing research.

Because the relationship of the researcher to his or her research is important to this study, it is necessary to say more about it. In positivist science, the neutral social scientist uses the scientific method in order to discover the laws of nature, human interaction, or whatever. It is an odd dynamic. For the researcher to be removed from participation in a situation—to be, in Merleau-Ponty's phrase, an "absolute spectator"—leads, according to Larry Spence, "to the strange situation in which social scientists literally know less and less about the detailed operations ... they profess to describe."[8] It is an odd dynamic that makes the researcher more ignorant.

Ignorance aside for a moment, it is the psychology of the situation that interests me most. Listen: "The traditional investigator tries to separate himself from the social context that he wants to study, even though such a separation is impossible and leads him to deny his own experience and knowledge. This separate or polarized perspective is *heroic*. . . . Heroic epistemology—in which evil, error, and ignorance haunt every attempt at knowing—result[s] in . . . [a] view of social processes that prescribes class distinctions and hierarchical forms for human organizations." [9]

Trigant Burrow, one of the first American psychiatrists and certainly one of the most interesting, was able to understand the process of this kind of research in social as well as personal terms. He wrote: "It is precisely this division of the individual into actor and onlooker, and its extension within the social mind to which we owe the birth of the hero. . . . This is the division which is insanity. This is the division that is the hero. As there can be no hero without an audience, there can be no insanity without an audience." [10]

To be a neutral, stand-apart-from, unbiased, heroic researcher is at best epistemologically wrong. At worst, if we are to believe Burrow, it is socially destructive and personally crazy. To do social research is, in part, to become immersed in the social/psychological context and to intelligently work on improving that context for everyone involved. Certainly Weber was right to claim that all research is value-infused. It simply makes sense to understand *which* values we believe are best. Also, it follows naturally that social knowledge is not, and should not be, judged by the measures of natural science.

Social knowledge is political. That is not meant to condemn it but rather to restore it to a central role in our society. While that may put more pressure on those who do research, it may also help make the research more useful and, in a word, better.

What Then, If Not What We Have?

It is, I am convinced, less than half of the job to do a critique, especially a critique of positivist social science. To actually do an empirical work a different way requires figuring out what is right from what is wrong. I keep thinking about medical doctors who practice; somehow, most research that tries to get beyond the problems of positivism is in the practice stage. What is needed, and what hopefully there will be more of, is more practitioners.

Let me repeat something from earlier in the chapter: What follows is something less than a formal epistemological statement and something much more than my personal fancy. It is a kind of mapping out of issues I understand to be of primary importance, in the context of how a great deal of social science research is currently done. Jean-Paul Sartre, William James, and Hannah Arendt form the core of what follows.

Put most simply, it is important to ask where one should begin when doing social research. Before taking up the question directly, I would like to offer the following thoughts:[11]

> ... as we attempt to reflect about the way in which life confronts us in immediate concrete situations, it presents an infinite multiplicity of successively and coexistently emerging and disappearing events, both "within" and "outside" ourselves. The absolute infinitude of this multiplicity is seen to remain undiminished.
>
> —Max Weber

> The stream of immeasurable events flows unending towards eternity.
>
> —Max Weber

> ... the assumption that the strict adoption of the principles of concept and theory formulation ... will lead to reliable knowledge of social reality is inconsistent in itself.
>
> —Alfred Schutz

> ... an *exhaustive* causal investigation of any concrete phenomenon in its full reality is not only practically impossible—it is simply nonsense.
>
> —Max Weber

> ... science is only genuine science when it proceeds from sense experience ... only when it proceeds from nature.
>
> —Karl Marx

And finally, the catch:

> ... philosophers as different as James, Bergson, Dewey, Husserl, and Whitehead agree that the common-sense knowledge of everyday life is the unquestioned but always questionable background within which inquiry starts and within which alone it can be carried out.
>
> —Alfred Schutz

At the very least—the stream of immeasurable events, the impossibility of exhaustive investigation, and the necessity of beginning research with everyday life events—it is important to work out ways of getting at, working with, and better understanding this reality. We will first consider Sartre.

By starting with Sartre one can begin to see the parameters of the basic assumptions, questions, and tensions that seem most important to working out a way to do research. First we will deal with his ideas about facts, realities, and truths; then with those concerning how to understand an individual; and finally with the tensions involved in these ideas. It should be obvious that this is a remarkably difficult and ultimately unanswerable set of topics. What is important to keep in mind is that the preciseness of the details of the following suggested solutions is not nearly as important as the *spirit* that informs the questioning.

To begin at the very focal point of research is to begin with the notion of a fact. It is sensible to agree with Sartre's argument that a human fact must be lived and produced by an individual.[12] Much, if not all, of what is said from here on is an explanation of that seemingly simple statement. Before looking at the implications of this starting place, the point is that the center of research is a person—a concrete individual—and his or her being in the world. Human fact is biography in a historical context.

Facts, in human events, are not isolated appearances; they must be understood as being bound and entwined to the whole of experiences and actions. Reality is not and cannot be a concrete totality of facts but is continually determined by relationships, functions, motives, ideologies, and so on.[13] Reality is a process: It is a becoming, never-ending movement. What we think of as truth, then, is the understanding of that reality. To quote Sartre: "For us, truth is something which becomes, it *has* and *will* have become. It is a totalization which is forever being totalized." [14]

In a very unadorned way, that vision of facts, realities, and truths is the primary basis of existentialist thought in our century. With such a view go all kinds of uncertainties and tensions that we live with daily. Part of Sartre's usefulness is that he presents a particular way of trying to understand an individual living in these times.

Given the collective ignoring, and the frequent demeaning of the individual by many modern methodologists (Sartre includes American behavioral scientists and many French Marxists), Sartre urges us to adopt an attitude that puts people—a person—at the center of our studies and concerns. His language is instructively striking: ". . . [we] ought to study real men in depth, not dissolve them in a bath of sulphuric acid." [15] Later Sartre instructs with sarcasm. He tells us what is obvious and what we ignore. He tells us that people are not symbols or myths[16] but are people—that it is entirely necessary and proper to anthropomorphize people.[17] We should, after all, recognize human properties in human beings.

According to Sartre, in order to begin to know this individual, this self in the world, we must know what is meant by the idea of a *project*. At its heart, the concept of a human project is tinged with an unknowable property, but it is possible to get at the spirit of the thought. The project has to do with *praxis:* with both an implied rejection of parts of the present and an acting upon "what has not yet been." [18] To quote Sartre: "Furthermore, to say what a man 'is' is also to say what he can be—and vice versa." [19]

One thing that should be clear is that in everything we have discussed, there is a sense of movement and incompleteness. There is a sense of struggle and creation. There is, in a *project,* a kind of beauty and mystery that should not be ignored:

> Only the project, as a mediation between two moments of objectivity, can account for history; that is, for human creativity.

> Finally, the project never has any *content,* since its objectives are at once united with it and yet transcendent. But its *coloration*—i.e., subjectivity, its taste; objectivity, its *style*—is nothing but the suppressing of our original deviations. [20]

It is possible to be more precise about our projects. They are, in part, the product of our past and future. [21] To know them, then, implies a sense of history and the vision of imagination. We come to our projects through needs, praxis, and transcendence. [22] It is through our projects that we reveal ourselves. In making this argument, Sartre wants to "reintroduce the unsurpassable singularity of the human adventure" [23] into our world.

This idea of project is an interesting and important one. I have included it not because it is a useful way to do research but because of its informing spirit. Regrettably, not only is the word *project* hopelessly confusing for those of us engulfed in the English language, but the notion itself does not seem to lend itself to empirical work.

The notion of aesthetics seems to provide a much better way to begin to understand a human life. Chapter 4, the chapter on wisdom, was an effort to begin with a life and see if the notion of one's aesthetic sense could help describe an individual's actions in the world. While *aesthetics* does turn out to be a richer term than *project* in a discussion of research, we should not be unmindful of Sartre's contribution. To understand the "human adventure" is critical to this research.

The task of such understanding is, of course, never complete and logically not completable. Contradictory as it may sound, in order to know our "unsurpassable singularity," we must be aware of literally a universe of facts. At its most basic point, the tension of knowing an individual in the world is that "the consequences of our acts always end up by escaping us, since every concerted enterprise, as soon as it is realized, enters into relation with the entire universe, and since this infinite multiplicity of relations goes beyond our intention." [24]

Put differently, people make history, but in a given environment under given conditions. We must look at, and try to know, how those prior conditions are acted upon by real people with real intentions that go beyond the present. To tie this with other parts of the discussion, in order to try to know reality, one must continually cross-reference and show the interrelatedness of biography with a particular historical period. It was reasonable, then, that this book begin with biographies: with individuals, with their personal backgrounds as well as their social context. In the research, it was important to get a clear sense of exactly who was doing what, and when.

Sartre deals with the broadest of categories, and the most particular. What he does so well is provide some direction, some important places to begin to look. The title of his book, *Search for A Method,* however, is not misleading. Sartre, in a sense, *is* searching for a method. The connotations of the idea are, in principle, too confining. If there are multiple realities, then the notion of *a* method is too narrow.

If the world is a flowing and constantly changing one for Sartre, it is ultimately chaotic for William James. James writes that the world "is a turbid, muddled, gothic sort of affair, without a sweeping outline and with little pictorial nobility." [25] Nature, our setting, presents us with no comfort. James explains: "The eeriness of the world, the mischief and the manyness, the littleness of the forces, the magical surprises, the unaccountability of every agent, these surely are the characters most impressive.... These communicate the thrills of curiosity and the earliest intellectual stirrings." [26]

To take James's view seriously will help us to understand the deeply rooted tension between our everyday experience of multiple realities and our everyday playing out of social and cultural regularities. This tension will be explored more fully after we work through the more relevant parts of James's thought.

At the most basic level, James tells us that there is one primal stuff of our universe.[27] The stuff in our head is the same as the stuff of a chair or a rug or a tree. From that general chaos, we sort things out and make certain kinds of distinctions that allow us to communicate better and make some sense of the world. We do live in a social setting and "... the artifice of plotting them [events, and so forth] on a common scale helps us to reduce their aboriginal confusion.... We thus straighten out the aboriginal privacy and vagueness, and can date things publically, as it were, by each other." [28]

There are interesting implications to that sorting out. For example, if we take James as correct, there is no objective/subjective split.[29] That is a distinction *we* make, and it is a distinction that we add to the world as we find it. That means that everything simply *is,* and we are continually adding to it.

As we progress—a minute at a time, or an hour or a day—we are in constant touch with bits and pieces of pure experience. At each moment, "The instant field of the present is always experience in its 'pure' state, plain unqualified actuality, a simple *that,* as yet undifferentiated into thing or thought. . . ." [30] We take in huge amounts of unreflected stuff; some we consciously consider, most we just let be. In the context of our research, those actions and events that were consciously related were the ones most carefully considered. Those events are facts of our lives.

But they are not the only facts of our lives. What is as interesting and as real as those facts is the relationships among them. More properly, the relationships we give events are as real and as important as the events themselves. According to James:

> The relations that connect experiences must themselves be experienced relations, and any kind of relation experienced must be accounted as "real" as anything else in the system.
>
> Knowledge of sensible realities thus comes to life inside the tissue of experience. It is *made;* and made by relations that unroll themselves in time.
>
> Life is in the transitions as much as in the terms connected; often, indeed, it seems to be there more emphatically, as if our spurts and sallies forward were the real firing line of the battle, were like the thin line of flame advancing across the dry autumnal field. . . . Mainly . . . we live on speculative investments, or on our prospects only.[31]

The implication for our own research was that what had to be understood somehow more than doubled. Not only was it necessary to know about an occurrence or an event, it was also necessary to keep in mind that the event had not one meaning but multiple meanings. In order to take an individual seriously, we had to know how that person's world was put together and how an event related to other events. In a sense, we can now better understand Charles Taylor when he writes that "human science looks backward. It is inescapably historical." [32]

It may be helpful to approach the whole idea a little differently. James calls his "a mosaic philosophy, a philosophy of plural facts." [33] Each of us arranges the events of his or her life in a mosaic. Each arrangement is individual; each forms the inner history of a person. We may think of events and experiences as tiles for our mosaics, and the relationships we make as the glue holding the tiles together. I argued earlier that this arrangement of facts may be the result of a preconscious sense of beauty.

We may reglue our mosaic: The way events are related may be

rethought, and a new pattern will necessarily appear. In a literal sense that means our world will be different; that what we see will be changed. There are many ways in which events may be related and may change. Three quick examples: (1) We may consciously initiate change (consciousness being an activity, the function of knowing); (2) events may appear close in time or space and connect that way; and (3) we may take a similar emotion to different events. The only constant is our ongoing uniting activities.

There are at least two important implications of those last statements that are helpful to remember. First, they may serve as a reminder that individuals can and do change. We do not simply flow in the world but bring to it—in James's terms—will and activity. The words that capture and describe will and activity give us a picture of why change is not easy: "The obstacle . . . the strain, the triumph, or the passive giving up . . . the swiftness or intensity, the movement, the weight and color, the pain and pleasure, the complexity, or whatever remaining characters the situation may involve." [34] It is possible to change, but it is not an effortless activity.

Second, while the discussion has been written in terms of the individual, there are "facts" we should not forget. Our culture—or any—constantly provides commonly held relationships. From the patterns of our speech to the patterns of our political and economic systems, we are silently (and sometimes not so silently) given directions on how to assemble our mosaics in fairly particular terms. We are told of the "proper" relationships of events. Frequently culture tries to lock us into a limited range of language, perceptions, dangers, chances, rewards, and punishments. Culture, our social/psychological context, may even make us crazy in spite of our playing by all of its rules.

Culture is holistic—and that idea is probably as close to an absolute as we can get. Yet, because we know that cultures can be changed and/or destroyed, we can dismiss as unrealistic and silly any quest for a social truth that is universal and everlasting. Even in the natural sciences, certainty has given way to statistical probability, and as we know more, the half-life of truth seems to become shorter and shorter.

As researchers—as people in the world—we must concede that much of the apparent certainty of the past is no longer available. We must live with the tension that revolves around chaos and personal values on the one hand, and the need to be social and social needs on the other. We must continually consider a world of multiple truths and realities; ongoing social/political/economic truths and realities, all of which are powerful and interrelated "facts." Finally, we must resign ourselves to studies of pieces of the whole.

The process of our world cannot stop. "Change itself is ... an unalterable concept ... all [other] abstract concepts are but as flowers gathered, they are only moments dipped out from the stream of time, snapshots taken, as by a kinetoscopic camera, at a life that in its original coming is continuous." [35] Of course, we can cut into life ("to apprehend reality's thickness ... in imagination by sympathetically divining someone else's inner life" [36]); and even with acceptance of the logical impossibility of our task, we may ultimately know much more than when we began. While searching and judging, it is wise to be sensitive to James's warning that logic is a useful idea, but not of value in our describing or understanding reality.

Schutz: Some Technical Help

Except for the second chapter, the preceding parts of the book are an effort to do empirical research in line with the above notions of reality. That we might make the research sharper, the decision was made to concentrate on a topic: on just what a college education/degree might mean. The advice of the philosophers was taken seriously, and the research began with the "unquestioned but always questionable background" of the "commonsense knowledge of everyday life."

The kind of advice gotten from philosophers is of a peculiar type. It is wonderfully suggestive, often remarkably insightful, but generally vague to the point of frustration. Right directions and correct actions are very different things. Most philosophers are best at facing us in the right direction. What has fascinated me is, once you get the direction right, how do you proceed? What do you do?

It may be helpful to repeat a bit of what has been done. The aim of the study was to understand the effects of post-secondary education on everyday life. To do that, it was necessary to suggest a way to approach the study of policy that began with an individual and "looked up." The individual's life served as the baseline—as the beginning reality—and the policy, the inclusion or exclusion of college, was understood as intruding on that life and affecting it.

The research was filled with sets of forces and facts in conflict. There were the personal choices each of us makes, and they formed a field of multiple and changing realities. There were also social forces, institutional pressures, and our political and economic system, which do give a kind of regularity to our reality. We are exposed to many of the same things. In the last chapter, some generalizations about how we might consider making decisions about higher education in different ways will be offered.

A great deal of effort was concentrated on being in sympathy with —and understanding as fully as possible—the inner life of the reality and thinking processes of those people with whom we talked. To do so, we used a mix of anthropology, sociology, linguistics, history, and psychology. There was no attempt to be neutral or passive. Both of these concepts are activities, and ones not helpful in examining social reality. Roughly speaking, there seemed to be a correlation between the levels of realities we examined, and success. The idea was to know what had happened, what was happening, what might happen; what all that had felt/was feeling/might feel like; and what sets of causes and results might be involved.

Those are all active questions that require active involvement and work before one even begins to get at them. My sense is that as you read the research part of the book, you were implicitly asked to actively question and be involved with the people interviewed. Further, much of the "truth" or insight of the book is rightfully the product of the reader.

There are two more parts to this chapter. The first is a discussion of how a technical problem got worked out. The second has to do with how to get a more clear understanding of how we can tie the individual into society. We will begin with Alfred Schutz.

Schutz, a phenomenologist, was the source of two ideas that were helpful in arranging the talks. He provided certain techniques of actually doing the work suggested by Sartre and James.

While it is unnecessary to repeat the similarities between Schutz and James, it is important to at least note our starting point. Schutz (with Henri Bergson and James) believed there were important distinctions between our unreflective taking in of the world (the inner stream of duration) and the realm of reflection (the spatial-temporal world). The first simply is. In our unreflective self there are no categories or concepts; we are even unaware of having grown older. The second, the realm of reflection, lifts experiences out of our inner stream and modifies and adds to awareness.[37]

In quite detailed ways, Schutz explores the differences between these two realms in which we almost constantly find ourselves. Of particular interest is his discussion of choicemaking, motives, and by implication, the meaning of actions. It is here that what has been done may be more clearly focused and its implications more clearly seen.

One of the aims of the study was to know as fully as possible why a person made the choice about post-secondary education he or she did. Ordinarily, we think back to a certain point of choice; (re)-construct options, logics, and the like; and explain why we did what we did in a reasoned, rational manner. Schutz argues that choices are not made in that fashion. In almost every way, that kind of explanation is not an accurate description of the choice-making process.

What Schutz (and the insight is properly Bergson's) believes is that much goes on *before* we reflect and consciously sort out phenomena. He writes that in the realm in which things are indistinguishable, we run "imaginatively ... through a series of psychic states in each of which it expands, grows richer, and changes ... until 'the free act detaches itself from it like an overripe fruit.'" [38]

More simply, what we think of as choices are, in their preconscious state, related, interrelated, and often merged. From a plural consciousness, there is a transformation of a single consciousness, and the "choice" is clear. [39] Our reconstruction of different "choices" is a product of our need for rules of good argument, logic, and what we rationally understand as common sense. Two implications of this insight should not be ignored.

First, it is clear that there are irrecoverable facts of our life that we carry around with us but are unable to articulate. They form our "intimate core," our "absolute personal privacy"; and, to quote, "That which is irrecoverable ... can only be lived but never 'thought'; it is incapable of being verbalized." [40] This is a true limit of empirical research.

The second implication, more optimistic, is that if we are interested in why people act as they do, there are particular ways in which we should go about our investigation. It is important that we focus our attention on certain motives. We should avoid accepting, as a full or accurate explanation, the placing of logic on an activity that is much more dense and complicated than that logic. What we are describing, simply, is a way to more fully reflect on and represent past experience. Schutz compares our "act of attention" to the parts of the stream of duration to a "cone of light." The light "illuminates already elapsed individual phases of that stream, rendering them bright and sharply defined. . . ." [41]

When we use our attention to illuminate the meaning of an act, there are two kinds of motives, Schutz tells us, that must be distinguished. The two are "in-order-to motives" and "genuine because-motives."

The in-order-to motive is helpful in explaining an act in terms of what was projected; it aids in our understanding the ideal of the result of the act. Before an activity begins, an individual has an image of the completed act, an image in the future perfect tense. For example, if I now wanted a cup of coffee, my image would be of the brewed hot coffee in a cup, and of its taste, smell, and the like. I would not think of the details of the muscular movements of standing up, taking one step after another to get to the kitchen, or moving my eyes to find the coffee, and on and on.

We do similar future perfect tense mapping with social projects. For instance, in our talks there were images of what individuals thought about being college graduates *before* they went to college. One goes to college in order to get a degree, but we wanted to know what that looked/felt like as a future perfect image. That image, in part, tells us much about the myth of a college education in our particular social context. One important way to understand meaning is to relate action to its context. One of its contexts is what was projected—its in-order-to motive.[42]

The genuine because-motive has to do with past, lived experiences. It is concerned not with anticipation but with experience; not with the process by which the act was constructed but with the act itself. "Genuine because-motives are pictured in the pluperfect tense; they are free from all pretentions or anticipations; they are simple memories and have received their perspective horizons, their highlights and shadows, from a Here and Now always later than the one in which the project was considered." [43]

For one to truly understand the meaning of genuine because-motives, it is necessary to begin with in-order-to motives. If that is not done, the possibility is high that memories will be placed within the context of logic, and any reconstruction done to find meaning will be lost. To be serious about how an individual places meaning on an action, genuine because-motives must be in the context of in-order-to motives.

Schutz insists on the phrase *genuine because-motives,* which, given his task, is certainly reasonable. The word *genuine* makes us focus on the individual's thought and meaning process. For Schutz, not-genuine because-motives reveal too much of what the logic of the culture imposes on the person. For our purposes, those culturally imposed meanings were important to know and were helpful in our generalizing about post-secondary education and its effects.

Getting from There to Here

We know from physics that it is impossible to know both the velocity and the exact position of an electron at the same instant. In a curious way, in the social sciences we seem to be unable to understand both the individual and the social/psychological context at the same time. There seems to be a real gulf between general laws of society (which Weber characterized as "most devoid of content [and] also least valuable" [44]) and the richness of lived reality. The conventional wisdom goes something like this: General laws tell us nothing of the uniqueness of a life; the study of a unique life cannot get us to the formulation of general laws.

The structure of this book reflects a conscious effort to move from the singular to the collective. Clearly, I made an attempt to do that in several ways, from taking each story in its historical context to showing how individuals react to common contextual pressures like politics, working, and organizations. In the above discussion of Sartre, James, and Schutz, the tension between the individual and his or her context was never ignored.

In the beginning of the book, there was a quote from Louis Hartz. In essence he makes the claim that a person does not escape a theory by refuting it; the only real escape is by creating new categories of thought. The problem, if that is true (and I believe it is), becomes one of how to do empirical work without counting, quantifying, modeling, and so on. What is required (and here I depart from Hartz a bit) is not new categories, which seem simply a new set of restrictions, but rather a different way to look at what is going on in our world.

What I found most useful in this particular context was the work of Hannah Arendt. Of special help was her book *The Human Condition*. It is full of insight and imagination about the current state of humanity in the post-industrial West. Surprisingly, in addition to its speculation, history, and occasional density of style, the book contains a commonsense explanation of how to understand the world. By linking individual to environment in the most intimate and meaningful ways, Arendt gives remarkably good advice to the empirical scientist.

It seems fair to begin with this social fact: ". . . we are all the same; that is, in such a way that nobody is ever the same as anyone else who ever lived, lives, or will live." [45] A seeming no-nonsense way of getting at the idea that we are all the same in our uniqueness. That uniqueness is tied to how we live our lives; it is tied to the who-we-are, and to how that who is understood.

We learn from Arendt that by speaking and acting, an individual discloses who he or she is: ". . . this disclosure of who somebody is, is implicit in both his words and deeds." [46] Put differently, "Human revelation is a nearly inevitable everyday occurrence; only mute passivity avoids it under normal circumstances." [47] It is here that the shift from the individual to the social is made.

Arendt argues that "the 'who' which appears so closely and unmistakably to others, remains hidden from the person himself, like the *daimon* in Greek religion which accompanies each man throughout his life, always looking over his shoulder from behind and thus visible only to those he encounters." [48] In a critical sense, then, we can never know who we are. It is possible to know who others are but impossible to know ourselves.

Action and speech, the ways in which we disclose ourselves to others, are critical ideas. One of the distinguishing features of our species is the ability to act, ". . . to take an initiative, to begin . . . to set something into motion." [49] Action, then, becomes a chain reaction. Here is the full social dynamic: "Since action acts upon beings who are capable of their own actions, reaction, apart from being a response, is always a new action that strikes out on its own and affects others . . . the smallest act in the most limited circumstances bears the seed of . . . boundlessness, because one deed, and sometimes one word, suffices to change every constellation." [50]

In other words, we all exist in a web of human relationships. Those relationships are, in part, ordered by a particular set of cultural/political/economic arrangements. But the who-we-are is constantly acting within this web of humanity. Our speech and our actions not only define who we are, but have an effect on those around us. The people who form the heart of this study all spoke and acted. They each reacted; they each were a "new beginning" that acted "into an already existing web where their immediate consequences" could be felt. Action and speech "start a new process which emerges as the unique life story of the newcomer, affecting uniquely the life stories of all those with whom he comes in contact." [51]

There are two things I want to note. First, the results of action are unpredictable. We each may initiate activity, but we can never control the outcome. The plurality of our human condition guarantees a plurality of reactions to any action. What we should not forget is that we are all responsible for the results of our actions, regardless of the outcomes. Second, the who-we-are is not known fully until we no longer produce the stuff of stories. We are incomplete until we die. It is then up to others to tell who we are; it is up to them to repeat our unique stories.

Trying to understand who we are and what we do in this way makes it impossible to concentrate wholly on either the individual or the society when we do empirical work. The two are tied in an absolute way. It is foolish to try imagining ways to do a study of individuals without paying careful attention to their history, culture, friends, family, work, and the like. It is absurd to think about making social policy without fully acknowledging that the meaning of a policy can be best calculated in terms of how people's everyday lives are affected.

Our potential as human beings is dependent, in part, on conditions that help our plurality to flourish, in order that the who-we-are can flourish. In this sense, our empirical science should be able to examine those institutions, myths, organizations, and general social and economic conditions in order to make judgments about them. People make judgments, behave, act, and react to these things daily. It would be nonsense to ignore what people say and do under the pretense of methodological purity or heroic separation.

There is no certainty that researchers' judgments will be fully acceptable or wholly correct. In fact, there is certainty that any judgment will be understood as wrong or dangerous or both to some or even many people. When we compare the plurality of humanity with the current state of research, the flowering of judgments is much more appealing than the stale, often putrid results of a positivist purity.

NOTES

1. *Moral* may seem a strong term. For an argument that clearly implies the relationship of research and morality, see the excellent work by Larry D. Spence, *The Politics of Social Knowledge* (University Park, Pa.: The Pennsylvania State University Press, 1978).
2. The scientific method, in short form: (1) stating a problem; (2) stating a hypothesis to explain the problem; (3) designing tests for the hypothesis; (4) predicting the results of each test; (5) conducting the tests and observing the results; and, finally, (6) making conclusions from the results.
3. Spence, *Politics,* pp. 287, 35.
4. Max Weber, " 'Objectivity' in Social Science and Social Policy," in Fred Dallmayr and Thomas McCarthy, eds., *Understanding and Social Inquiry* (Notre Dame: University of Notre Dame Press, 1977), p. 27. Emphasis in the original.
5. Ibid., pp. 31–32. Emphasis in the original.
6. For good statements of the connections, see Dwight Waldo, *The Administrative State: A Study of the Political Theory of American Public Administration* (New York: The Ronald Press Company, 1948), and Sheldon Wolin, *Politics and Vision* (Boston: Little, Brown and Company, 1960).
7. Spence, *Politics,* pp. 22–23.
8. Ibid., p. 25.
9. Ibid., p. 260. Emphasis added.
10. Trigant Burrow, "The Heroic Role: An Historical Retrospect," *Psyche,* vol. 6, no. 25 (1926). Quoted in Spence, *Politics,* p. 260.
11. In order: Weber, " 'Objectivity,' " p. 24; Weber, ibid., p. 33; Alfred Schutz, "Concept and Theory Formation in the Social Sciences," in Dallmayr and McCarthy, p. 232; Weber, " 'Objectivity,' " p. 29; Karl Marx, quoted in Spence, *Politics,* p. 47; and Schutz, "Concept," p. 232.
12. Jean-Paul Sartre, *Search for a Method* (New York: Vintage Books, 1968) p. 14.

13. Ibid., p. 25.
14. Ibid., p. 30.
15. Ibid., pp. 43–44.
16. Ibid., p. 53.
17. Ibid., p. 157.
18. Ibid., p. 92.
19. Ibid., p. 93.
20. Ibid., pp. 99 and 106, respectively.
21. Ibid., p. 133.
22. Ibid., p. 171.
23. Ibid., p. 176.
24. Ibid., p. 47.
25. William James, *Essays in Radical Empiricism and A Pluralistic Universe* (New York: E. P. Dutton & Co., Inc., 1971), p. 143.
26. Ibid., p. 132.
27. Ibid., p. 5.
28. Ibid., p. 231. Also see Alfred Schutz, *The Phenomenology of the Social World* (Chicago: Northwestern University Press, 1967), p. 47.
29. James, *Essays,* p. 7.
30. Ibid., p. 40.
31. Ibid., pp. 25, 32, and 46–47, respectively.
32. Charles Taylor, "Interpretation and the Sciences of Man," in Dallmayr and McCarthy, *Understanding,* p. 130.
33. James, *Essays,* p. 24.
34. Ibid., p. 87.
35. Ibid., p. 232.
36. Ibid., p. 24.
37. Schutz, *Phenomenology,* p. 47.
38. Ibid., p. 67.
39. Ibid., p. 68.
40. Ibid., p. 53.
41. Ibid., p. 70.
42. Ibid., p. 94.
43. Ibid., p. 95.
44. Weber, " 'Objectivity,' " p. 30.
45. Hannah Arendt, *The Human Condition* (Chicago: The University of Chicago Press, 1958), p. 8.
46. Ibid., p. 178.
47. Robert Waterman, *Political Action: Dialogues With Hannah Arendt* (Berkeley: Unpublished Dissertation, 1978), p. 65. This is essential reading for a full appreciation of Arendt's work.
48. Arendt, *The Human Condition,* pp. 179–180.
49. Ibid., p. 177.
50. Ibid., p. 190.
51. Ibid., p. 184.

But What Do You Do?

... like the same coat that new might have fitted a thousand men, yet after one man has worn it for a while it fits no one else....

—**William Faulkner**

The rest was a question of gear; of running machinery; of economy; and involved no disputed principle.

—**Henry Adams**

Once the underpinnings of this study were determined —once the philosophic issues were settled and the topic was picked—there were an enormous number of practical problems that we needed to solve.* There was something slightly wrong with simply presenting the research design. While there was one, and while

* Much of the basic thought that went into this chapter is the result of of what Ken Dolbeare and I worked out. It is both foolish and impossible to sort out who thought of what. I am certain some of the phrases are his, even though I am responsible for what has been written. In terms of this chapter, it would be wrong to say, "Ken was a great help." At the research/talk stage, each of us was half the project.

There is no reason to believe Ken remembers the details as I did, nor can one assume he agrees with my conclusions. Further, in the course of the chapter, *we* means both of us; *I* means just that.

it was a productive one, I thought it would be more helpful to explain something of the process we went through in making it; what we discovered to be helpful and what we found to be mistakes. That way, there could be a more complete answer to the "But What Do You Do?" question.

It was clear from our philosophical perspective that we should begin with the experience of an individual. To do that, we could not be "scientists" in the normal sense; instead, we had to somehow investigate various actions and experiences with each person. In our talks there were very few formal questions that we had prepared in advance. We decided that we could outline topics, suggest relationships, or relate stories, but only to set the stage for a talk.

By taking this approach, we rejected the idea of doing a study in which we gathered replicable material. As you saw in earlier chapters, some of the issues that were important to some individuals were not mentioned by others. That is less a shortcoming of the study than it is an important fact of human plurality. In the course of our talks, we made no attempt to seek responses to a specific set of questions.

One goal was to get to know people well enough to begin to see and feel what they saw and felt. During the period of the interviews, we were in constant contact with each other in order to do an on-going analysis of what seemed to lie behind what was being said and otherwise communicated. It was an extraordinarily difficult task at the time, especially when we had spent only a few hours with a person.

As we got some practice and began to know people better, we often surprised ourselves with our ability to anticipate responses. Now, a few years past the talks, and with complete transcripts in front of me, different realities seem equally clear. I am convinced our private discussions (i.e., those among the interviewers) were important as they kept us in the middle between two destructive extremes: doing an overly analytic analysis and being overwhelmed by an individual's everyday experiences.

I have written in terms of talks we had instead of interviews in order to discover a set of "facts" about each individual. We wanted to provide a setting in which a person's unique stories would be the central focus. As teachers who were very involved with lecturing at the time, we found that no simple task. The urge for us to complete others' thoughts with our own words and to impose our ideas and views on their actions was great.

After a short time two things happened. First, each person's story began to have an integrity and a uniqueness that was compelling. Much of our early identification with a person's story and most of our unnecessary interruptions almost naturally ceased. Second, we decided to be interviewed, ourselves. It made sense to go through what the others were going through. We were the subjects of the same number of talks as the rest of the people, and we had many of the same reactions they did. (We were always amused that, after the first talk, the person being interviewed would ask, quite nervously, "Did I tell you what you wanted to know?" To our surprise, the question proved irresistible. Both of us asked it, and we *knew* better. We knew that everything said was just right because we were not looking for anything specific.)

Inexperience and Overconfidence

We knew that we wanted to understand a person's life, and the impact of post-secondary education on that life; and we wanted to know those things as fully as possible. We decided to work with what we considered a small group of people and determined that twenty-five was the best number.

The best advice we got about interviewing was that we should do as many interviews as we could ourselves. That way, we could have a better idea of what was going on, and certainly we could get a fuller understanding of the people than if we just read words of a transcript. Also, the presence of two of us helped the flow of the conversation and enabled us to later check each other's interpretations of what had gone on. The work was as exhausting as it was exciting.

Twenty-five people were too many. We settled finally on fifteen, and that included ourselves.

It made sense to talk with people with lower- or lower-middle-class origins. The assumption was that post-secondary education was the traditional path to the American middle class. We decided that if there was a myth of college education, it would probably be most alive here. Looking back, I am uncertain if that was a wholly accurate assumption. Only one person was of a "higher" class, and she certainly had been seriously involved in the myth. The age group we selected was thirty to forty-five, but one person was older. None was younger. Finally, we kept away from people who were closely tied to the educational community. You have seen the range of occupations, incomes, and formal education we ended up with.

After getting an initial list of names and doing some preliminary screening, we found the people we contacted surprisingly willing to do the talks. We did a form of overkill in explaining that our intentions were honorable. We gave people a long, written description of the project; then we provided even more details about the research in a conversation. The only thing we would not share was the identity of the person who had given us each participant's name. We also talked about ourselves: discussed what we taught, and on and on. It was gratifying that all but one person agreed to take part. As a very nice unintended consequence of our eagerness to be honest, we began the process of demystifying our professional status.

It seems clear, in retrospect, that our genuine enthusiasm for the research, our wonderment (still in principle) of the uniqueness of each individual's story, and our conspicuous inexperience were all helpful.

All of our talks were tape-recorded. We tried to have them typed within a week, as it was important for us to read the last interview to prepare for the next. The pressure on the typists, who were simply first-rate, was probably unfair. We consulted with them frequently for advice, as they were obviously in close touch with what was going on. The average conversation was about two hours long and filled about fifty typed pages. At the end, each person had between three hundred and four hundred pages of transcript.

We gave each person a copy of his or her interviews. I can think of only one or two who read them. Spouses, living partners, and even one brother seemed more interested in seeing what had been said than the participants.

Not surprisingly, there were substantial differences from the actual conversation to the taped word to the written word. My initial urge was to argue that things fell off from the spoken word down to the typed transcript. In one sense that is certainly true. However, a different kind of information becomes available when one can carefully go over a whole range of talks and ideas. It was important both to have personally done the talks and to have then had time to "see" the talks and think about them.

Most of the conversations took place in a private setting—a great many of them in my living room. There were few interruptions: We were able to silence the telephone but had less luck with my dog. After some initial awkwardness, and after our professional status was no longer an issue, the whole idea of an "interview" faded. The conversations were most like the best ones we have on a daily basis.

With good results—but for the wrong reason—we engaged an associate interviewer, a woman with several years' experience in various helping professions. She was a great asset to us. We had believed, cleverly, we thought, she would be most helpful with the female members of the project. That was not always the case. We found that her occasional presence as one of the two-member team changed the dynamic and the responses of the participants, whether male or female, in revealing and interesting ways. She did a great deal of work, and my guess is that we would not have had the time or energy to carry out the study without her.

The Plan

Basically, the in-order-to motives and genuine because-motives discussed in the last chapter were the keys to setting up the talks. We had to understand what each individual said, and that required establishing the context and reaching back and forth from the past to the future with each. We set up a series of eight conversations. The first six were conducted in a period of from six to eight weeks beginning in mid to late summer. The next one was six months later, and the last after another six months. In the last two, we sought particularly to fill any gaps that study of the transcripts had revealed —to complete any stories left unfinished—and we wanted to see if we could judge what the passage of time did to change people and their self-understanding. In most cases, the last session was conducted on a small-group basis—the first time that members of the project met each other.

Session One

This was essentially for fact-finding. We simply sought a basic biography, from genealogy to present circumstances. Our problem was to follow a broad outline and not get stuck on interesting and, in many cases, amazing stories. We learned to get the basic facts about post-college lives first, and then go back and have each person recall parents, grandparents, childhood, and growing up.

Session Two

We asked each person to describe—roughly—what an ordinary day was like. We were also interested in the kinds of connections the individual had with the world. For example, there was generally some discussion about what a person read (if anything), what restaurants he or she went to, who his or her friends were, what a person's neighborhood was like. This was a vague talk, in part because we had no context in which to understand the meanings of what was being said. But the information proved very useful in the fifth and sixth sessions, when we were able to explore a day in some depth.

Sessions Three and Four

These were more pointed talks in that they covered sets of times in greater detail. Depending on the experience of the individual, we did grade school and high school in session three, and post-secondary in four; or grade school in three, and high school and a few years beyond in four. Our general aim was to find out what the individual had thought to be important during those years.

It is critical to note that these talks were never time-bound or topic-bound. Reflections and memories take on fuller meaning when they are related to other reflections or other people. For example, it seems natural for a person to talk about his or her childhood and relate that to his or her children. To recall James, the glue that holds events together is as meaningful and real as the events themselves.

Session Five

This was done in the person's home and included the husband or wife or housemate (if that individual was agreeable). An effort was made to put the person in his or her actual physical setting, and to try again to understand what a typical day was like. In these talks, the first two interviews were critical as they provided at least an outline of what to think about. We shared with the participant a kind of intimacy that was striking, and we knew things that the living mate frequently did not know. In a strange way, I found it a little awkward.

These were often very good talks. The motives and meanings that much of our research revolved around began to become clearer. We knew enough—after eight to twelve hours of talk—to catch glimpses of the world through the person's eyes. While we had no intentions of talking in cause-and-effect terms, it did seem that a kind of understanding was reached, a kind of payoff for the preceding work.

Session Six

This was the last of the first set of talks. It was a bit of a review and an exploring of questions we had about the first five talks. In most cases, everyone was very tired by this time.

Session Seven

In December and January, after the preceding talks, we got together again. In Sartre's terms, we were interested in how the events of the world were affecting these people, in how history was being made in history. We were surprised that January Blues, Post-Christmas Depression, Worldwide Slump, and the like did not seem to be a fact of many people's everyday lives. The optimism of the participants was impressive.

In these talks, we were more likely to ask opinions and discuss ideas than previously. For example, instead of discussing the items in the news, it often made more sense to talk about the idea of news, newspapers, T.V., and so on.

Session Eight

These talks took place in early June and were not very much like those that had preceded. We wrote a short statement—actually, four questions—that we thought formed important concerns of our discussions. We asked the participants to consider the questions, and then—in groups, at night, and with food and drink—we asked for their evaluations of the project. They became, in a self-conscious way, co-participants and co-analysts. They generally gave us more not-genuine because-motives than in all the previous sessions put together. The four questions we had worked so hard on were fairly useless.

With the last talks, we had more than we could read, think about, and understand. As you know, I decided to use the information provided by only twelve of the participants. One did not finish all of the talks, and I felt uncomfortable "doing" either Ken or myself.

On one level, we had too much; on another, it seems a shame that we will no longer see and talk with those people. In a world of unlimited funding, it would be fun to return to the Northwest on a yearly basis and see how each person is doing—learn what factors are more or less important, and see if and how change takes place.

After the Plan

There is little I can add about the research. There were times of panic when I was confronted with—or was I confronting?—stacks and stacks of typed transcripts. Fortunately, our design was close enough to our philosophy so that I was never tempted to "retrieve data" in a systematic and "scientific" way. Counting and quantifying, even with five thousand pages of data, were out of the question.

While it was difficult to make a research plan from a philosophy, it proved even harder to write a book that remained fairly true to both. The old state-the-problem, state-the-hypothesis, etc., way of doing research dies hard. In the end it seemed silly to have gotten to the book-writing stage and not carry out the logic of the study. Once the logic was decided, the integrity of the work, as I understand it, seemed intact.

All that is left is the advice to policymakers. After all, this is a work of public policy analysis, and it is only fair that the analysis be given, in part, in terms of advice. So, on to the last chapter, where some literature will be reviewed, some insights from earlier chapters will be recalled, and specific thoughts on college will be revealed.

11 The Concluding Concluding Chapter

... fantasy may serve a curious purpose for the American political mind, for it may well be the only technique whereby it can seize any kind of perspective other than the liberal perspective which has governed it throughout its history.

—Louis Hartz

"... circumstances are modified precisely by men, and the educator must himself be educated."

—Sartre, quoting Marx

A friend of mine at a New York hospital recently told me of the possibility that science will be able to sever completely the human mind from the rest of the body and with appropriate tubing, machinery, and pumps, keep the brain alive indefinitely with no connection to the heart. My comment was that it was really not new—we have been doing it for years at Amherst.

—Robert Ward

This, the concluding concluding chapter, is important for at least two reasons. First, there is still the literature of the field to review and assess. Second, and of more importance, there are the conclusions themselves. We can begin to see if the method I have tried to work out is worth pursuing; if this different kind of empiricism will lead us to a different—and more helpful and realistic—analysis. To change the old line just a little: I have seen the results, and I believe that they work.

Basically, the chapter has three parts. The first is a review of the liberal context of education in the United States. At the level of ideology, it seems wrong to try and understand America without knowing something about liberalism. We will study the ideas of John Stuart Mill, Louis Hartz, and Diane Ravitch.

The second section begins with a brief history of higher education in America. The history serves as a background for the current debates about higher education. This section contains a review of the literature of the fight—which is an accurate way of presenting a review of the literature of the field.

The final third will deal with the research I have presented, and how we might think about it in relation to what we now have. What will be clear is that when research is conducted in this way, basic questions need to be redesigned, and our range of actions may be radically expanded. The conclusions, then, will definitely conclude.

The Liberal Context

Liberalism, the particular ideological context of education in America, will be reviewed in a kind of descending order. We will begin with an overview of liberalism, by offering the thought of the English philosopher John Stuart Mill. We will then move to America and look at the work of Louis Hartz. Finally, we will see liberalism in action in education, through study of a work by Diane Ravitch. Mill, of course, gives us the classic statement of liberalism.

To understand liberalism, a person must understand individualism and competition. Those two elements are at the heart of the matter. They form the fabric of liberty, truth, freedom, education, and government for the liberal. When Mill writes that "among the works of man which human life is rightly employed in perfecting and beautifying, the first in importance surely is man himself," [1] we should take him seriously.

For Mill, the articulate liberal, "the only freedom which deserves the name is that of pursuing our own good in our own way, so long as we do not attempt to deprive others of theirs or impede their efforts to obtain it." [2] He believes that "... the sole end for which mankind are warranted, individually or collectively, in interfering with the liberty of action of any of their number is self-protection. That the only purpose for which power can be rightfully exercised over any member of a civilized community, against his will, is to prevent harm to others. . . . Over himself, over his own body and mind, the individual is sovereign." [3]

Freedom and liberty are not that clear-cut for Mill, but certainly the above statement is the driving force for those concepts. Later, we will take up Mill's refinements.

Given the supremacy of the individual, it is no surprise that the nature of truth in liberalism is the result of the interaction of individuals. More accurately, truth is the result of competition. Of this, Mill had few doubts: ". . . the only way in which a human being can make some approach to knowing the whole of a subject is by hearing what can be said about it by persons of every variety of opinion, and studying all modes in which it can be looked at by every character of mind. No wise man ever acquired his wisdom in any mode but this; nor is it in the nature of human intellect to become wise in any other manner." [4]

A person who knows "only his side" of a matter, "knows little." It is necessary to know the other side, or sides, and to hear it not from one's "own teacher," but from "persons who actually believe them, who defend them in earnest and do their very utmost for them." [5] It is critical to keep this competition up, because "both teachers and learners go to sleep at their post as soon as there is no enemy in the field." [6] And sleeping people cannot get at the truth.

Truth depends on conflict: ". . . on every subject on which difference of opinion is possible, the truth depends on a balance to be struck between two sets of conflicting reasons." [7] Getting at the truth is no easy matter: "Truth, in the great practical concerns of life, is so much a question of the reconciling and combining of opposites that very few have minds sufficiently capacious and impartial to make the adjustments with an approach to correctness, and it is has to be made by the rough process of a struggle between combatants fighting under hostile banners." [8]

In an interesting sense, this truth by conflict has a way of triumphing. Although truth does not always triumph over persecution, Mill does believe that "the real advantage which truth has consists in this, that when an opinion is true, it may be extinguished once, twice, or many times, but in the course of the ages there will generally be found persons to rediscover it. . . ." [9] One of these "rediscoveries" is bound to come at a time of "favorable circumstances," and at that time the truth will triumph.

There is more to the liberal argument than this. There is a moral dimension, which is more complicated as the pulls of society are taken into account.

Mill is appalled by social intolerance: ". . . the price paid for this sort of intellectual pacification is the sacrifice of the entire moral courage of the human mind." [10] "The greatest harm done is to those who are not heretics, and whose whole mental development is cramped and their reason cowed by the fear of heresy." [11]

If that is Mill's plea for the common folks, his plea for the elite is even stranger: "I insist thus emphatically on the importance of genius and the necessity of allowing it to unfold itself free by both thought and practice. . . . Originality is the one thing which unoriginal minds cannot feel the use of." [12]

The use of originality is that "of opening their [the common people's] eyes." Mill writes that "the honor and glory of the average man is that he is capable of following that initiative; that he can respond internally to wise and noble things, and be led to them with his eyes open." [13] It seems, then, that in a liberal society, the competition that leads to the truth is carried on with an elite bias.

Just as Mill is against social intolerance, he is also against most governmental actions: "But the strongest of all the arguments against the interference of the public with purely personal conduct is that, when it does interfere, the odds [are] that it interferes wrongly and in the wrong place." [14] It is here, with the topic of governmental "interference," that we can get a sense of how Mill refines his notions of freedom and liberty. There are limits.

Mill states and restates that the individual, as long as he or she is not interfering with others, should be left alone. That means that people may triumph in an unhindered way, and that the "disappointed competitors" have no "immunity" from suffering. What follows are Mill's conditions for liberty, and for its restriction.

"If he displeases us, we may express our distaste, and we may stand aloof from a person as well as from a thing that displeases us; but we shall not therefore feel called on to make his life uncomfortable. We shall reflect that he already bears, or will bear, the whole penalty of his error . . . instead of wishing to punish him, we shall rather . . . [show] him how he may avoid or cure the evils his conduct tends to bring upon him." [15]

Yet, if "the evil consequences of his acts do not fall on himself, but on others; . . . society, as the protector of all its members, must retaliate on him, *must inflict pain on him* for the express purpose of punishment, and must take care that it be sufficiently severe." [16]

At this point the liberal knife is in; Mill then twists it: "No person is an entirely isolated being; it is impossible for a person to do anything seriously or permanently hurtful to himself without mischief reaching at least to his near connections, and often far beyond them . . . [even if] a person does no direct harm to others, he is nevertheless . . . injurious by his example, and ought to be compelled to control himself for the sake of those whom the sight or knowledge of his conduct might corrupt or mislead." [17]

Put a little differently, "...if society lets any considerable number of its members grow up...incapable of being acted on by rational consideration of distant motives, society has itself to blame for the consequences." [18]

It is in this context that we can fully see education in liberalism: "Hardly anyone, indeed, will deny that it is one of the most sacred duties of the parents...after summoning a human being into the world, to give to that being an education fitting him to perform his part well in life toward others and toward himself." [19]

Education is the competitive center where one can prepare for the individualism of society as well as learn how to get at the truth. It is also a place where one can become capable of "being acted on by rational consideration of distant motives." It is a place, one assumes, to learn about liberty and its limitations. Finally, it is education that might teach a person to respect genius.

There is more than a hint that the parent who fails to educate his or her child is committing the kind of act that is detrimental to others. Put directly, to fail to educate is to invite punishment.

Mill provides us with a clear idea of the major themes in liberal thought. By reading him, we are able to recognize many things that are commonsense to us. This nineteenth-century Englishman tells us much about ourselves.

What is now important is to see how liberalism traveled; how we here in the United States live with liberalism. After all, the history of America and of England differs in important ways. We must know more than J. S. Mill to understand our liberalism.

Our Liberalism

There are several interesting and defensible ways in which to understand—in broad terms—the dynamics of the United States. I believe the single best explanation of its political, economic, and social forces comes from the "consensus" theorists. The best of these theorists, to me, is Louis Hartz. It is important to note there are omissions and serious shortcomings in the concensus theory. It is far from perfect, but I repeat it here because it helps us to get at the foundation of much of our thought and action.

The core of the consensus theory is this: The United States is a nation founded on classical Western liberalism. For our entire history, the vast majority of citizens have taken that basic philosophy for granted and have tended to treat all problems as technical problems and not moral ones. The consensus theorists argue that we are absolutists philosophically, and it follows naturally that we are pragmatic in our everyday decisions.

We know, of course, that there have been and are those who are not liberals. They have, in most cases, been either systematically ignored or destroyed. The roots of this have to do with the liberalism of John Locke and with our "absolute and irrational attachment" [20] to him.

To appreciate our attachment to Locke, we must first understand that Americans, finding themselves in an environment different from Locke's, transformed his work to suit the different place. John Locke developed his liberal thought during a time of transition. It was a time when feudalism was coming to an end and liberalism and capitalism were coming into their own.

There are two parts to Locke's argument: There are both an implied defense of the state and an explicit limitation of it. Because of the many oppressive private organizations in feudalism, Locke set up the state to "become the only association that might legitimately coerce them [the citizens] at all." [21] But that was implied, and because there was no feudal tradition in America, there was seemingly no need to utilize that half of Locke's argument.

The limitation of the state, Locke's explicit argument, was based on the concept that free individuals in the state of nature did well enough without it. This part of Locke was readily adopted in the United States and helped further the notion of individualism.

What is so striking is the degree of agreement on many of these principles, and the ignoring or suppressing of other ideologies. Hartz writes that "this then is the mood of America's absolutism: the sober faith that its norms are self-evident." [22] What we will see clearly, when we take up the work of Diane Ravitch, is the belief that what *we* believe is simply commonsense, while what *they* believe is slavishly ideological. It is a wrong belief.

What makes the consensus notion tricky, in addition to the fact that it is difficult to understand one's own ideological biases, is the very nature of our beliefs. Gunnar Myrdal wrote that "America is . . . conservative. . . . But the principles conserved are liberal and some, indeed, are radical." Further, the "radicalism and conservatism have been twisted entirely out of shape by the liberal flow of American history." [23]

It seems a true contradiction for us to somehow be repressive in a belief that is freeing. When Santayana wrote that "even what is best in America is compulsory," [24] he stated the contradiction clearly.

The results of this basic consensus are common: the attachment to the Constitution and to the law; a political party system that caters to one ideological position; and the American philosophy, which is pragmatism. These, and many other things, depend on an underlying and substantial agreement on basic principles.

As mentioned earlier, there are problems with the theory. While Hartz talks about challenges to liberalism, he does so only in order to tell how they were crushed or ignored. The rich history of diverse thought in America is seemingly doomed by liberal definition. According to this theory, it is lost in fact and will stay lost in the future.

Also, there is a profound problem with the viability of liberalism in an economic and organizational world that is anti-liberal. We are far from the state of nature that formed the key to Locke's sovereign individual, and we are almost as far from the state of America that existed when liberalism was taking hold.

In many ways I agree with Hartz that "the master assumption of American political thought, the assumption from which . . . American attitudes . . . flow [is this]: the reality of atomistic social freedom. . . ." [25] A world of giant bureaucracies and complex organizations simply does not foster individualism. As important, a world of huge private businesses and equally huge government does little to encourage capitalism.

While our liberal consensus may still be a fact, there are other powerful facts seriously challenging it.

It is in this muddle, this time of profound but often hidden tension and change, that our interviews took place and that policy recommendations must be made.

Before going on, let me be as clear as I can about liberalism. There is much to commend many of its aims, just as there is much to fear in irrational attachments to it. If one is a liberal, of the kind Mill and Hartz describe, then it is important that he or she come to terms with the belief and current reality. The old virtues are at war with the world we are becoming. That means at least one of two things: Either people must give up the old virtues (and I doubt that will happen), or people must rethink how the world is to become and they are going to act. The latter is not easy to do.

Before we take up those themes in further detail, there is one more part to this section: education and liberalism. In a very important sense, we saw the ties in the thought of John Stuart Mill. What I would like to do is turn to a contemporary writer and consider how liberalism is played out in the discussion of American education.

Making It Real: Liberal Scholarship

There is a literature on the relationship between education and politics, culture, and the economic system. In one way or another, that relationship has always been acknowledged in the United States, but it has been only relatively recently—the mid-1950s—that scholars have concentrated on the matter. By the sixties and seventies the role of education within its context became a central focus in much of the literature.

There have been bloody battles (if academic fights can be called bloody) about just what schools have done, do, and should do.

While trying to figure out the best way to present this particular strand of thought, I came across a book by Diane Ravitch titled *The Revisionists Revised*.[26] In it she presents a critique of those who are, roughly speaking, on the political left in the education debate. It soon became clear to me that one could learn much from Ravitch, not so much from her critique as from her mind-set.

What we have is the work of a bright person who has done most of her homework. The book is useful because it is a fine example of liberal thought turned to educational matters. It is an example of how liberalism can be mistaken for Self-Evident Truth, and how one's own biases can be mistaken for an Impartial Reporting of The Facts.

What follows, then, is a discussion of some things to consider when you are reading about liberalism tied to schooling.

The Good, the Bad, and the Biased

Anyone connected with higher education certainly knows that there is a continual concern with standards. It is such a sacred concept that we invoke it on almost any occasion. We all fear lowering our standards. It is not very unusual for personal feuds to be covered with the shield of standards, and for academic revenge to be carried out with the sword of standards.

In her book Ravitch mentions inappropriate ways of studying history and education. She gives us standards. She cautions against "zealous commitment," "ideological asides," a "researcher's ideology," and a "moralistic presentist" approach. Basically, she is against "radical revisionists," those who, in her terms, "offer moralistic condemnation instead of understanding, hindsight instead of insight." [27]

There is not much question that there is some merit in what she writes. After all, we have all read stuff we consider just awful because of the writer's bias. What I would like to argue is that the *idea* of bias is not what is troubling; it is the idea of the *wrong* bias that we resent. It is not that Ravitch is against bias—she is against the radicals' bias. Let me relate her to liberalism. Let us, in other words, review her ideological bias.

Liberals believe that "political participation is stimulated by the dispersion of education," and that "as more people participate . . .

[and] express their interest ... [then] the freest possible exercise of human reason would contribute to the establishment of a good society." Further, "Liberals tend to believe that American society has become more open, more inclusive, and more democratic over time, *not accidentally or inevitably, but because of political action by those who sought these goals.*" [28] Indeed, the liberals have been "bound up with the spirit of reform, a sense that education could be consciously arranged to make American society more open, more just, and more democratic." [29]

The liberals tell us that "the appropriate analytical question is not whether there is a gap between ideal and practice, but whether the gap is growing larger or smaller." [30]

And just what is the ideal? "Theirs was an optimistic, individualistic outlook ... anyone could overcome his original circumstances by his own effort ... a young man should have no bounds other than his own ability and energy ... heredity and authority counted for little ... society ought to be open, democratic, and malleable. These were the values of a society bent on self-improvement, a society with fluid class lines, a society where Horatio Alger stories would become popular...." [31]

We learn that "the most important fact" is that public schools are popularly controlled, that school politics are an extension of democratic politics, and that the electorate will not "long support a school system that openly subverts its wishes, values, and interests." [32]

The other virtues of liberalism include "blurring and compromising" conflicting demands, consensual politics, and a democratic decisionmaking process, as well as stability and civility. There are also the concept of equal opportunity, the idea of equal rights before the law, and the assumption that "the individual is the basic unit of society, not the group."[33]

This is the set of values Ravitch uses to see and judge the world. Liberalism, like all ideologies, is a certain configuration of biases. Because we live in a liberal society it is easy to forget that we are ideologues. Liberalism is not only a way to critique scholarship, it is also a way to do scholarship. Of course, there are costs. The virtues of liberalism are not universal, and their application may be destructive.

One of the central debates about schooling concerns whether it might be understood as discriminating (in a variety of ways) to minorities. Ravitch reviews many facts about the integration of immigrants and blacks. She also discusses American Indians. The history of this last minority, she believes, "most nearly fits the radical concept of schooling as a tool of coercion and imposition." [34]

But Ravitch will admit to no such thing. The Indians, she claims, were hostile not so much to schooling as to cultural suppression. That pluralistic policies were enacted in the 1930s and the 1960s, suggests to her "a policy of cultural respect," and, "ultimately, Indian assimilation on terms set by Indians."

Ravitch writes that "where educational policy was coercive, where it was toward the Indians ... it was least successful in promoting education, assimilation, or social harmony. It would appear that the best way to promote these ends is in an atmosphere of cultural pluralism and individual freedom." [35]

Here, liberalism is blind to its own set of values. Nowhere do we find the suggestion that "individual freedom" is an extraordinarily loaded political value. We are not reminded that liberal individualism is directly opposed to the traditional values of Indian tribal life. In the innocent implication of the universality of individualism, remarkable violence is done to the structure of Indian life and to the particular world of each person involved.

If Indians are assimilated by being made to believe in individual freedom, it is dead wrong to argue "Indian assimilation on terms set by Indians."

Contexts, Studies, and Conclusions

It is fair to consider what might be done after all of those lessons about what not to do. Rightly, Ravitch tells us we must remember the context in which action and thought take place. While doing this, she again educates us with careful application of her ideological biases.

In a curious rendering of John Dewey and George Counts, Ravitch writes that they were highly influential because they were not "radical enough" for their present critics. She implies that it is necessary to be politically "central" in order to be academically "central."

This is, of course, bad advice. Had Dewey *not* been ahead of his times, he would have never been "central" in important ways.

The point is that context, and a writer's relationship to it, are fundamental. Ravitch rightly believes that the "intellectual, emotional, and political currents" of the times "furnished the climate" favorable for the radicals to write their revisionist books.[36] What we are never told, and what we must construct, is the times in which Ravitch herself wrote.

By implication, she wrote in a neutral, ahistorical time that gave rise to nonbiased scholarship. We know that there has never been such a time, nor has there been such a kind of scholarship. But Ravitch will concede no such thing. She writes that a study should be grounded in "a realistic appraisal of American politics and disciplined by historical craftsmanship. . . ." [37]

Clear enough. Now all we have to do is conclude our three-hundred-year fight about what a "realistic appraisal" of our politics would be and impose binding standards on our historical craftsmanship, and we will be all set to do an acceptable study.

Given all of that, what does Ravitch know, and what does she conclude?

In a clever argument, she turns a radical argument on the radicals. She claims that the radicals have tried to prove that all previous reforms were wrongheaded, or worse. So, the twist: "If reformers in the past have been power-hungry, manipulative, and devious, why trust reformers of the present?" [38]

Of course, she is only clever by half: If reforms were so positive in the past, why not trust the contemporary reformers?

It seems like an out-of-fashion dance: The Academic Twist, Twist.

After her careful appraisal of radicals, Ravitch naturally gives us liberal conclusions. She just wishes that the radicals would show "some slight appreciation for the democratic-liberal values that preserve their freedom to publish a call to revolution against democratic liberalism." [39]

We are reminded to think about a teacher as a "rather ordinary citizen with a complicated job to do." We are told that schools are "limited institutions" that sometimes fail to meet "realistic expectations" but that at other times succeed "beyond realistic expectations."

What we must do is "judge them by reasonable standards. . . ." [40]

There it stands, a tribute to our liberalism. The velvet glove of the liberal ideology is so smooth and comforting, it is easy to forget that only those with a great deal of power can conclude that an unspecified "reasonableness" is the answer. That is what liberalism is about in the United States; that is the ideological context of education in America.

History and Context

At the end of the 1970s, at a state university in the East, the provost was forced out by an extraordinarily angry faculty. The provost was beginning to institute changes that would make the university more responsive to training people for jobs. The faculty resisted the changes in a rare show of unity. The whole affair was bitter and ugly.

After he was forced out, the provost gave an interview that was essentially a lecture to the faculty about the state of higher education that covered how economics would inevitably change the university. He ended by saying that the faculty could not alter the fact of the bad news by killing the messenger. If the incident had not happened I suppose I would have tried to image it as a very good illustration of an ongoing tension in higher education.

We have seen, in earlier chapters, some of the effects of higher education on individuals. We saw the effects, in part, in terms of the myth. It is now necessary to take a step back, that we might get a sense of the history of higher education in the United States and see how education is understood by those who think and write about it. The history will be brief.

In a sense, vocational education has always been a part of higher education in America. There was Harvard, the first college in the colonies, intent on serving. A commencement address in the 1670s made the purpose of Harvard plain enough: "The ruling class would have been subjected to mechanics, cobblers, and tailors; . . . the laws would not have been made by *senatus consults,* nor would we have rights, honors, or magisterial ordinance worthy of preservation, but plebiscites, appeals to base passions, and revolutionary rumblings, if these our fathers had not founded the University. . . ." [41]

Harvard did vocational training: an educated clergy and a political elite.

Certainly that is not quite what we consider vocational training today, but we should realize the purposiveness of early colleges and their clear class—if not exactly vocational—aims. While Latin seems far from such training today, it was just right three hundred years ago.

Harvard did not please everyone. Benjamin Franklin wrote that the rich sent their sons to Harvard "where, for want of suitable Genius, they learn little more than to carry themselves handsomely, and enter a Room genteely. . . ." [42] For that reason and even better ones, new colleges were begun.

By 1837, a college president concluded that " 'our busy, restless, speculating, money-making people' required colleges as scattered and mobile as the American people themselves." [43] That same year, in another part of the country, a college education was recommended for the "formation of lasting friendships and associations . . . among those who are to constitute no small portion of our future leaders." [44]

As Harvard was helped by the Commonwealth of Massachusetts, so every state was helped by the establishment of land-grant colleges. More than an official endorsement of higher education, it was a very real action to bring certain kinds of vocational colleges to each state. The link between learning and prosperity was seen, approved, and acted upon.

By the last quarter of the nineteenth century, "graduates discovered that a college education as a social investment was now of less importance than a college education as a personal investment." [45] Not surprisingly, Henry Adams said it best by quoting a classmate: "The degree of Harvard College is worth money to me in Chicago." [46]

When Theodore Roosevelt dedicated a new law building at the University of Chicago at the turn of the century, he put higher education in its American setting: "We need to produce, not genius, not brilliancy, but the manly, commonplace, elemental virtues." [47] In 1940, the president of a university told the incoming freshmen, "I want you to learn to be an American." [48]

I introduced this section as a brief history of higher education in the United States. Let me now be more accurate. The above represent important themes in higher education, and we can see that those themes have been with us since the colonists started the first colleges. Much history has been left out and much left unsaid, but the purpose is to concentrate on certain themes.

What we can see is the constant vocational/social/patriotic/political pull of higher education. While we know that there have always been academics in the academy—Thorsten Veblen is a fine example—the purpose of the above is to remind us of those other parts of our educational tradition—those parts that, I believe, helped create the myth of higher education in America.

As we have seen, the ideological context is liberalism. Richard Hofstadter wrote that "in earlier days, after all, it had been our fate as a nation not to have ideologies but to be one." [49] Liberal, and, with it, capitalistic reality, was built into the structure of institutions of higher education. Liberal soil grows liberal schools.

Included in our liberalism were "the two basic ancestral pieties of the people—evangelical faith and populistic democracy." [50] They combined to form a strong current of anti-intellectualism. The place of the heart and instinct in religion, and the belief in equality of democracy, had a common enemy in a rationalistic, scientific, intellectual elite. Not only was there something unequal about intellect, there was, in the pursuit of science, a seemingly direct challenge to religion. Evangelicalism fostered "anti-authority, anti-aristocracy, anti-Eastern, [and] anti-learning." [51]

As noted earlier, once questions of value are agreed upon, it is natural to become concerned with questions of technique. Hence, pragmatism; hence, American "know-how"; hence, a world of technology and technical training. "In the main, America took its stand with utility, with improvement and invention, money and comfort. It was clearly understood that the advance of the machine was destroying old inertias, discomforts, and brutalities, but it was not so commonly understood that the machine was creating new discomforts and brutalities, undermining . . . esthetic sensitivities." [52]

The tension between technocrats, or specialists of any kind, and generalists is neither new nor an exclusively American problem. Max Weber saw it clearly around the turn of the century: "The modern development of full bureaucratization brings the system of rational, specialized, and expert examinations irresistibly to the fore.... The bureaucratization of capitalism, with its demand for expertly trained technicians, clerks, et cetera, carries such examinations all over the world. ...

"Behind all the present discussions of the foundations of the educational system, the struggle of the 'specialist type of man' against the older type of 'cultivated man' is hidden at some decisive point. This fight is determined by the irresistibly expanding bureaucratization of all public and private relations of authority and by the ever-increasing importance of expert and specialized knowledge. This fight intrudes on all intimate cultural questions." [53]

Fifty years later, the Frenchman Jacques Ellul wrote that "education . . . is becoming oriented toward the specialized end of producing technicians; and, as a consequence, toward the creation of individuals useful only as members of a technical group, on the basis of the current criteria of utility—individuals who conform to the structure and the needs of the technical group." [54]

Not long after Ellul made that observation, the Cold War was brought sharply into the educational focus when Russia put a satellite into space. The federal government, with a history of land-grant colleges and the G.I. bill, became deeply involved with funding scientific research on college campuses.[55] Everything seemed to come together: There was money, there was national interest, there were students who had been taught that a college degree was necessary. The conditions did not last into the 1970s.

There was less money, there was a real debate about the national interest, and there were students (the last of the "baby boom") who were disruptive. The debate over what higher education was about began to consume the academy.

Where We Are

I do not intend to imply that the meaning of an education suddenly became a topic; I simply mean that there was an increased focus on the topic. Less money and more trouble helped force us to reconsider just what we do at the university and, even more difficult, to consider the whys behind the what. The debate is not as public as it was in the early seventies; but with tight budgets and declining enrollments, it has turned grim and sometimes vicious.

In the first chapter—as much for fun as for making a point—I listed titles of studies concerned with the meaning of a college education. On the whole, they were statistical studies that seemed concerned with the economic aspects of education. The story about the provost who proposed converting his university to a more vocational orientation certainly speaks to the economics of the situation. Lifelong learning, in a technological society, serves at least two functions: First, the individual can "retool" when he or she becomes technologically obsolete, and, second, lifelong learning implies lifelong income for the university.

Certainly there are other reasons to return to college, but the pull towards economic necessity is strong. For example, in 1975 the then United States Commissioner on Education, Terrel Bell, said that a college that chose to devote itself to teaching the liberal arts was "kidding itself . . . to send young men and women into today's world armed only with Aristotle, Freud, and Hemingway is like sending a lamb into the lion's den. It is to delude them as well as ourselves." [56]

Let me present the sentiment in clear administrative terms: "In these schools the enrollment market dominates budgeting . . . for most of them most of the time, the budgeting problem is one of finding a set of allocations that produces an educational program that attracts enough enrollment to provide the allocations." [57]

One part of the debate, then, revolves around the following dynamic. In order for colleges to stay in business, they must attract consumers. To do that, they must make the consumer understand that there is a payoff in getting a degree. Given our "busy, restless, speculating, money-making people," it seems natural enough that the payoffs can be understood in terms of money and prestige.

The implication of the dynamic is that a liberal arts education does not pay. In the world of lions and lambs, Aristotle is a lamb.

There is a middle ground between vocational training and liberal arts. For example, Steven Muller writes that "it is *not* true that higher education is useless unless it pays our in dollar-earning potential, or that liberal education is only a myth." [58] Yet, he acknowledges that "we live in a society so sophisticated technologically that it depends on a vast and complex range of highly developed skills."

Muller's middle ground involves "an expanded system of higher education." He believes we need "post-secondary education for the majority of all jobs and [we need] differentiated schools teaching an expanding variety of specialized skills."

Finally, "The American future depends on a higher learning that teaches both civilization and specialized skills. While open to all, it should separate out those who fail to perform as students. Some institutions should be openly reserved only for the intellectually gifted." So speaks Muller, a college president (Johns Hopkins) who did his best to come to terms with specialization and civilization.

In a little different way, Caroline Bird adds to the debate. To read the title of an essay she wrote is to know her point of view: "College Is a Waste of Time and Money." [59] First we will look at the money part of the time and money equation.

Bird tells us that in 1972, the Census Bureau reported that a man who finished four years of college could expect to earn $199,000 more in his working years than a man with just a high school diploma. But if, in 1972, a Princeton-bound student put the $34,181 that his four years of college was going to cost into a savings bank, and that money earned 7.5 percent interest compounded daily, he would have $1,129,200 when he retired at the age of 64. In comparative terms, he would have "$528,200 more than the earnings of a male college graduate, and more than five times as much as the $199,000 extra the more educated man could expect to earn between 22 and 64...." [60]

She continues her attack on the economic payoff theory by citing evidence that the most important variable in income is the status of the wage earner's family. People from high-status families have higher incomes than those from low-status families. That is true even if they have the same amount of education and enter the same occupations.[61]

Even when college graduates do better, Bird is not ready to acknowledge the importance of college. "College graduates are superior and desirable because they are superior and desirable to begin with ... gifted students can do at least as much for Podunk (or Harvard) as Podunk or Harvard can do for gifted students." [62]

To show the problem with the payoff part of college does not really present a full critique of college. There are still all of those people in college, people Bird sees as sad. They are in college, she says, because it is the place to be, or because their parents want them to be there, or because college allows them financial support without working. At best, for as many as 75 percent of the students, college is "a social center, a youth ghetto, an aging vat, and at worst a young folks (rhymes with old folks) home, a youth house (rhymes with poor house) or even a prison." [63]

The good news, for Bird, is that through college, a person may get out of an intolerable home situation, may avoid a dull 9-to-5 job, and may gain practice at being independent while retaining the security of continued financial support. But, of course, that is not very good good news.

The whole idea of the institutionalization of college-as-the-thing-to-do is upsetting for Bird. It requires that everyone, no matter his or her abilities, submit to four years of academic rigor. For her, it "violates the fundamental egalitarian principle of respect for the differences between people." [64]

Things are bleak, according to Ms. Bird: "My unnerving conclusion is that students are sad because they are not needed. Somewhere between the nursery and the employment office, they become unwanted adults. No one has anything in particular against them. But no one knows what to do with them either. We already have too many people in the world of the 1970s, and there is no room for so many newly-minted 18-year olds. So we temporarily get them out of the way by sending them to college where in fact only a few belong." [65]

There is, beyond technology, payoffs, and even sadness, the argument for a liberal arts education. We can see it clearly in the writings of Robert Hutchins and Robert Paul Wolff.

In a short but influential book, *The Higher Learning in America,* Hutchins attacks three causes of confusion in higher learning. "The first of them is very vulgar; it is the love of money." [66] Higher learning and job training are different enterprises.

"Even more important than the love of money as a cause of our confusion is our confused notion of democracy." [67] Basically, Hutchins wants the university to be left to academics. After all, he argues, we cannot expect those without the proper training to understand the workings of higher education.

To money and democracy he adds "an erroneous notion of progress." Hutchins believes that the pursuit of progress has led to a kind of empiricism that has "taken the place of thought as the basis of research, took its place, too, as the basis of education . . . thus the modern temper produces that strangest of modern phenomena, an anti-intellectual university." [68]

For Hutchins, the reformulation of the university must be as thorough as it is necessary. His vision:

If we can revitalize metaphysics and restore it to its place in the higher learning, we may be able to establish rational order in the modern world as well as in the universities.

The higher learning is concerned primarily with thinking about fundamental problems. . . . I have used the word metaphysics to include not only the study of first principles, but also all that follows from it . . . the principles of change in the physical world . . . the philosophy of nature . . . the analysis of man and his productions in the fine arts including literature.[69]

In many ways, Robert Paul Wolff ties the defense of a liberal arts education into a neat, understandable package. Wolff writes that there are three ways in which to look at an undergraduate education. It, the education, may be viewed as an extension of high school. Just as easily, it may be seen as the opening stage of a professional training. Wolff opts for number three: "... there ought to occur an intellectual, cultural, and emotional experience which is *neither* a mere continuation of what went before, *nor* a mere foretaste of what is to follow. ... I am deeply committed to a belief in the unique and irreducible character of undergraduate education. ..." [70]

The argument for a liberal education, for a unique undergraduate education, is not an argument for the training of intellectuals. But Wolff believes that "the life of the mind should be the possession of every man and woman," and that is exactly what a proper undergraduate education should encourage.

A payoff is offered by Wolff, and he uses his own experience as an example.[71] He tells us that his understanding of mathematical logic ultimately enabled him to criticize technical arguments offered by defense intellectuals during the Vietnam war. His knowledge of Kant was the source of his "analysis of the foundations of the authority of the state."

While the argument is not that everyone must have a doctorate to be able to act in the world, certainly those who act should know fundamental concepts. So, Wolff writes that a course in theoretical economics is better preparation for the student than a course on poverty; a course in logic "will pay off more handsomely than a seminar on the philosophy of war."

Simply stated, to learn the solutions to present problems will not help the student to identify and solve future problems. If that is so, one must remember that "the original and important intellectual work always proceeds at a considerable distance from immediate problems, and for that reason frequently seems 'irrelevant' and abstract." [72]

We come full circle with the following argument by James O'Toole on the value of a liberal education:

> ... one is inevitably drawn to traditional liberal education as the most relevant form of career education. All we know for certain about the future is that it will be ... filled with unpredictable change ... the people most able to adapt to the vicissitudes of social life have been most liberally educated ... for the liberally educated, learning has always been a way of life. The person best able to cope with change is the one who has the broadest background and is thus the most flexible.[73]

In one sense what I have written about the debate in higher education draws the traditional battle lines but lacks the reality of the first part of the book. There was a time, while I was preparing to write this chapter, that I thought it possible to understand about higher education by reading autobiographies and edited books about how people thought about their education. It was wonderful fun: I read that Walter Cronkite missed class a great deal and got awful grades. I found that Jane Addams was quite remarkable. I learned that she "became ill and despondent" after she graduated, and that breakdowns of that sort were common among women who tried to break out of traditional roles. My hunch was confirmed that Margaret Mead was probably always an interesting person.

I read about former college presidents and successful women, and found out a lot of things. But I did not learn as much from them as I did from the people I interviewed, and I came to realize that the debate on education—liberal arts vs. vocational training—was lively and ongoing but simply the *wrong* debate. The traditional battle lines are all that need to be mentioned. Given the broader activities of society, the particular location of the line moves. More war gets us more technology; more money and more leisure time gets us more liberal arts, and on and on. There are variations on the theme, but the theme is the same.

Let me change the battle metaphor. What we have seen is two sides of a coin. The same coin. The problem is that it is the wrong coin.

If That's Not Right, What's Left?

There is one more important argument. It has to do with political education in a liberal democracy. This particular subject is considered in a collection of essays in a book titled *The Philosophy of Education*.[74] I mention the book because it is a serious and effective attempt to explain the ties that bind democracy, liberalism, and a liberal education.

The essay that concerns us here is "Education, Democracy, and the Public Interest," by Pat White. What White sets out to show is that in a democratic society, there is *one thing* that "a democrat is compelled to regard" in the public interest. That one thing is "an appropriate political education."

After some discussion, we learn that "a policy in the public interest is one which benefits every member of a given public under the description member of the public. It is not necessarily the policy which is best for any individual considered as an individual." [75] If that is so, then it is important to know just what "benefits every member"; we must know what needs to be learned.

Here is one key: "Living in a pluralistic democracy obliges people to *tolerate* variety but they do not have to positively value it." At least as important is the knowledge of "how to operate the democratic institutions." White is more specific about these points.

An individual, as a member of "one or more of the diverse groups in the society," has to learn to relate, through the group (or groups), to the government. Along with that, groups must tolerate other groups. In other words, a person must learn about pluralism and pressure groups—and the rules of that game.

In addition to tolerance and technical information, White's democrat must learn other values, such as fraternity and justice. Together they form the underlying principles of democratic institutions.

All of this is best gotten in a liberal arts education. Again, White is explicit:

> The liberally educated man is not characterized by items of knowledge he possesses ... but by the fact that he can think in these various ways, knowing, for instance, what a truth of mathematics is as distinct from a truth of science ... he is able to think in these various forms of thought and not because of any particular stock of items of knowledge he may possess.

> ... all citizens in a democracy do not need to have ... *all* the relevant knowledge for making *all* the political decisions in the society ... as long as citizens can check that all relevant interests are being considered, i.e., as long as the government is accountable to the people.[76]

A good liberal arts education enables a citizen to judge the government; to check and hold the government accountable.

White deals with the one other example of what a political education might be. It comes from Robert Paul Wolff's essay "Beyond Tolerance." Wolff's argument is quoted by White in the following way: "There is a need for a new philosophy of community, beyond pluralism and beyond tolerance. . . . It is indeed the greatest virtue of society, which supports and enfolds the individual in a warm, affective community stretching backwards and forwards in time and bearing within itself the accumulated wisdom and values of generations of human experience. . . . The only hope is for man to huddle together and collectively create the warm world of meaning and coherence which impersonal nature cannot offer."[77]

After questioning some of Wolff's references, White gets to what she considers the most important point: "He ... deal[s] with problems like the preservation of natural beauty, public order, and the cultivation of the arts which are not the special interest of any identifiable social group." In fact, to encourage people to be concerned with what is in the public interest "would not itself be sufficient for a political education in the public interest in a democracy." The

White idea is this: "The political education in any given society must appropriately match the political system if the system is to be maintained." [78]

The underlying assumptions of the arguments White has presented to here are one or another variation on the theme of the purpose and the structure of education in a liberal state. White and Wolff, while in disagreement about particulars, seem to agree on the rules of the debate itself. By that I mean they concede a great deal to the common interpretation of what our pluralistic society is like and what higher education has to offer.

It may be helpful at this point to repeat some questions that were the guiding principles of this study. If research is carried out in a different manner; if we begin not with institutions, policy processes, decisionmakers, or huge, statistically significant populations, but with individuals who are affected by policies—if we do that, what will we learn? Will we find out things we did not know, and will we be able to get conclusions and policies that are not only different from, but also better than what we now have? Will a different kind of research result in a different set of rules?

In Chapter 9 I presented the intellectual background, and throughout the book I have made judgments about what seems to be going on. Indeed, the structure of the book was made to reflect the structure of the inquiry itself; stories were presented from which conclusions could be made. Now, I have made an attempt to set the academic context—and we can see not only what our interviewees know, but also what is being written and thought about in higher education. My earlier claim was that the debate is the wrong one: It is now time to present that argument in more detail.

Education as Structure

The structure of higher education in the United States fits nicely with the structure of society. Organizationally, for example, it is hierarchical.

Imagine yourself about to start college—or better yet, recall the earlier interviews in which people talked about entering college. Nervous, excited, ready to take the next appropriate step in growing up. As a first-year student, you find structurally that upperclasspeople, graduate students, every level of professor, and various kinds of administrators from department heads to registrars to deans to presidents to boards of regents outrank you. Moreover, everyone who holds a job in the school knows more than you do.

A first-year college student has moved into the real world writ small: Here is a hierarchy, and you begin at the bottom.

We have seen people react differently to the structure. Bill flunked out within the first semester his first time around. The school was just too big. Carol found aid and comfort in a sorority. The step from high school to college is, structurally, a big one, and hierarchy is only a part of it.

There is also the structure of classes and learning. After all, each individual has his or her classes, his or her schedule. While we normally think of this as an increase of freedom for the individual—and surely it is—it also carries other values.

Sara remarked that her education was "just like penny candy—a little history, a little geography, a little, you know, whatever. . . ." It is important to see what that means in terms of structure.

As a normal undergraduate in a typical program of study, a student will have five professors each semester. From each one, that student learns a version of the truth on which to write papers and be tested. He or she competes for grades. The sum of these small competitions adds up to the grade point average, which serves as a way to judge which job a person may get, or even which professional or graduate school he or she may attend.

In this penny-candy way, college fosters individualism and is the jewel in the crown of divide and conquer. A student is made to divide himself or herself into parts: a history of Western civilization part; an English part; a foreign language part; a science part; a social science part.

Five courses, five truths, five selves.

There is a third way of understanding structure. It may seem a little off the point, but it is important. We can get at it by considering different types of professors.

We know about the kindly senior professor lost in another world in a different age; the socially concerned young faculty member who is nervous and intense. There is the I-hope-I-get-tenure teacher who is ever-so-careful about everything; there is the professor who represents himself or herself as a neutral seeker of truth, and the one who always claims to be telling you the truth.

There are those who love to teach and those who are good at it and those who are just awful. In the words of the interviewee, we saw various examples.

But it is foolish to be misled by style, because all of us teachers have this in common: *We are not unbiased.* Each of us has preferences, from the books we choose to teach to the questions we choose to ask on exams. Each professor teaches his or her point of view. If college is the liberal marketplace of ideas, only professors get to have an idea.

The structure of college is such that the student learns, quite naturally, many visions of the truth. In the end, that makes it very difficult to see the world in any kind of unified way, or to know who you are in it.

One of Willy's basic criticisms about the university was that "it wasn't well enough organized." While at one level that is certainly true, at a more fundamental level Willy was all wrong. Higher education is structured to produce liberal citizens. Whether they have a liberal arts or a vocational focus, our institutions of higher education are set up, in White's terms, to "appropriately match the political system."

Education and Our Democracy

Earlier we read of the virtues of pluralism and democracy. Not only have writers been able to make good sense of them conceptually, but others have proven them empirically by using the methods of ordinary social science. We are members of groups, groups do make demands on and put pressure on the government; but rarely do these groups kill or maim each other. From the top, it all looks fine down there. Alexis de Tocqueville certainly put it in the most appealing and poetic way, while James Madison conceptualized it in a more base manner.

From the people we talked with, we see that the reality of pluralism is very different from the theory. There is another name for the way our political system works: cross-cutting cleavages. (That name has always conjured up images of some kind of weird sexual violence to me. The image, as will be clear, is not altogether wrong.) The theory, roughly, is something like this: We all belong to many different groups, most of which do and want different things.

For example, we want good neighborhood schools, but we also want lower property taxes. Or, we want less pollution but at least two cars; a better environment but fewer governmental regulatory agencies; more equality but more than our share economically. We can see more closely how the crosses and the cuts feel to the college-educated.

Liz: ". . . you've been educated to believe that there's something you can do about things, that you *don't* have to accept things as they are; then they've got you in a double bind. Because you're not getting it, and you can sit around and blame yourself for not getting it instead of somebody else, and say, 'It's their fault I'm not—I'm powerless. I think we *are* to blame to some extent if we don't try to do—I mean, there are things we *can* do."

While unhappy, Liz had the makings of an ideal citizen. She could catch herself between two powerful ideas—just who is to blame anyway?—and end up with no power, believing it her own fault. A good liberal learns not only to *argue* both sides of an issue, but to somehow *believe* both sides as well.

As we saw in the realm of politics, it is easy to live with contradiction. *Chuck:* ". . . poor old Nixon. He was wrong . . . I think Nixon was guilty. But it was minor compared to his responsibilities. . . . Now, I'm still for Nixon." It all may not matter a great deal anyway when we think about the context of differences in American politics. *Bill:* "It strikes me that there's not that much difference between the Democrats and Republicans."

Those involved with politics find it frustrating and difficult. Again, *Bill:* "It would require an awful lot of effort on the private citizen's part to keep track of what's going on." And: "I used to think that I could have that much personal power. But I don't think so anymore, . . . except on a very small, tiny scale." And finally: ". . . I should, in any small way that I can, leave the world a better place. I feel a social responsibility. But I've not been able to figure out how exactly to do it."

These, I believe, accurately reflect the reality of our citizenship. In a systemic way, the dynamic certainly leads to stability; yet it seems much less than even reasonable on an individual basis. Higher education reflects the political system; so it is safe to assume that those with college degrees are at least as stuck as those without degrees.

With all of the cross-pressures, it seems natural to sit in the middle of any single issue. It is normal to vote for the person running for office who also stands dead in the center. People in politics muddle through because people who elect them muddle through. Increasingly, as the interviews reflect, there seem to be dynamics that make muddling through ineffective in public as well as private life.

There is a problem, and a very big one at that, that seems to emerge from the stories: The world can whip almost everyone who takes it on. There is Carol talking about professionals: "I'm getting hooked up to a bureaucracy [that can be] . . . devastating personally." There is Willy, trying to invent: "What they really want is a well-written report, which doesn't have to say anything as long as it's thick enough. You can't say in those reports, this is *great!* This is real *good!* You have to say, this seems to show promise."

Bill summed it up: "I see man as being such a—in a sense, a fool and tampering so much with natural processes . . . man, at the end, is gonna be erased."

At an everyday level, the fix seems to be on. The world is too complex, messy, overwhelming, confused, and technologically sophisticated to attack on its own terms. Even statistically, and in grand ways, we are failing, for:

1. The majority of people in the majority of elections do not vote.
2. More than half of the hospital beds in America are filled by schizophrenics.
3. Our family life is falling apart: To get married is to prepare to get divorced.
4. A very small percentage of people owns a very large percentage of wealth.
5. Our current energy policy will possibly result in our flattening the state of Colorado and melting the state of Pennsylvania.

People taught to believe in considering everything, and in a sense to believe everything (hence, nothing), will somehow see both sides of these facts.

From the data, it appears that higher education does little to help us out of these messes. Far from arguing that education—and the educated—are no good and do no good, what I would like to argue is that education—and the educated—can do much better.

To Suggest

Much of the burden of the chapter on epistemological underpinnings was to point out that the world simply looked—and indeed was—different when one started with what Weber called natural events and not with ready-made conceptualizations.

If I understand correctly; if indeed there was a great deal of struggling to do the right thing on the part of those we talked with; and if each of us sorts out the world in different aesthetic ways, then it is necessary to restructure our colleges and universities so that they both allow us to be our best selves and help us make more sense and do better in and with the world.

We need, I think, to make each school more distinct; to use a more loaded term, more pure. Both faculty and students would be better off if what was taught and learned was somehow connected with belief and outlook. By integrating material instead of dividing it, we would have a better chance of making sense of our lives and of social issues.

What seemed missing in the lives of those we talked with was a perspective on a world that too often seems bizarre and out of control. Robert Waterman suggests that we think less in terms of a search for truth and more in terms of a search for a viewpoint. Philosophy and science teach us that there is no Truth in any absolute sense, and it is important that we acknowledge that insight in practical ways.

The bias of our pluralism, in the final analysis, is economic. Those groups with a great deal of wealth generally are able to get a great deal of power. That is the way pluralism should be taught and learned in a liberal college or university if higher education is going to reflect society. But if we go past the bias of the theory, and past even the power of the wealthy, what we find is the diversity of tastes, values, and visions of the good at an everyday level.

Reason dictates a multiplicity of "pure" institutions. It is easy to imagine the existence of Marxist University, where everything from finance to fine arts is taught. One could just as easily conceive Ultra-Conservative University, Freudian University, Capitalist University, even Liberal University.

Two quick examples may be helpful. First, we can imagine Corporate/Capitalist University. It would be structured, in many ways, as most schools are now—only more so. Economics would span Adam Smith to Milton Friedman; politics would cover Thomas Hobbes to Ronald Reagan. The people in history could concentrate on the end of feudalism and the rise of nationalism and capitalism in Europe, the settling of the American West, the industrial revolution, and the like.

The spirit of the place, the guiding principle, would be competition. Competition for grades, for the best dorm rooms, for the most prestigious social group, for the most successful and famous professors, for class offices, and on and on. In a seeming contradiction, the most popular courses would be in organization behavior, yet there would be few team sports.

Certainly a student might study other viewpoints, but only to critique them. One could study the failures of socialism, the bad examples of anarchy, the corruptions of Communism.

Certain skills would be taught. One would take many tests, learn to write clearly and simply, interact warmly, shake hands firmly. Learn what the bottom line is in every situation, and know that the *real* bottom line is that polyester is only middle management.

It is fair that you think this corporate/capitalist example is less than serious. While I mean to engage in stereotypes and to have a little fun, the point should not be missed: Structure, ethics, ideology, and outlook should be coordinated. Further, this coordination should be thought out and should be as complete as possible. In the end this kind of education has a better chance of helping the individual than what now goes on.

The second example is that of Socialist University. We can easily envision a different structure, one in which many—if not most—matters would be decided collectively.

The ideology and analyses in each class would lean to the left. The problems of rampant individualism would be seen through examples from literature, politics, popular culture, agriculture, and economics. People would be horrified. In most courses there would be group assignments and an emphasis on sharing.

The hierarchy would be flattened out, and formal position would be less highly regarded than personal attributes.

There would be team sports.

The spirit of the place would be one of cooperation. If the stereotype held true, probably most people would wear blue jeans. There would be an effort to have everything used be union-made.

It would be wrong to think that this kind of structure and education would be inferior to any other kind. It would simply be *different.* Like Corporate/Capitalist University, it would be very attractive to some, and almost repulsive to others.

Our study has shown that people who do best in the world—best in their own terms—are those who have a sense of what they think is most beautiful, what is aesthetically most pleasing. That sense, when developed, is a critical cord that ties a life together. That aesthetic sense is translated into what can be a beautiful life.

There are many aesthetics; so should there be many kinds of colleges. The debate about technical training versus liberal arts really misses the point. We need to rethink the whole idea of what education adds to—or subtracts from—any single person. It is time that a college education provides a chance for a student to really begin to understand and practice what that student thinks best.

For higher education to flourish, for it to provide a basis for different kinds of lives for different types of people, then courses, structure, ideology, and social concerns must come together in a more intelligent way. There is no reason why a university could not teach an anarchist type of industry or a socialist way of doing business.

The distinctions within higher education now are ones of public or private, prestigious or plain, liberal arts or professional, parochial or non-parochial, large or small, expensive or not so expensive. But most schools of higher learning are structured in the same way, have the same notions of the truth, and have similar effects on their students.

Like all restructuring, to change one thing implies to change other things. For students to make informed choices about college, it might be best for eighteen- and nineteen-year-olds to spend their time learning about different viewpoints. The last year of high school and the first of college might merge to form a truly transitional time.

The suggestion seems to tug at once at our best and our worst instincts. It surely is not "liberal" education as we know it. John Stuart Mill would be hard-pressed to call it a marketplace of ideas at work, a place where the truth will be worked out in conflict. Even though we know that in the academy, academics fight for *power* so that their *ideas* will win, instead of the other way around; the very hint that we should deny the prospect of the marketplace is annoying.

The vision that comes to the liberal mind has to do with authoritarianism; it is a vision that has been honed to the point of being rightfully and truly horrifying to us in the twentieth century. One way to understand authoritarianism is to see that it means imposing one thing on everyone. That is what makes liberalism so beguiling. We impose liberalism on everyone, yet there are so many good and anti-authoritarian things about it.

Our best instincts acknowledge (and certainly this study shows), that we are not all alike, and that we should glory in our human diversity. Reasonably, that could mean that by the time we are young adults, we should begin to learn a way to look at, judge, and live in the world. It is at this point that pluralism and liberalism are pushed to their fulfillment, and we may get a nation of more active citizens.

If our public institutions are, as we are told, open and accountable, and if liberalism is, as we are told, the natural home of diversity, then there is no reason to believe that people who are educated in different ways, with differing viewpoints, will be doomed to failure. We have gotten where we are today—over-organized and personally without power—in part because of the way we have been educated. One can assume that there are equally powerful versions of the truth.

If an individual is not "liberal" in terms of understanding a kind of basic tolerance by the time he or she is out of public schools, a college education will have, at best, only an incremental effect. Equally important, if an individual comes into college with that underlying tolerance, it will be difficult to turn that person into an authoritarian. The existence of diverse but distinct institutions does not mean we will be forever pulled apart.

With a diversity of institutions it is possible that an interesting assortment of organizations and economic forms might emerge, and that a greater number of people would be better off in the world. One could more easily recognize friends and spot foes. In an increasingly chaotic and tyrannizing world, that is a useful ability.

To restructure higher education this way might prepare a person to be a citizen in the best sense. The marketplace of ideas is switched from the university to the public realm. The individual might actually enter the world in general, and the political realm in particular, *with a vision, with an idea.*

We might be able to begin, in individual and collective ways, to make the world beautiful in many beautiful ways. That, it seems to me, gives the people who are the heart of this study the respect due them. It also gives higher education, if it were to become more thoughtful and serious about itself, a task it may achieve someday.

NOTES

1. John Stuart Mill, *On Liberty,* ed. Currin V. Shields, © 1956 by the Liberal Arts Press, Inc., p. 72. Reprinted by permission of the Bobbs-Merrill Co., Inc.
2. Ibid., pp. 16, 17.
3. Ibid., p. 13.
4. Ibid., p. 25.
5. Ibid., p. 45.
6. Ibid., p. 52.
7. Ibid., p. 44.
8. Ibid., p. 58.
9. Ibid., p. 36.
10. Ibid., p. 40.
11. Ibid., p. 41.
12. Ibid., p. 79.
13. Ibid., p. 81.
14. Ibid., p. 102.
15. Ibid., p. 96.
16. Ibid., p. 97. Emphasis added.
17. Ibid., pp. 97, 98.
18. Ibid., p. 100.
19. Ibid., p. 128.
20. Louis Hartz, *The Liberal Tradition in America* (New York: Harcourt, Brace, and World, Inc., 1955), p. 6.
21. Ibid., p. 60.
22. Ibid., p. 58.
23. Ibid., p. 50. The first is quoted by Hartz; the second is Hartz.
24. Quoted by Hartz, ibid., p. 57.
25. Ibid., p. 62.
26. Diane Ravitch, *The Revisionists Revised* (New York: Basic Books, 1978). Reprinted by permission of Basic Books, Inc.
27. Ibid., pp. 22, 153–154, 103, 127, 56.
28. Ibid., p. 7. I underscored these lines because later (pp. 88, 90), Ravitch says that that you cannot make those judgments.
29. Ibid., pp. 8–9.
30. Ibid., p. 11.
31. Ibid., p. 14. Horatio Alger stories are interesting in part because the heroes are *lucky.*

32. Ibid., pp. 35, 16.
33. Ibid., p. 96.
34. Ibid., p. 63.
35. Ibid., p. 72.
36. Ibid., p. 35.
37. Ibid., p. 163.
38. Ibid., p. 167.
39. Ibid., p. 154.
40. Ibid., p. 173.
41. Frederick Rudolph, *The American College and University: A History* (New York: Vintage Books, 1962), p. 18.
42. Ibid., p. 20.
43. Ibid., p. 49.
44. Ibid., pp. 60–61.
45. Ibid., p. 65.
46. See Henry Adams, *The Education of Henry Adams* (Boston: Houghton Mifflin Co., 1973).
47. Rudolph, *The American College,* p. 65.
48. Ibid., p. 58.
49. Richard Hofstadter, *Anti-Intellectualism in American Life* (New York: Vintage Books, 1963), p. 43.
50. Ibid., p. 127.
51. Ibid., p. 80. These points have been noted in many places. Certainly Hofstadter presents the case clearly and in detail.
52. Ibid., p. 238.
53. Hans Gerth and C. Wright Mills, eds., *From Max Weber: Essays in Sociology* (New York: Oxford University Press, 1972 reprint), pp. 241, 243.
54. Jacques Ellul, *The Technological Society* (New York: Vintage Books, 1964), p. 349.
55. For one such study, see Nathan Pusey, *American Higher Education, 1945–1970* (Cambridge, Massachusetts: Harvard University Press, 1978).
56. Terrel Bell, "Does the Small Private College Have a Future?" Speech to the Council of Small Private Colleges, Washington, D.C., January 14, 1975.
57. Michael Cohen and James March, *Leadership and Ambiguity* (New York: McGraw-Hill, 1974), pp. 101–102.
58. This and the following are from Steven Muller, "Colleges in Trouble," *Psychology Today* 8, no. 12 (May 1975): 81.
59. Caroline Bird, "College Is a Waste of Time and Money," *Psychology Today* 8, no. 12 (May 1975). This essay conveys the essence of Bird's book, *The Case Against Colleges* (New York: David McKay Co., Inc., 1975).
60. Bird, "College," p. 32.
61. This is from Christopher Jencks's study, *Inequality.*
62. Bird, *Case,* p. 123. Also see John Keats, *The Sheepskin Psychosis* (Philadelphia & New York: J. B. Lippincott Co., 1963).

63. Bird, *Case,* pp. 3, 4.
64. Bird, "College," p. 32.
65. Ibid., p. 31.
66. Robert Maynard Hutchins, *The Higher Learning in America* (New Haven: Yale University Press, 1936, 1976), p. 4.
67. Ibid., p. 13.
68. Ibid., pp. 26, 27.
69. Ibid., pp. 105, 6, 7.
70. Robert Paul Wolff, *The Ideal of the University* (Boston: Beacon Press, 1969), p. 15.
71. Ibid., p. 78.
72. Ibid., p. 79.
73. James O'Toole, "Education, Work, and Quality of Life," in Dyckman Vermilye, ed., *Lifelong Learners—A New Clientele for Higher Education* (San Francisco: Jossey-Bass, 1974), p. 20.
74. R. S. Peters, ed., *The Philosophy of Education* (London: Oxford University Press, 1973).
75. Pat White, "Education, Democracy, and the Public Interest," in Peters, *Philosophy,* p. 223.
76. Ibid., pp. 235, 234.
77. Ibid., p. 230. Quoting Wolff from Robert Paul Wolff, B. Moore, Jr., and H. Marcuse, *A Critique of Pure Tolerance* (Boston: Beacon Press, 1965).
78. White, "Education," pp. 232–233.

Notes after Ending

I know of no writer who, having finished a book, is not faced with either second thoughts, additional thoughts, or others' thoughts. In the majority of cases, time, will, and stubbornness conspire to keep things written as they are. That, or there are countless revisions and no final manuscript. In this case the conspiracy failed, but instead of full revisions, I would like simply to add some ideas and clarify certain decisions.

First, while I try to make a strong case for a particular kind of understanding, I do not mean to argue that all other kinds are useless. In fact, we can learn certain things from quantitative studies, case studies, and formal modeling. My argument is that when these other methods are used exclusively, we get a truly warped and wrongheaded view of the world.

Further, it is my sense that the kind of study just presented is in a real way prior to other kinds of studies. The insights and facts from here may be important data in the construction of other studies.

Finally, to finish this first point, it should be clear that I do not believe that mine is the only way in which to view reality. There can be no single way to see multiple realities. Of course I like my way best, and am attracted to what I understand to be its virtues, but I cannot argue that it is the only view.

Second, there was a conscious decision to be fairly restrictive in my comments most of the time. The truth is that the book could have been much longer had I detailed my thoughts about every story and listed the many interpretations that might be made from point to point.

These restrictions were a result of my belief that each person's story should not be limited by my comments or insights. Hannah Arendt counsels us that speech and action have countless meanings and ramifications. The less I impose, the better chance the reader will have to make his or her own interpretations, and to come to particular as well as general meaning. The personal likes, dislikes, and judgments of the reader do, in fact, count.

The book was written, in part, to be discussed. All books form some kind of relationship with the reader; so it seems natural to ignore stupid books, or boring ones, or those that are offensive. But this book was written so that its readers could discuss it. The stories of the book, and the book as a story, are now public and are meant to be discussed.

I clearly did exercise judgments about what to include and exclude, as well as to what to say about the stories. I simply decided not to impose a great many Final Truths on any particular life or story.

Third, this book is meant to provide some advice to administrators. When I began the study I was in favor of a liberal arts education (as opposed to a technical education), and I suspect I still am in certain ways. I had assumed that the conclusions of the study would confirm my unexamined belief.

Once I realized that very little in the study supported my assumptions, and once I realized that the changes I was going to suggest might sound fairly radical, I was faced with this question: Isn't advice supposed to be "practical"? In a talk I gave to some academics, the whole point of practicality was pushed in a remarkable way. This group of professors, at a state university, argued essentially that funding was the critical variable in the pursuit of knowledge.

What that group was trying to teach me was a kind of bottom-line theory about the search for truth: Pleasing those who allocated funds was what mattered most in academic affairs. There was a kind of dual dynamic: People believed that was so, and people would say it out loud in public. I was honestly stunned.

Of course being stunned is not very interesting. It occurred to me that what was at stake, in an important sense, was the notion of practical advice (not to mention academic freedom and similar topics that are not considerations in this book). Normally, we think that practical suggestions have something to do with budget reform, with technology making administration more efficient, and with either centralization or decentralization helping to cut costs.

We all too rarely consider how these "practical" suggestions affect the equally "practical" problems of the meaning of college to the student. Organizational form and functioning are clearly tied to their effects on those in the organization. That is as true for IBM as it is for Big State U. It is wholly *impractical* to divide means and ends, or functions and forms.

There is another issue in this bias about practicality, and it has to do with administrators. I am unconvinced that all college administrators are simply mindless bureaucratic wolves dealing with sheepskins. To isolate administrators from everything on campus but "business" is to really make them the enemy of the academic process.

On a fairly regular basis we see that bureaucrats can be forced into a position of acting like bureaucrats—and are capable of making life unpleasant for everyone. That, I am convinced, is an important definition of *impractical*. What I am arguing is that it is necessary to reexamine the whole structure of education and rethink the whole idea of *practical*.

Fourth, there is the matter of focus. This was not meant to be a narrowly focused study in the tradition of trying to understand the effect of one policy on a particular population. The effort to know one small thing is fine, but something gets lost when there are so many little studies and so few that are broad in scope. Those small studies, remarkably enough, rarely seem to be cumulative; they do not add up to anything more than a number of small studies.

While I understand this to be a relatively short piece, I meant to limit it in size and not in scope.

Thinking back to the beginning of these additions, I failed to consider another problem: Endless Notes After Ending.

The prospect does not interest me.

Eighteen Useful Books

Adams, Henry. *The Education of Henry Adams*. Boston: Houghton Mifflin Company, 1973.

Arendt, Hannah. *The Human Condition*. Chicago: The University of Chicago Press, 1958.

————. *Men in Dark Times*. New York: Harcourt, Brace and World, Inc., 1968.

Barrett, Cyril, ed., *Wittgenstein: Lectures and Conversations on Aesthetics, Psychology and Religious Belief*. Berkeley: University of California Press, 1972.

Bergson, Henri. *The Creative Mind: An Introduction to Metaphysics*. New York: Citadel Press, 1946.

Gerth, Hans, and C. Wright Mills. *From Max Weber*. New York: Oxford University Press, 1946.

Hartz, Louis. *The Liberal Tradition in America*. New York: Harcourt, Brace and World, Inc., 1955.

Hofstadter, Richard. *Anti-Intellectualism in American Life*. New York: Vintage Books, 1963.

Hutchins, Robert. *The Higher Learning in America*. New Haven: Yale University Press, 1976 edition.

James, William. *Essays in Radical Empiricism and a Pluralistic Universe*. New York: E. P. Dutton & Co., Inc., 1971.

Mill, John Stuart. *On Liberty*. Indianapolis: Bobbs-Merrill, 1956.

Peters, R. S., ed. *The Philosophy of Education*. London: Oxford University Press, 1973.

Read, Herbert. *To Hell with Culture.* New York: Schocken Books, 1964.

Rudolph, Frederick. *The American College and University: A History.* New York: Vintage Books, 1962.

Sartre, Jean-Paul. *Search for a Method.* New York: Vintage Books, 1968.

Schutz, Alfred. *The Phenomenology of the Social World.* Chicago: Northwestern University Press, 1967.

Spence, Larry. *The Politics of Social Knowledge.* University Park, Pa.: Pennsylvania State University Press, 1978.

Waterman, Robert. *Political Action: Dialogues with Hannah Arendt.* Berkeley: Unpublished Dissertation, 1978.

1 2 3 4 5 6 7 8 9 0